Mr CIBBER OF DRURY LANE

NUMBER 143 OF THE
COLUMBIA UNIVERSITY STUDIES IN ENGLISH
AND COMPARATIVE LITERATURE

$\mathcal{M}^{r}$ $\mathcal{C}ibber$

OF DRURY LANE

By RICHARD HINDRY BARKER

COLUMBIA UNIVERSITY PRESS

New York : Morningside Heights : 1939

Copyright 1939

COLUMBIA UNIVERSITY PRESS, NEW YORK

Foreign Agents: Oxford University Press, Humphrey Milford, Amen House, London, E.C. 4, England, and B.I. Building, Nicol Road, Bombay, India; Maruzen Company, Ltd., 6 Nihonbashi, Tori-Nichome, Tokyo, Japan.

Manufactured in the United States of America

PREFACE

In preparing this life of Colley Cibber I have received invaluable assistance from members of the English Department at Columbia University, and I desire especially to record my obligations to Professor Oscar James Campbell, Professor George Sherburn, and Professor Ernest Hunter Wright. Professor Sherburn supplied me with much important information about Pope and other eighteenth-century figures, from which I trust I have profited. I must add that my researches in the British Museum and the Public Record Office were made possible by the Trustees of Columbia University, who awarded me a Columbia University Fellowship for the year 1929-30.

In the footnotes I have attempted to indicate my other obligations, and if I have not mentioned all the recent studies of Cibber, it is because I have tried to rely as far as possible only upon primary sources. I have referred to Robert W. Lowe's edition of Cibber's *Apology* simply as *Apology,* and in my quotations I have taken the liberty of modernizing spelling and punctuation.

Columbia University   R. H. B.
May, 1939

CONTENTS

Mr CIBBER OF DRURY LANE

I. EARLY YEARS

- I -

COLLEY CIBBER's father, Caius Gabriel Cibber, was born in Flensborg, Slesvig, in 1630. He was the son of a cabinetmaker—a court cabinetmaker, it is said—and at an early age he attracted the attention of the Danish king, who sent him to Italy to study art.[1]

The name may originally have been Sieber, which is close to Sievert and Siewert, German names found in Friesland and Holstein. If so, Caius Gabriel possibly changed the spelling while he was in Italy to make it resemble Cibo, the name of an ancient Italian family whose coat of arms he is known to have borrowed.[2]

From Italy Caius Gabriel went to London, possibly by way of the Netherlands. For several years he worked in Long Acre at the shop of the mason-sculptor John Stone, but he ultimately became his own master. He is described as the first artist of his profession in England "without the additional labor of an artisan," [3] and it is said that when he came into his own he was able to restrict himself almost entirely to the production of statues and busts. His works include a statue of Sir Thomas Gresham for the Royal Exchange, a bas-relief for the London Monument, a mermaid for the Leathersellers' Company, a set of statues for Trinity College, Cambridge, another set for the Duke of

[1] Harald Faber, *Caius Gabriel Cibber, 1630-1700. His Life and Work* (Oxford, 1926), pp. 3-4.

[2] *Ibid.*, p. 3; Albert Heintze, *Die Deutschen Familiennamen,* ed. Paul Cascorbi (7th ed., Halle, 1933), p. 439. In 1697 Cibber placed over his wife's grave in the Danish Church a monument on which were the Cibber (Cibo) and Colley coats of arms. On January 20, 1703, his son Colley Cibber thus advertised in the *Daily Courant* for a watch that he had lost: "In or near the old playhouse in Drury Lane, on Monday last the 19th of January, a watch was dropped, having a tortoise-shell case inlaid with silver, a silver chain, and a gold seal ring, the arms a cross wavy and chequer. Whoever brings it to Mr Cibber at his house near the Bull-Head Tavern in Old Spring Garden at Charing Cross shall have three guineas reward." The cross wavy was the Colley and the chequer the Cibo coat of arms.

[3] E. Beresford Chancellor, *The Lives of the British Sculptors* (London, 1911), p. 61, quoted in Faber, *Caius Gabriel Cibber,* p. 8. (In the notes which follow I have given the place of publication only in the case of works not published in London.)

Devonshire's estate at Chatsworth, and a Danish Church in Wellclose Square. But his most famous work was undoubtedly his gate-piece for Bedlam Hospital—two monumental figures representing Raving and Melancholy. Obviously reminiscent of the "Day" and "Night" of the Medici Chapel, they were singled out for particular praise in the eighteenth century, when the influence of Michelangelo was at its height. Roubiliac never went near Bedlam without stopping to admire them, and Pope mentioned them in the first lines of the *Dunciad*.[4]

Some ten or fifteen years after his arrival in London, Cibber—now a widower—married Jane Colley, a member of an old family from Glaston in Rutlandshire. The Colleys were apparently well known in their county. They traced their descent as far back as William of Wykeham's sister, and for several generations they had served as sheriffs and Members of Parliament. Sir Antony Colley, Jane Colley's grandfather, had been a zealous Cavalier during the Civil War and had contributed so liberally to the King's cause that he had reduced his estate from £3,000 to about £300 a year. But after the Restoration the family was still moderately wealthy, for when Jane Colley married, her father was able to give her a dowry of £6,000.[5]

Colley was the first child of this marriage. He was born on November 6, 1671, and christened after his maternal uncle, who was the last male heir of the Colley family.[6]

The Cibbers later had two other children, Lewis and Veronica. Lewis is described by his brother as a person of lively parts, with a good deal of natural wit and humor. He was educated at Winchester and New College, and later ordained by Dr Compton, Bishop of London. But there appears to have been very little piety in his disposition. Dr Young told Spence that at Winchester Lewis was thought loose as well as ingenious, and that his conduct was so immoral that even Colley used to reprove him. "He was a vile rake afterwards and in the greatest distress." Once, Young continues, he approached Dr Burton for a small loan, remarking "that he did not know any sin he had not been guilty of but one, which was avarice; and if the doctor would give him a guinea, he would do his utmost to be guilty of

---

[4] Faber, *Caius Gabriel Cibber*, pp. 5-8, 43.
[5] *Ibid.*, p. 17; Cibber, *Apology*, ed. Robert W. Lowe (1889), I, 8-9.
[6] *Apology*, I, 7-8.

that too."[7] He died in 1711, "from too great a disregard to his health."[8]

Little is definitely known about Colley's earliest years except what he himself tells us in his autobiography. He was born in a new and fashionable suburb of London—Southampton Street, which at its northern end faced Southampton or Bloomsbury Square, one of the show-places of the metropolis. While he was still very young he saw King Charles II playing with his dogs and feeding his ducks in St James's Park, and once his father took him to the chapel in White-hall, where he saw the Duke of York as well as the King. He later remembered that the Duke was present throughout the service.[9] But there seem also to have been unpleasant experiences during his child-hood which he himself fails to record. About 1673 his father "chanced to have a gent[leman] lodge with him that practised gaming, [who] drew him into play that ruined him to the degree that when he cut the basso-relievo on the Monument in the City he then was a prisoner in the King's Bench and went backwards and forwards daily on that account."[10] Cibber borrowed considerable sums of money—from his brother-in-law Edward Colley as well as from others—but several years passed before he quite extricated himself from debt. Between 1673 and 1678 he was in the Marshalsea Prison.[11] Colley's life may not have been profoundly affected, but it is difficult to avoid thinking that he knew enough about the family calamity to hold his father responsible. In his autobiography he clearly expresses his contempt for his father—the contempt of the successful for the unsuccessful man—and this feeling may easily reflect the experiences of his early childhood.

In 1682 Colley was sent to the free school of Grantham in Lincoln-shire.[12] It was near Glaston, the home of his mother's family, and while he was there he probably became acquainted with old family friends. His second play, *Woman's Wit*, is dedicated to a kinsman,

[7] Joseph Spence, *Anecdotes, Observations, and Characters of Books and Men*, ed. Samuel Weller Singer (1820), p. 377.

[8] *Apology*, I, 57; also Faber, *Caius Gabriel Cibber*, pp. 19, 74.

[9] *Apology*, I, 7, 30.

[10] Vertue MSS., quoted in Faber, *Caius Gabriel Cibber*, pp. 19-20.

[11] Faber, *Caius Gabriel Cibber*, pp. 20-21.   [12] *Apology*, I, 9.

Samuel Adams of Wolverton, who had, Colley says, taken care of his brother Lewis.

At Grantham, as at Drury Lane in later days, Colley was generally unpopular. He was a bright student and a lively companion, but he had at the same time many extremely irritating qualities. Once, he tells us, he was whipped for his theme, though the master said that "what was good of it was better than any boy's in the form."[13] The punishment was seldom so severe, for Colley, an assiduous flatterer, was soon in the master's good graces; but he often experienced the ill-will of his schoolfellows, who were hurt by his sharp tongue and annoyed by his self-complacence. He was once pummelled by a boy larger than himself while his particular friend looked on and cried, "Beat him soundly!" It later appeared that he had alienated his friend by jeering him before the other boys of the school.[14] An even more illuminating incident took place in February, 1685. The King had just died, and the master asked the form to write an appropriate funeral oration. But Colley alone felt himself qualified for the task. "This oration," he says, "such as it was, I produced the next morning: all the other boys pleaded their inability, which the master taking rather as a mark of their modesty than their idleness, only seemed to punish by setting me at the head of the form: a preferment dearly bought! Much happier had I been to have sunk my performance in the general modesty of declining it. A most uncomfortable life I led among them for many a day after! I was so jeered, laughed at, and hated as a pragmatical bastard (schoolboys' language) who had betrayed the whole form that scarce any of 'em would keep me company; and though it so far advanced me into the master's favor that he would often take me from the school to give me an airing with him on horseback while they were left to their lessons, you may be sure such envied happiness did not increase their good-will to me."[15]

Strangely enough, however, he learned nothing by the experience, for when, two months later, the master offered to give the boys a holiday if one of them would produce an ode on the coronation, Colley again volunteered. The ode achieved its purpose, but Colley's self-complacency so much annoyed the other boys that they left him out of a coronation-day party which he was particularly anxious to attend.[16]

[13] *Ibid.*, I, 10.   [14] *Ibid.*, I, 10-11.   [15] *Ibid.*, I, 31-32.   [16] *Ibid.*, I, 32-33.

Colley finished his course at Grantham at the age of sixteen, and his father, who intended him for the church, sent him to stand election to Winchester College. "My being by my mother's side a descendant of William of Wykeham, the founder," Cibber says, "my father (who knew little how the world was to be dealt with) imagined my having that advantage would be security enough for my success, and so sent me simply down thither without the least favorable recommendation or interest but that of my naked merit and a pompous pedigree in my pocket. Had he tacked a direction to my back and sent me by the carrier to the mayor of the town to be chosen Member of Parliament there, I might have had just as much chance to have succeeded in the one as the other. But I must not omit in this place to let you know that the experience which my father then bought at my cost taught him, some years later, to take a more judicious care of my younger brother, Lewis Cibber, whom, with the present of a statue of the founder of his own making, he recommended to the same college. This statue now stands (I think) over the school door there, and was so well executed that it seemed to speak—for its kinsman. It was no sooner set up than the door of preferment was open to him." [17]

Unsuccessful at Winchester, Colley hastened to London, arriving in time to see a play before his mother could demand an account of his traveling expenses. " 'Twas about this time," he says, that "I first imbibed an inclination, which I durst not reveal, for the stage." [18] But Colley had only a few months to cultivate this new inclination before he was summoned to Chatsworth, where his father was working on the estate of the Earl of Devonshire. It had been decided that he was to be sent directly to Cambridge, where his father had friends, but in the meantime he was to be removed from the temptations of London and kept under his father's eyes. He set out for Chatsworth, but before he could complete the journey the Revolution began. At Nottingham he found his father in arms, and he was easily persuaded to take his father's place in the force that the Earl of Devonshire had raised to fight for the Prince of Orange. He spent the winter under the Earl, waiting for resistance that was never offered. He was one

[17] *Ibid.*, I, 56-57. The completion of the statue is announced in the *Post Boy* of July 24-27, 1697.
[18] *Apology*, I, 58.

of the men who advanced a few miles on the London road, met the
coach of Princess Anne, and escorted it back to Nottingham. On the
night of Her Royal Highness's arrival, Lord Devonshire gave a
banquet and it was Colley's privilege to wait at table on the second
guest of the evening in the order of rank, the future Duchess of
Marlborough.[19] "Being so near the table," he wrote many years later,
"you may naturally ask me what I might have heard to have passed in
conversation at it; which I should certainly tell you, had I attended
to above two words that were uttered there, and those were, 'Some
wine and water.' These, I remember, came distinguished and observed
to my ear, because they came from the fair guest whom I took such
pleasure to wait on. Except at that single sound all my senses were
collected into my eyes, which during the whole entertainment wanted
no better amusement than of stealing now and then the delight of
gazing on the fair object so near me. If so clear an emanation of
beauty, such a commanding grace of aspect struck me into a regard
that had something softer than the most profound respect in it, I
cannot see why I may not, without offence, remember it; since beauty,
like the sun, must sometimes lose its power to choose and shine into
equal warmth the peasant and the courtier." [20]

When the campaign was over Colley returned to Chatsworth and
drew up a Latin petition to the Earl of Devonshire asking for a place
of some sort. ("My father," Colley says, characteristically attributing
the move to his father's meanness, "my father thought that a little
court favor ... might give him a chance for saving the expense of
maintaining me, as he had intended, at the university.") [21] The Earl
promised to make provision for the young man—indeed he later mentioned a post in the office of the Secretary of State when a proper
vacancy should occur—and Colley obediently went to London. He
remained in the Earl's household for five months, waiting, not too
impatiently, for his post and enjoying for the first time complete freedom in the city. He revisited the park and the playhouse, learned to
admire Mountfort and Nokes, saw more of the gay life about Covent
Garden, and soon conceived an overpowering desire to adopt the
stage as a profession. "The distant hope of a reversion," he decided,

[19] *Ibid.*, I, 58-61, 67-68.   [20] *Ibid.*, I, 68-69.   [21] *Ibid.*, I, 73.

"was too cold a temptation" for a spirit so impatient as his; he wanted "immediate possession of what [his] heart was so differently set upon." And so, against the wishes of his parents, he left the Earl's household and joined the company at the Theatre Royal.[22]

- 3 -

"The first thing that enters into the head of a young actor," Cibber says, "is that of being a hero. In this ambition I was soon snubbed by the insufficiency of my voice, to which might be added an uninformed meagre person (though then not ill made) with a dismal pale complexion. Under these disadvantages I had but a melancholy prospect of ever playing a lover with Mrs Bracegirdle, which I had flattered my hopes that my youth might one day have recommended me to. What was most promising in me then was the aptness of my ear, for I was soon allowed to speak justly, though what was grave and serious did not equally become me."[23]

But even the aptness of his ear did not at once bring him to the attention of the patentees, and for the usual six months he remained in the company as an unpaid probationer. He listened and learned, picked up odd pieces of theatrical gossip, and watched famous men who came to the theatre. In the spring of 1690, for example, he saw Dryden at the reading of *Amphytrion,* and he was surprised to notice that Dryden's delivery was cold, flat, and completely unaffecting.[24] On another occasion he overheard Nokes giving an account of some table-talk, while a gentleman who stood near was so much deceived by Nokes's manner that he asked him if he was rehearsing for a new play.[25] But finally, after nine months of study and observation, Colley was taken into the company and given his first part. He got a salary, though he owed it—so the story goes—to his own blundering incompetence. Assigned to carry a message to Betterton in some play or other, he became so nervous when he saw the audience that he threw the whole scene into confusion. "Who is the young man who made the blunder?" Betterton asked. "Master Colley," replied the prompter. "Master Colley! Then forfeit him." "Why, sir," said the prompter, "he

[22] *Ibid.,* I, 73-74.
[23] *Ibid.,* I, 182-83.
[24] *Ibid.,* I, 113.
[25] *Ibid.,* I, 142.

has no salary." "No?" replied the old actor. "Why then put him down ten shillings a week and forfeit him five." And accordingly Master Colley was entered, for the first time, in the treasurer's books.[26]

This beginning was certainly not auspicious, and for several seasons the young man was confined to short and insignificant parts. He was a commander who delivered a few short speeches, a courtier who was quickly killed, a servant in a comedy.[27] But he gradually improved enough to show that he was not quite the fool that Betterton had thought him. In 1692—or possibly earlier—he gave so good a performance as the Chaplain in *The Orphan* that the audience applauded, and Goodman afterwards described him as an actor of considerable promise[28] and in 1694 he was selected to substitute for Kynaston as Lord Touchwood in *The Double Dealer*. The Queen had commanded a performance of the play, and Congreve offered Cibber the part at the very last moment. "The flattery of being thus distinguished by so celebrated an author," Cibber says, "and the honor to act before a queen, you may be sure made me blind to whatever difficulties might attend it. I accepted the part and was ready in it before I slept; and the next day the Queen was present at the play and was received with a new prologue from the author, spoken by Mrs Barry.... After the play Mr Congreve made me the compliment of saying that I had not only answered but had exceeded his expectations and that he would show me he was sincere by his saying more of me to the masters. He was as good as his word and the next pay day I found my salary of fifteen was then advanced to twenty shillings a week. But alas!" Cibber adds, "this favorable opinion of Mr Congreve made no farther impression upon the judgment of my good masters."[29]

[26] Thomas Davies, *Dramatic Miscellanies* (1783-84), III, 417-18.

[27] Casts in George Powell, *Alphonso King of Naples* (1691); Thomas D'Urfey, *Bussy D'Ambois, or the Husband's Revenge* (1691); Thomas Southerne, *Sir Anthony Love, or the Rambling Lady* (1691); etc.

[28] *Apology*, I, 183. The date is fixed by the fact that Mountfort figures in the incident; Mountfort was murdered December 9, 1692.

[29] *Apology*, I, 185-86; Public Record Office, L.C. 5/151. The entry in the Lord Chamberlain's warrant-book reads: "1693 Jan^r 13 ye Q a Box & a Box for ye Maids of Hon^r double Daler." Allardyce Nicoll, in *A History of Restoration Drama, 1660-1700* (2nd ed., Cambridge, England, 1928), p. 314, interprets 1693 as 1692/3, though on p. 356 he gives October, 1693, as the month in which *The Double Dealer* was produced. In Congreve, *Works* (1923), I, 21, note, Montague Summers suggests that 1693 is a clerical error for 1694. The obvious interpretation of the entry is that 1693 means 1693/4.

In 1695, the year of the division of the companies, Cibber got his second important part, that of Fondlewife in *The Old Bachelor*. Powell, the principal actor at Drury Lane, had given out the play and announced that he himself would mimic Betterton (now at Lincoln's Inn Fields) in the part of Heartwell. He had sent for play-books and assigned the other parts when suddenly he was reminded that there was no one in the company to substitute for Doggett, whose brilliant Fondlewife had been principally responsible for the play's success during the previous season. But Powell was determined to let nothing stand in his way, and accordingly sent for young Cibber, who had been heard to remark that he himself would like to play Fondle-wife. "If the fool has a mind to blow himself up at once," Powell said, " let us e'en give him a clear stage for it." Cibber, however, was not entirely unprepared, for he had made a careful study of Doggett's performance in the part, and when evening came he was ready to give an exact imitation.[30] "At my first appearance," he says, "one might have imagined by the various murmurs of the audience that they were in doubt whether Doggett himself were not returned, or that they could not conceive what strange face it could be that so nearly resembled him; for I had laid the tint of forty years more than my real age upon my features and to the most minute placing of an hair was dressed exactly like him. When I spoke the surprise was still greater, as if I had not only borrowed his clothes but his voice too. But though that was the least difficult part of him to be imitated, they seemed to allow I had so much of him in every requisite that my applause was perhaps more than proportionable." [31] In short, the appearance was a distinct triumph for the young actor; but again the patentees were so little impressed that they refused to trust him with other parts of the same type.

- 4 -

Disheartened by his disappointments at the theatre, Cibber turned with relief to the pleasures of the town. He frequented taverns and bagnios, coffeehouses and gaming houses; he joined the disorderly company at the Rose and listened to the wits at Will's. Many years later Dr Johnson asked him if, during his visits to the famous coffee-

[30] *Apology*, I, 204-8.   [31] *Ibid.*, I, 208.

house, he had ever seen Dryden. "O Lord!" he replied, "I was as well acquainted with him as if he had been my own brother." But when he searched his memory he could recall only that Dryden was a "decent old man, arbiter of critical disputes." "You are to consider," said Johnson afterwards, "that Cibber was then at a great distance from Dryden, had perhaps one leg only in the room, and durst not draw in the other." [32] But Cibber was certainly there, however badly in later years his memory may have served him.

It was not long before he picked up the vices and affectations of his companions. He bought a periwig and became a fop; he learned to drawl and take snuff, to strut and cock his cravat strings. He had his intrigues, he quarreled, and though not distinguished for courage he occasionally fought a duel; one hears, for example, of a "rancounter at the Bath" and of a "pinking" of his "corps in the Piazzas"; [33] and forgetting the misfortunes of his father, he went to the Groom Porter's and staked his small income at the tables.

The Groom Porter's, the licensed gambling hall of the seventeenth and eighteenth centuries, is described by Pepys, who visited it one evening in 1668.

They begun to play at about eight at night [Pepys notes in his diary], where to see how differently one man took his losing from another, one cursing and swearing, and another only muttering and grumbling to himself, a third without any apparent discontent at all ... to see two or three gentlemen come in there drunk and putting their stock of gold together, one twenty-two pieces, the second four, and the third five pieces; and these to play one with another and forget how much each of them brought, but he that brought the twenty-two thinks that he brought no more than the rest: to see the different humors of gamesters to change their luck when it is bad, how ceremonious they are as to call for new dice, to shift their places, to alter their manner of throwing, and that with great industry, as if there was anything in it ... to hear their cursing and damning to no purpose, as one man being to throw a seven if he could, and failing to do it after a great many throws, cried he would be damned if ever he flung seven more while he lived, his despair of throwing it being so great, while others did it as their luck served almost every throw: to see how persons of the best quality do here sit down and play with people of any, though meaner; and to see how people in ordinary clothes shall come hither and play away one

[32] Boswell, *Life of Johnson,* ed. George Birkbeck Hill (Oxford and New York, 1887), III, 71-72 and note.
[33] *Visits from the Shades, or Dialogues Serious, Comical, and Political* (1704), p. 23.

hundred, or two, or three hundred guineas without any kind of difficulty: and lastly to see the formality of the groom porter, who is their judge of all disputes in play and all quarrels that may arise therein, and how his under-officers are there to observe true play at each table, and to give new dice, is a consideration I never could have thought had been in the world had I not now seen it.

"Brisband pressed me hard [to venture]," Pepys adds, "and tempted me with saying that no man was ever known to lose the first time ... but I did refuse." [34] Cibber, who visited the Groom Porter's in the next generation, was less cautious. He ventured as heavily as his salary would permit, and when, some years later, he became manager of Drury Lane it was apparently not uncommon for him to lose £200 or £300 in a single evening. Once he is reported to have thrown away more than £1,000, "very near the whole sum he was master of at that time to support a large and increasing family." [35] But by this time he was too old a gamester to feel the loss keenly. After a run of bad luck, Davies says, he would return to the theatre, hum over an opera tune, and go on the stage not well prepared to act.[36]

Possibly connected with his losses at the Groom Porter's is a letter which he wrote to the Lord Chamberlain between April 19 and December 26, 1697.[37] He pointed out that he was in prison at the suit of a certain Mrs Lucas, and he petitioned the Lord Chamberlain for the immunity which was traditionally granted to actors at the Theatre Royal:

To the Right Honorable Robert Earl of Sunderland, Lord Chamberlain of His Majesty's Household, etc.
The humble petition of Colley Cibber, one of His Majesty's sworn comedians.
S h o w e t h   That your petitioner was the 16th instant (without any leave from your lordship) arrested at the suit of Jane Lucas, and carried to the prison of the Gatehouse, where he now remains a prisoner at her suit.

That your petitioner having always been and still being willing to submit to such order herein as your lordship shall think fit to give, and at the same time (as far as in him lies) to justify the privilege of His Majesty's servants.

[34] Pepys, *Diary,* ed. Henry B. Wheatley (London and New York, 1893-99), VII, 245-46.
[35] *The Laureat, or the Right Side of Colley Cibber, Esq.* (1740), p. 123.
[36] Davies, *Dramatic Miscellanies,* III, 450-51.
[37] The Earl of Sunderland was Lord Chamberlain between these dates.

Your petitioner therefore humbly prays that the said Mrs Lucas and her attorney and bailiffs may be brought before your lordship to answer their contempt and to show cause why they refuse to discharge your petitioner from prison. And your petitioner, as in duty bound, shall ever pray, etc.[38]

The outcome of the appeal is unknown, but Cibber was probably released, reprimanded, and ordered to come to a settlement with Mrs Lucas. He apparently did so, for it is clear that he did not remain in prison.

At the Rose, at the theatre, and at the Groom Porter's Cibber met the fine gentlemen of the town, and it was soon his good fortune to form an intimate friendship with one of them—Henry Brett, who was later to play a curious part in the history of Drury Lane. Brett was heir to an estate in Gloucestershire; but the estate was heavily mortgaged and he himself had been obliged to seek his fortune in the drawing-rooms of London. One night shortly after the production of *Love's Last Shift,* he came to the greenroom at Drury Lane, drawn partly by the charms of the theatrical "nymphs" who were there to be seen and partly by "a more sincere passion" for the full-bottomed periwig which, as Sir Novelty, Cibber wore in the play. Brett began by praising it; went on to rally himself on the folly of desiring so extravagant an article of dress; and finally suggested a bottle at a tavern, where the price might more conveniently be discussed. The bargain was struck, the bottle brought the two fops closer together, and before the evening was over their acquaintanceship had ripened into intimacy.[39]

In the dedication to *Richard III* (1700) and again in the *Apology* (1740) Cibber eloquently describes the advantages conferred upon him by this first distinguished friend of his youth. Brett had introduced him to men of the highest quality and sponsored him in social circles where, without Brett's protection, he would never have been tolerated. Furthermore the man of pleasure had condescended to take an interest in theatrical affairs. He had left a company of fine gentlemen in order to attend a reading of *Richard III,* and a few days later he had ignored the advances of a fine lady in the next box in order to go behind the scenes and make a few suggestions about one of

[38] L.C. 7/3. I have not attempted to reproduce Cibber's abbreviations.
[39] *Apology,* II, 34-37; *Dictionary of National Biography* (1921-22), article Henry Brett.

Richard's soliloquies. But the obligations were not entirely on one side, for in 1700 Cibber was able to help his friend in an affair of the utmost consequence. Brett was courting a lady whose fortune, estimated at £12,000 or £25,000, was large enough "to disencumber him of the world and make him every way easy for life." [40] He had won her sympathy, it is said, when he had been arrested by bailiffs opposite her windows, and he had later been introduced to her by Sir Thomas Skipwith, one of the patentees of Drury Lane.[41] The rest of the story is best told by Cibber himself:

While [Brett] was in pursuit of this affair, which no time was to be lost in (for the lady was to be in town but for three weeks), I one day found him idling behind the scenes before the play was begun. Upon sight of him I took the usual freedom he allowed me to rate him roundly for the madness of not improving every moment in his power in what was of such consequence to him. "Why are you not," said I, "where you know you only should be? If your design should once get wind in the town, the ill-will of your enemies or the sincerity of the lady's friends may soon blow up your hopes, which in your circumstances of life cannot be long supported by the bare appearance of a gentleman." . . . After twenty excuses to clear himself of the neglect I had so warmly charged him with, he concluded them with telling me he had been out all the morning upon business, and that his linen was too much soiled to be seen in company. "Oh, ho!" said I, "is that all? Come along with me, we will soon get over that dainty difficulty." Upon which I hauled him by the sleeve into my shifting-room, he either staring, laughing, or hanging back all the way. There, when I had locked him in, I began to strip off my upper clothes and bade him do the same; still he either did not or would not seem to understand me, and continuing his laugh cried, "What! is the puppy mad?" "No, no, only positive," said I; "for look you, in short, the play is ready to begin, and the parts that you and I are to act today are not of equal consequence; mine of Young Reveller (in *Greenwich Park*) is but a rake; but whatever you may be, you are not to appear so; therefore take my shirt and give me yours; for depend upon't, stay here you shall not, and so go about your business." To conclude, we fairly changed linen, nor could his mother's have wrapped him up more fortunately; for in about ten days he married the lady. In a year or two after his marriage, he was chosen a Member of that Parliament which was sitting when King William died. And upon raising of some new regiments, was made lieutenant-colonel to that of Sir Charles Hotham. But as his ambition extended not beyond the bounds of a park wall and a pleasant retreat in the corner of it, which with too much expense he had just

[40] *Apology*, II, 39. [41] *Dictionary of National Biography*, article Henry Brett.

finished, he within another year had leave to resign his company to a younger brother.[42]

The estate which Cibber mentions was Sandywell Park in Gloucestershire, later sold by Brett to Lord Conway; the lady was Anne Mason, divorced wife of the Earl of Macclesfield, and reputedly the mother of Richard Savage.[43] Cibber became a frequent visitor at Sandywell Park, and for years is said to have been on the best terms with his hostess. Boswell reports that he "had so high an opinion of her taste and judgment as to genteel life and manners that he submitted every scene of his *Careless Husband* to [her] revisal and correction." The biographer adds that the plot of the comedy was suggested by an incident which occurred in the Brett household. "Colonel Brett was reported to be too free in his gallantry with his lady's maid. Mrs Brett came into a room one day in her own house, and found the colonel and her maid both fast asleep in two chairs. She tied a white handkerchief round her husband's neck, which was a sufficient proof that she had discovered his intrigue; but she never at any time took notice of it to him." [44]

- 5 -

In his second or third year at Drury Lane Cibber became acquainted with a family of musicians by the name of Shore. The father, Matthias Shore, was a trumpeter, who since 1685 had been Trumpeter in Ordinary to His Majesty and since 1689 Sergeant Trumpet. He was known as a curmudgeon who exacted rigorously the fees of his office. His sons William and John were also trumpeters, and his daughter Katherine was a pupil of Purcell's for singing and harpsichord.[45]

Cibber's first friend among the Shores was apparently John, already a popular performer at Drury Lane and especially famous for the trumpet obbligatos written for him by Purcell. He is said to have improved the technique of trumpet playing to such an extent that he was able to get from the instrument a tone as sweet as that of the oboe. He later succeeded his father and elder brother as Sergeant Trumpet, and in 1715 became lutanist to the Chapel Royal. He died,

---

[42] *Apology*, II, 39-42.   [43] *Dictionary of National Biography*, article Henry Brett.
[44] Boswell, *Life of Johnson*, I, 174, note.
[45] Grove, *Dictionary of Music and Musicians*, ed. H. C. Colles (1928), article Shore; L.C. 5/149.

it is said, at the advanced age of ninety, shortly after he had married a lady who, according to one account, was his maid, and according to another, a widow with a dowry of £15,000. His character is not easy to make out, but it is known that he had a passion for puns. He never gave a concert without producing a tuning-fork which he had invented and remarking: "I have not about me a pitch-pipe, but I have what will do as well to tune by, a pitch-fork." Like his father, he was careful to collect his fees, and he so frequently had to sue for them that he became extremely eccentric and possibly insane. But these misfortunes belong to his later years, and when Cibber first met him he was no doubt, as Sir John Hawkins says, a man of humor and pleasantry.[46]

One day as Cibber entered the Shore house, he passed by a room in which John's sister was singing and accompanying herself on the harpsichord. He stopped to listen; "his ear was immediately charmed; on which he begged to be introduced, and at first sight was captivated. Nor," continues his daughter, who tells the story, ". . . was [Katherine] less delighted with the sprightliness of his wit than he was with the fund of perfecion with which art and nature had equally endowed her. In short, a private courtship began and ended in a marriage against her father's consent, as Mr Colley Cibber was then rather too young for a husband in the old gentleman's opinion."[47]

Too young perhaps, but certainly too poor; for Cibber's income at this time was only 20 shillings a week (from the theatre) and £20 a year (from the estate of his uncle Edward Colley).[48] The marriage took place on May 6, 1693,[49] and Shore immediately spent the money he had intended to leave his daughter in building a large houseboat on the Thames later known as the Folly. It was used as tavern, concert-hall, brothel, and place of general amusement.[50] In 1696 Shore

[46] Grove, *Dictionary of Music and Musicians*, article Shore; Charles Burney, *A General History of Music* (1782-89), III, 499, note; Sir John Hawkins, *A General History of the Science and Practice of Music* (1853), II, 752, note; L.C. 5/151, 5/154, 5/159; Charke, *A Narrative of the Life of Mrs Charlotte Charke*, Constable's Miscellany (1929), pp. 26-27, 69-70.

[47] Charke, *Narrative*, p. 69.

[48] *Apology*, I, 184; Faber, *Caius Gabriel Cibber*, pp. 17-18.

[49] *Notes and Queries*, 11th series, IV (July-December, 1911), 366.

[50] Charke, *Narrative*, p. 69; J. E. B. Mayor, *Cambridge under Queen Anne* (Cambridge, England, 1911), p. 371; Tom Brown, *Amusements Serious and Comical* (New York, 1927), pp. 123-24; Edward Hatton, *A New View of London* (1708), II, 785.

apparently relented, for he made a will leaving Katherine a third of his property. But inasmuch as he refers to her as Katherine Shore and not as Katherine Cibber, it seems clear that he was not yet entirely reconciled to his son-in-law.[51]

For several years the Cibbers were apparently so poor that Katherine was compelled to go on the stage. In 1694 she sang Purcell's song "The Genius of England" in the second part of D'Urfey's *Don Quixote,* while her brother John played the trumpet obbligato; [52] and in 1695–96 she acted Galatea in Settle's *Philaster,* Orinda in Mrs Manley's *The Lost Lover,* and Hillaria in her husband's *Love's Last Shift.* Later she had an opportunity to sing as well as to act in the parts of Olivia in *Woman's Wit* (1697) and Biancha in *Sauny the Scot* (published in May, 1698, and probably revived not long before).[53] She was clearly not an actress of the first rank, for none of her parts are very exacting; but she remained on the stage as long as her husband needed the small salary that she made.

The subsequent history of the Cibber family, as far as we know it, is concerned largely with legacies. In 1700 they inherited money from Edward Colley,[54] in the same year or shortly afterwards from Matthias Shore,[55] and in 1713 from William Shore and his wife Rose.[56] The last of these legacies is particularly interesting because it precipitated a family quarrel in the course of which Cibber found himself in a position not unlike that of his own sentimental heroes, Lord Wrong-love and Sir Charles Easy. William Shore left his money to his wife and after her death to Mrs Cibber and the Cibber children, specifically directing that the bequest of £30 a year to Mrs Cibber should be "for her own separate use." Rose left *her* money to Elizabeth, one of Cibber's daughters, and instructed her executors to spend it, if circumstances warranted, for Elizabeth's maintenance and education. She also left Elizabeth a pearl necklace, a diamond cross, and three suits of Flanders lace headcloths. But the terms of the two wills were not carried out, chiefly, it seems, because Cibber insisted on claiming all

[51] Matthias Shore's will, Somerset House.
[52] Grove, *Dictionary of Music and Musicians,* article Shore.
[53] Edward Arber, *Term Catalogues, 1668-1709* (1903-6), III, 65.
[54] Faber, *Caius Gabriel Cibber,* pp. 17-18.   [55] Matthias Shore's will.
[56] The rest of the paragraph is based on Public Record Office, Chancery Decrees and Orders, 1713 A, p. 634; 1733 A, p. 183; Masters' Reports, Vol. 335 (1716). I have been unable to find the bills and answers in the case.

the money concerned, and his wife was finally obliged to file suit in the Court of Chancery. Cibber defended himself by arguing that he was a poor man. He had no real estate, he insisted, and his income was so small that he could not afford to set aside money for his old age. He agreed that his wife had a right to the £30 a year, but he felt that the other bequests should be used to maintain and educate the children. His statements were not strictly true, for his income at this time was at least £1,000 a year, but at the hearing (July 13, 1714) his arguments were sustained and he was given the right to spend his children's money during their minorities.

In Cibberian comedy a family quarrel of any sort is always followed by a scene of reconciliation, but in Cibber's own case one cannot be quite sure that such a reconciliation took place. Direct evidence is lacking, but not long afterwards one hears—though not perhaps on the best authority—that Cibber was grossly neglecting one of his daughters. He allowed her to go about "very bare in clothes"— so bare, in fact, that his fellow managers felt obliged to offer her a private benefit. But when the benefit was given Cibber himself kept the profits "rather than let his child have necessaries." [57] On the other hand, Charlotte Charke—possibly the daughter in question—gives a pleasant picture of the Cibber family life between 1715 and 1725. She assures us that she herself was well cared for and extremely well educated, and she speaks of attractive summer residences occupied by the family at Twickenham and Hampton (the former the lodging house later purchased by Horace Walpole for the famous Strawberry Hill).[58] Later, Charlotte says, her mother, who was afflicted with asthma, retired to Uxbridge near Hillingdon, "an agreeable retreat my father had taken a lease of for some years." [59] But Charlotte herself is not a very reliable authority, and too much importance can easily be attached to her remarks. It remains—and perhaps always will remain— doubtful to what extent her father's domestic life followed the pattern of his comedies.

[57] *Weekly Journal, or Saturday's Post,* March 1, 1718.
[58] Charke, *Narrative,* pp. 19-28; Horace Walpole, *Works* (1798), II, 399.
[59] Charke, *Narrative,* p. 28.

II. FIRST PLAYS

- I -

DISCOURAGED by his slow progress at the theatre and convinced that he would never get good parts until he should write them for himself, Cibber began work on a comedy, *Love's Last Shift*. He probably sketched the plot and began filling in the dialogue in the winter of 1694–95,[1] but in the spring of 1695 he put his manuscript aside to write two less ambitious pieces, a prologue for the reopening of Drury Lane and an elegiac poem on the death of Queen Mary.

The prologue was composed at the last minute when none of the other prologues offered at the theatre proved satisfactory. It was accepted and Cibber bargained for the privilege of delivering it himself. But the patentees insisted on giving it to Powell, the leading actor of the company, who accordingly appeared before the curtain on the opening day, April 1, 1695.[2] "Every line that was applauded," Cibber says, "went sorely to my heart when I reflected that the same praise might have been given to my own speaking, nor could the success of the author compensate the distress of the actor. However, in the end it served in some sort to mend our people's opinion of me, and whatever the critics might think of it, one of the patentees (who, it is true, knew no difference between Dryden and D'Urfey) said, upon the success of it, that insooth I was an ingenious young man. This sober compliment (though I could have no reason to be vain upon it) I thought was a fair promise to my being in favor." [3]

The *Poem on the Death of Our Late Sovereign Lady Queen Mary* followed D'Urfey's *Gloriana*, Congreve's *The Mourning Muse of Alexis,* and other elegies written for the same occasion. It was pub-

---

[1] *Apology*, I, 212.
[2] Leslie Hotson, *The Commonwealth and Restoration Stage* (Cambridge, U. S. A., 1928), p. 311.
[3] *Apology*, I, 196.

lished in June, 1695,[4] and dedicated to Cibber's former patron, now
Duke of Devonshire. "The succeeeding piece," Cibber wrote, "though
it be my first attempt in poetry, never gave me the usual pain and
cowardice of a young beginner; for I knew my reputation was as
safe under the protection of so great a name as my person under your
successful conduct at the time of His Majesty's happy landing."

The *Poem* conclusively demonstrates that the future laureate of
England had no talent for verse. Little more than an exercise in the
manner of Cowley, it is full of conventional language and frigid conceits. The best lines attempt the epigrammatic:

> For each religion did its faith enjoy,
> She one defended, but did none destroy,
> Unless to bring the day destruction be,
> When bigots wander in obscurity.

> Religious discord she might well prevent,
> For in example she was argument.

The worst attempt eloquence without ever rising above the common-
place:

> Look down, bright saint, from thine ethereal seat,
> And view the pious ruins of thy state,
> Assuage the torrent of our monarch's woe,
> Which o'er his drowning reason seems to flow,
> Return the hero's part that reigned in thee,
> When thou in smiles didst meet mortality,
> Teach him thy early fate, like thee, to bear,
> Nor let him woman in his griefs appear.

But perhaps one should not be too critical. At the time the poem
served its purpose—it was published, it was not unfavorably received,
and the young actor was encouraged to complete the manuscript of
his first play.

– 2 –

Love's Last Shift is a play which belongs to two traditions—the
tradition of the comedy of manners, which culminated in the work

---

[4] Arber, *Term Catalogues,* II, 559. Most of the other poems on the Queen's death
appeared earlier; see advertisements in the *London Gazette,* January 28-31 to May 16-20,
1695.

of Etherege and Congreve, and the sentimental tradition, which flour-
ished during the Elizabethan period in the bourgeois drama of Hey-
wood and reappeared during the Restoration in the work of such
writers as Shadwell, D'Urfey, and Mrs Behn.[5] The sentimental aspect
of the play has been emphasized—possibly overemphasized—by Croissant, who calls Cibber a deliberate reformer,[6] and by Bernbaum, who
credits him with the first significant expression of confidence in the
goodness of human nature.[7] But Croissant and Bernbaum are certainly
right in calling attention to the historical importance of the play, for
it is indeed a landmark in the history of English comedy. It came out
at a time when taste was changing—when wit and cynicism were
becoming less acceptable, when priggish characters, emotional scenes,
and obtrusive morality were beginning to appear. It was more sentimental than any earlier Restoration play; it was a brilliant success on
the stage; it probably influenced Steele, Vanbrugh, and Farquhar as
well as Cibber himself in later years. Hence in our time it has not
unnaturally come to be regarded as the first sentimental comedy.[8]

The main plot concerns the marital differences and ultimate reconciliation of a husband and a wife—Loveless and Amanda. In the early
scenes Loveless is a typical Restoration character. He is a Gargantuan
rake, coarser if anything than the Rover of Mrs Behn, entirely un-
troubled by the promptings of conscience. His servant reproaches him
for throwing away a pearl necklace on a Venetian strumpet and he
replies: "Why, sirrah, I knew I could not have her without it; and I
had a night's enjoyment of her was worth a pope's revenue for't."
"The world to me," he continues, "is a garden stocked with all sorts
of fruit, where the greatest pleasure we can take is in the variety of
taste: but a wife is an eternal apple-tree; after a pull or two you are
sure to set your teeth on edge." [9] Amanda, the eternal apple-tree, be-

---

[5] For the early history of sentimental comedy, see Nicoll, *Restoration Drama,* pp. 251-
67; also Kathleen M. Lynch, "Thomas D'Urfey's Contribution to Sentimental Comedy,"
Philological Quarterly, IX (1930), 249-59.

[6] DeWitt C. Croissant, *Studies in the Work of Colley Cibber,* reprinted from the
Bulletin of The University of Kansas, Humanistic Studies, Vol. I, No. 1 (Lawrence,
1912), p. 44.

[7] Ernest Bernbaum, *The Drama of Sensibility* (Cambridge, U. S. A., 1915), pp. 1-2,
72-77.

[8] Perhaps the most interesting recent discussion of the play is in F. W. Bateson,
English Comic Drama, 1700-1750 (Oxford, 1929), pp. 20-26.

[9] Cibber, *Love's Last Shift, or the Fool in Fashion* (1696), I, i.

longs to an entirely different tradition. She is represented as a "good" character; more properly perhaps she is not a character at all, she is simply an embodiment of virtue. Her conversation is sober, edifying, and dull, never for a moment deviating into wit. "All the comfort of my life," she says, "is that I can tell my conscience I have been true to virtue." [10] She is, in short, the typical pathetic heroine of sentimental fiction.

In the first scene Loveless returns from abroad. We learn that he left Amanda some eight years before and spent the intervening time whoring, drinking, and gaming in the capitals of Europe. His estate is now completely gone and he is compelled to borrow money from a friend in order to provide a dinner and a "brace of whores" for himself and his man. Amanda hears of his arrival and enters a plot (devised by Young Worthy) to win back his affections. She lures him to her apartment, appears before him as a lady of pleasure, and admits him to her bed for the night. (He fails to recognize her, partly because he believes her dead and partly because her face has been changed, though not for the worse, by smallpox.) In the morning she lectures him, awakens his sympathy, and finally tells him who she is. Loveless trembles and turns from her, "confounded" with guilt, but at last he finds words to express his emotion:

LOVELESS. I have wronged you. Oh! rise! basely wronged you! And can I see your face?

AMANDA. One kind, one pitying look cancels those wrongs for ever. And oh! forgive my fond presuming passion; for from my soul I pardon and forgive you all: all, all but this, the greatest, your unkind delay of love.

LOVELESS. Oh! seal my pardon with thy trembling lips, while with this tender grasp of fond reviving love I seize my bliss and stifle all thy wrongs for ever.   [Embraces her.]

AMANDA. No more; I'll wash away their memory in tears of flowing joy.

LOVELESS. Oh! thou hast roused me from my deep lethargy of vice; for hitherto my soul has been enslaved to loose desires, to vain deluding follies and shadows of substantial bliss; but now I wake with joy to find my rapture real.—Thus let me kneel and pay my thanks to her whose conquering virtue has at last subdued me. Here will I fix, thus prostrate sigh my shame, and wash away my crimes in never-ceasing tears of penitence. [11]

The whole scene is shamelessly sentimental, but—if a late tradition recorded by Tom Davies is trustworthy—it was very successful on

[10] *Ibid.*, I, iii.   [11] *Ibid.*, V, ii.

the stage. "Honest" tears were shed, and "never were spectators more happy in easing their minds by uncommon and repeated plaudits" [12]— plaudits which undoubtedly help to explain Cibber's later excursions into sentimental comedy.

Of the other characters, only one—the Elder Worthy—is sentimental; the rest belong entirely to the comedy of manners. Narcissa and Hillaria are typical coquettes; Young Worthy is the familiar fortune-hunter who has decided to purge out his wild humors with matrimony but who has "taken care to see the dose well sweetened with a swinging portion"; [13] Sir Novelty Fashion—the character written by Cibber for himself—is the most familiar of all, the type of Sir Fopling Flutter and Sir Courtly Nice—the "coxcomb that loves to be the first in all foppery." We first see him in the garden of Sir William Wisewou'd, paying extravagant compliments to Hillaria, but Narcissa flatters him and he immediately turns to her. "Pray, madam," he says, "how do I look today? What, cursedly? I'll warrant with a more hellish complexion than a stale actress at a rehearsal.—I don't know, madam— 'tis true—the town does talk of me indeed—but the devil take me, in my mind I'm a very ugly fellow." [14] He is of course fishing for more compliments and the ladies obligingly give him an opportunity to display his clothes. He discusses his suit with its ribbon trimming, his buttons which "are not above three inches diameter," his sleeves which reach but to his knuckles.

HILLARIA. Nay, I confess the fashion may be very useful to you gentlemen that make campaigns; for should you unfortunately lose an arm or so, that sleeve might be very convenient to hide the defect on't.

SIR NOVELTY. Ha! I think your ladyship's in the right on't, madam.

[Hiding his hand in his sleeve.]

NARCISSA. Oh! such an air! so becoming a negligence! Upon my soul, Sir Novelty, you'll be the envy of the beau monde.

His vanity is perfectly transparent, but he poses as a modest man. "Ladies," he says, "stop my vitals! I don't believe there are five hundred in town that ever took any notice of me." The outlines are drawn with a good deal of delicacy, and one feels that Sir Novelty is a real character. But the impression is immediately destroyed. He

[12] Davies, *Dramatic Miscellanies* (1783-84), III, 412.
[13] Cibber, *Love's Last Shift*, I, i.
[14] *Ibid.*, II, i, for quotations in this paragraph.

grows rude, he makes vulgar boasts, he stoops to pick up a fan and tumbles flat on his back. It is apparent that Cibber was interested less in creating a consistent coxcomb than in displaying himself as an actor in a variety of moods. He is capable of a few deft lines; but only a few. He writes for the actor and the audience, he cannot resist even the rough-and-tumble of farce.

Character Cibber cannot portray, but he is usually at his best in working up "big" climactic scenes. In the fourth act, for example, he is very effective in the scene in which Sir Novelty courts his kept mistress Flareit (whom he mistakes for Narcissa), while the fine ladies and gentlemen of the play, including Narcissa herself, look on from a place of concealment. "Generous creature," he begins, "this is an unexampled condescension, to meet my passion with such early kindness. Thus let me pay my soft acknowledgments." [15] And he kisses her hand.

FLAREIT. But will you never see the common creature Flareit more?
SIR NOVELTY. Never! never! Feed on such homely fare after so rich a banquet?
FLAREIT. Nay, but you must hate her too.
SIR NOVELTY. That I did long ago for her stinking breath. 'Tis true, I have been led away; but I detest a strumpet: I am informed she keeps a fellow under my nose, and for that reason I would not make the settlement I lately gave her some hopes of: but e'en let her please herself, for now I am wholly yours.
FLAREIT. Oh, now you charm me! but will you love me ever?
SIR NOVELTY. Will you be ever kind?
FLAREIT. Be sure you never see Flareit more.
SIR NOVELTY. When I do, may this soft hand revenge my perjury.
FLAREIT. So it shall, villain!
[*Strikes him a box on the ear and unmasks.*]

Sir Novelty holds his cheek, then realizing that he must brazen it out, "walks unconcerned." Flareit "snatches Young Worthy's sword and runs at him"; he "draws and stands upon his guard"; "Young Worthy takes the sword from her and holds her." "Let her come, let her come, gentlemen," exclaims Sir Novelty. But she abruptly retires, muttering the sentence later paraphrased and made famous by Congreve, "He shall find no fiend in hell can match the fury of a disappointed woman."

[15] *Ibid.*, IV, i, for quotations in this paragraph.

The scene is pure farce and Sir Novelty is a typical buffoon. But the first of the Loveless-Amanda scenes is even better, reminiscent indeed of the most exciting and amusing episodes in the Beaumont and Fletcher romances. The stage is half darkened as Loveless and his man Snap enter Amanda's house, conducted by Amanda's servant Sly. "Where the devil will this fellow lead me?" asks Loveless. "Nothing but silence and darkness—sure the house is haunted and he has brought me to face the spirit at his wonted hour!" [16] But a moment later he sees "a table, light, a night-gown, and a periwig lying by." He undresses and sits down to a meal which mysteriously arrives, while Snap hides under the table, solacing himself with a bottle of wine. A woman announces that "my lady" has been unavoidably detained, but almost immediately my lady appears, "loosely dressed." "Look up, my lord," she exclaims as she throws herself into her husband's arms, "and bless me with a tender look; and let my talking eyes inform thee how I have languished for thy absence." But when he answers, she pretends to realize that he is not "my lord," and calling her servants, she orders them to toss him in a blanket and turn him out of doors. Loveless, however, persuades her that one man is as good as another, and on these terms she accepts him for the night. When husband and wife have retired, Snap emerges from under the table and makes advances to Amanda's woman. To get rid of him, she leads him to a dark entry, opens a trapdoor, and pushes him into the cellar. But when she tries to shut the door, he catches hold of her and pulls her in, and they too remain together until morning.

The dialogue, except in the sentimental scenes, closely follows the traditions of the comedy of manners. But it is frothy rather than epigrammatic, deliberately shocking rather than cynical. It lacks the polish and the insight which one associates with the wit of Congreve and Etherege. "Ah! Will," says Loveless to Young Worthy, "you'll find marrying to cure lewdness is like surfeiting to cure hunger, for all the consequence is you loathe what you surfeit on and are only chaste to her you marry." [17] The remark follows an accepted formula, and may have been, no doubt was, extremely amusing on the stage; but it scarcely stands the test of quotation. Epigrams of the same sort are frequently given to the fine ladies and gentlemen of the play,

[16] *Ibid.*, IV, ii-iii, for quotations in this paragraph.   [17] *Ibid.*, I, i.

but few of them are successful and few are dramatically appropriate. In the park scene of the fourth act, Narcissa, Hillaria, and the two Worthys saunter down the walks and thus comment on the persons they meet:

> NARCISSA. Protect me! How can you see such a medley of human stuffs as here is without venting your spleen?—Why look there now; is not it comical to see that wretched creature there with her autumnal face, dressed in all the colors of the spring?
>
> ELDER WORTHY. Pray who is she, madam?
>
> NARCISSA. A thing that won't believe herself out of date, though she was a known woman at the Restoration.
>
> YOUNG WORTHY. Oh! I know her, 'tis Mrs Holdout, one that is proud of being an original of fashionable fornication and values herself mightily for being one of the first mistresses that ever kept her coach publicly in England.
>
> HILLARIA. Pray who's that impudent young fellow there?
>
> ELDER WORTHY. Oh! that's an eternal fan-tearer and a constant persecutor of womankind; he had a great misfortune lately.
>
> NARCISSA. Pray what was it?
>
> ELDER WORTHY. Why, impudently presuming to cuckold a Dutch officer, he had his foreteeth kicked out.
>
> OMNES. Ha, ha, ha! [18]

This is no doubt lively vulgarity, but one realizes at once that Narcissa and Hillaria are talking out of character. Elsewhere in the play they are represented as fine ladies, and here they are given the manners of the tavern and the brothel. It is curious that Cibber, who was soon to become famous for his scenes from high life, should in his first play have shown so little regard for the niceties of polite conversation.

As a whole the play is capital entertainment, but it has, one need scarcely point out, little relation to life or to art. It is a highly seasoned theatrical dish, compounded of naughtiness and sentimentality. The naughtiness is deliberate, it never expresses a point of view, and the sentimentality is too obviously insincere to be either edifying or convincing.

When Cibber finished *Love's Last Shift*—probably in the autumn of 1695—he read it to the dramatist Southerne, who good-naturedly recommended it to the patentees. It was produced, and on the night

[18] *Ibid.,* III, ii.

of the first performance Southerne took Cibber by the hand and said:
"Young man, I pronounce thy play a good one; I will answer for its
success if thou dost not spoil it by thy own action." [19] The evidence
suggests that Cibber did not, for the play became the sensation of the
year. The author of the *Comparison between the Two Stages* (1702)
describes it as the philosopher's stone, and goes on to say that "it did
wonders." "It's often acted nowadays," he continues, "and by the help
of the author's own good action it pleases to this day." [20]

Outside the theatre there were indeed a few unfavorable comments. Congreve remarked that the play had in it a great many things
that were *like* wit that in reality were *not* wit,[21] and Dryden was probably thinking of Sir Novelty Fashion when he ridiculed the beau of
the contemporary stage:

> You laugh not, gallants, as by proof appears,
> At what his beauship says, but what he wears;
> So 'tis your eyes are tickled, not your ears.
> The tailor and the furrier find the stuff,
> The wit lies in the dress and monstrous muff.
> The truth on't is, the payment of the pit
> Is like for like, clipped money for clipped wit.[22]

But on the whole critical opinion was distinctly favorable. The Earl
of Dorset congratulated Cibber by saying "that it was the best first
play that any author in his memory had produced, and that for a young
fellow to show himself such an actor and such a writer in one day
was something extraordinary." [23] The Earl of Dorset was perhaps too
good-natured to be entirely frank, but other critics were equally

---

[19] *Apology*, I, 213.   [20] *A Comparison between the Two Stages* (1702), p. 25.
[21] *Apology*, I, 220.
[22] John Dryden Jr., *The Husband His Own Cuckold* (1696), epilogue by John Dryden Sr. In *Restoration Drama*, p. 355, Nicoll gives January 1695/6 as the date of *Love's
Last Shift*, probably on the authority of Cibber himself (*Apology*, I, 213). But Cibber
had no memory for dates and probably adopted January, 1695, because the preface to
the first edition of the play was written in that month. On p. 360 Nicoll gives 1695
as the date of *The Husband His Own Cuckold*, on what authority I do not know. The
dedication—dated "Rome, August the 20th, 1695, New Style"—was (according to the
preface) written the summer before the play was published. *Love's Last Shift* was first
advertised in the *London Gazette* of February 10-13, 1696, *The Husband His Own
Cuckold* not until the issue of July 9-13; see Sybil Rosenfeld, "Dramatic Advertisements in the Burney Newspapers 1660-1700," *P. M. L. A.*, LI (1936) 123-52. It is
probable, therefore, that *Love's Last Shift* appeared before young Dryden's play.
[23] *Apology*, I, 214.

enthusiastic. Gildon (1699) spoke highly of the plot, describing it as new, surprising, and admirable. "Some of the critics," he says, "will have it founded on a very great improbability, viz. on Loveless's not knowing his wife . . . yet the beauty of the incident and the excellent moral that flows from it abundantly outweigh the fault." [24] The *Comparison between the Two Stages* (1702) also praises the play "for purity of plot, manners, and moral," [25] while Davies (1784) discusses it in terms which suggest Bernbaum and Croissant. "The first comedy acted since the Restoration," he says, "in which were preserved purity of manners and decency of language, with a due respect to the honor of the marriage bed, was Colley Cibber's *Love's Last Shift, or the Fool in Fashion.*" [26] Davies also argues that the play was the first modern comedy in which men and women of high quality were represented on the stage and given language and manners suitable to their rank and birth.[27] Davies once expressed this opinion in conversation with Dr Johnson, and Boswell, who was present, records that Johnson refuted him by pointing to several such characters in comedies before Cibber's time.[28] Johnson was undoubtedly right in saying that gentility did not originate with Cibber, but the particular type of moral-genteel character which Davies had in mind was indeed distinctively Cibberian, though it first appeared, not in *Love's Last Shift*, but in *The Careless Husband*.

Soon after the production of the play it was rumored that Cibber had not written but stolen it. The charge was frequently repeated throughout his lifetime,[29] and as late as 1742 an anonymous pamphleteer suggested that the real author was a certain R—rs, a relation of Cibber's who wrote the prologue.[30] But since the play bears the marks of Cibber's hand on almost every page, his own statements on the subject in the preface and in the *Apology* must be taken at their face value.

[24] Gerard Langbaine and Charles Gildon, *The Lives and Characters of the English Dramatic Poets* (1699), p. 20.
[25] *Comparison between the Two Stages*, p. 25.
[26] Davies, *Dramatic Miscellanies*, III, 409.   [27] *Ibid.*, III, 414.
[28] Boswell, *Life of Johnson*, ed. Hill (1887), II, 340.
[29] *Visits from the Shades*, pp. 25-26; John Dennis, *Original Letters, Familiar, Moral, and Critical* (1721), p. 140.
[30] *Sawney and Colley* (n. d.), p. 8 and note.

- 3 -

Elated by the success of *Love's Last Shift,* and eager to exploit his newly discovered talent, Cibber wrote a second comedy for production during the winter of 1696-97. It was originally called *Woman's Wit, or the Devil to Deal With,* [31] but the sub-title was later changed to *The Lady in Fashion,* probably to suggest a parallel, which is actually very slight, between the characters of Leonora and Sir Novelty.

The play was a complete failure, largely, Cibber himself admits, because of the haste with which it was written. "My first hindrance," he says in an introductory note to the first edition,

my first hindrance was want of time; for rather than lose a winter (the profits of my other [play] being so considerable) I forced myself to invent a fable. Now my first was spontaneous and consequently more easy: the one was the kindly product of my fancy, this of my judgment.... Another inconvenience was that during the time of my writing the two first acts I was entertained in the New Theatre, and of course prepared my characters to the taste of those actors; and they having the two most experienced, I might there (without discouraging the people of this house) have expected a more masterly performance.[32] In the middle of my writing the third act, not liking my station there, I returned again to the Theatre Royal, and was then forced as far as I could with nature to confine the business of my persons to the capacity of different people; and not to miss the advantage of Mr Doggett's excellent action, I prepared a low character which (though I dare not recommend it to the reader) I knew from him could not fail of diverting; I have seen him play with more success, I own, but ne'er saw any man wear a truer face of nature; and indeed the two last acts were much better performed than I could have proposed in that other house; the difference is only this, had it been there I had proposed some scenes more of a piece with the former acts: but however, the performance of the whole was better than my expectation from so thin, and I may add, so uncertain a company.

The lack of spontaneity which Cibber mentions is everywhere apparent in the play. The dialogue is flat, the character-drawing perfunctory, and the plot so improbable as to be utterly unconvincing. The acts written for Betterton's theatre develop a threadbare story of

---

[31] L.C. 7/3, printed in Nicoll, *Restoration Drama,* pp. 343-44.

[32] As published the play contains several jibes at Drury Lane: "There's brass for you! The rogue would make an admirable player in the old house." "Odsbud, I can no more resist him than a patentee can a pretty wench when she demands an unconscionable salary in the playhouse." Both speeches come from Act I.

intrigue, featuring the beautiful but heartless Leonora, who toys with the affections of Lord Lovemore. Longville tries to expose her by making love to her himself, while his friend Lovemore stands concealed behind a curtain, but Leonora evades the trap and completely outwits her adversary. Later the two friends fight a duel and Longville falls, but it soon appears that the pistols were not loaded. Further complications ensue when Leonora alters one letter, misdirects another, and appears before Longville in disguise. Act IV and much of Acts III and V are devoted to grossly farcical characters—Major Rakish and his son Young Rakish, acted by Penkethman and Powell, and the schoolboy Mass Johnny, acted by Doggett. The Rakishes are rivals in love and companions in debauchery; Mass Johnny plays tricks on his mother, Lady Manlove, and tries to marry Lettice, her maid. These scenes are even less acceptable to modern taste than those involving Leonora and Longville, but they seem to have been much more successful on the stage. In 1702 they were revived as an afterpiece, *The School-Boy, or the Comical Rivals,* and acted until the second half of the eighteenth century.[33]

Despite the failure of *Woman's Wit,* the season of 1696-97 was a memorable one for Cibber. In the autumn the young architect John Vanbrugh wrote, as a sequel to *Love's Last Shift,* his now famous comedy *The Relapse.* It has been called an answer to Cibber's play and indeed to some extent it is.[34] Loveless soon forgets his virtuous resolutions and falls in love with the beautiful and pliant Berinthia; later—in one of Vanbrugh's most daring scenes—he goes in the dark to Berinthia's chamber and carries her, softly screaming, to the couch in the closet. The incident is intentionally cynical, and so too is the characterization. Berinthia is quite unlike the innocent and somewhat insipid coquettes of Cibber: she is a lecherous widow who lives with Amanda, intrigues with Loveless, and acts as bawd for Worthy, whose mistress she has been. "I that love cards so well," she says in soliloquy, "—there is but one thing upon earth I love better...."[35] Sir Novelty

---

[33] Langbaine and Gildon, *English Dramatic Poets,* p. 20, and Nicoll, *Restoration Drama,* pp. 206, 267, find resemblances between *Woman's Wit* and two earlier plays— James Carlisle, *The Fortune Hunters* (1689), and William Mountfort, *Greenwich Park* (1691). But Cibber's indebtedness appears to be slight; see Croissant, *Studies in the Work of Colley Cibber,* pp. 17-18.

[34] Bernbaum, *Drama of Sensibility,* pp. 77-78.

[35] Vanbrugh, *Works,* ed. Bonamy Dobrée and Geoffrey Webb (1927), I, 68.

Fashion appears in the play under his new title of Lord Foppington, but in Vanbrugh's hands he has undergone a significant transformation. He is not so much a fool as a deliberate charlatan, who stuffs his periwig with extra ounces of hair because he thinks that it pays. He shows an almost sinister ugliness of temper in his relations with his brother as well as in his amours. "Dear Loveless," he begins in the drawing-room scene of the second act, "I am overjoyed to see you have braught your family to tawn again; I am, stap my vitals—[*Aside.*] Far I design to lie with your wife." [36] The brutal frankness of the aside would be quite out of place in Cibber, whose treatment of character is much more genial. Lord Foppington, in short, is a distinct creation. He is one of the last and one of the greatest triumphs of the Restoration spirit, suggested perhaps but not really anticipated by Sir Novelty in Cibber's play. [37]

The Relapse was brought out in November 1696, [38] and Cibber was of course chosen for the part of Lord Foppington. All authorities agree that he did it brilliantly—so brilliantly, in fact, that even the patentees of the theatre were now convinced that he was one of their finest actors. The year before they had admired his Sir Novelty Fashion, but they had not been sufficiently sure of his ability to trust him with other good parts. When they saw him as Lord Foppington, however— saw him trying on the suit with the immoderately low pocket and admiring himself before the mirrors, saw him preciously taking snuff from his fashionable snuffbox, saw him bickering with Foretop over the periwig that was so large, Pope tells us, that it was usually carried on the stage in a sedan chair [39]—they could doubt no longer, and they soon permitted him to take over Sparkish, Sir Fopling Flutter, Sir Courtly Nice, and the other fops of the Restoration theatre.

The Grisoni portrait of Cibber as Lord Foppington suggests that he entered completely into the spirit of the character, portraying as perfectly as Vanbrugh's text the vulgar impostor affecting the foppery

---

[36] *Ibid.*, I, 36.

[37] Bateson, *English Comic Drama, 1700-1750*, p. 25, remarks that Sir Novelty's "fopperies and affectations are merely a deliberate experiment in self-advertisement." The remark applies to Lord Foppington but not, I think, to Sir Novelty.

[38] Hotson, *Commonwealth and Restoration Stage*, pp. 307, 377.

[39] Pope, *Works*, ed. Whitwell Elwin and William John Courthope (1871-89), IV, 116, note. Pope is probably wrong in suggesting that the periwig was carried on the stage in *Love's Last Shift*.

of the fashionable world. But one can perhaps read too much into a picture and it is safer to refer to descriptions of Cibber's acting, of which the best—Aaron Hill's—belongs to a later period.

As to his person [Hill says], his shape was finely proportioned yet not graceful, easy but not striking. Though it was reported by his enemies that he wanted a soul, yet it was visible enough that he had one, because he carried it in his countenance; for his features were narrowly earnest and attentively insignificant. There was a peeping pertness in his eye, which would have been spirit had his heart been warmed with humanity or his brain been stored with ideas. In his face was a contracted kind of passive yet protruded sharpness, like a pig half roasted; and a voice not unlike his own might have been borrowed from the same suffering animal while in a condition a little less desperate. With all these comic accomplishments of person, he had an air and a mind which completed the risible talent, insomuch that, when he represented a ridiculous humor, he had a mouth in every nerve and became eloquent without speaking. His attitudes were pointed and exquisite, and his expression was stronger than painting; he was beautifully absorbed by the character, and demanded and monopolized attention; his very extravagances were colored with propriety; and affectation sat so easy about him that it was in danger of appearing amiable.[40]

Having learned that he could not write under pressure, Cibber devoted two years to his third play, *Xerxes*. But his industry was ill-repaid, for the play proved to be as worthless and as unsuccessful as *Woman's Wit*. It owes something to Dryden and something to Otway, but like many tragedies of the period, it never rises above melodrama. In the first act Xerxes returns from Greece, celebrates victories he has not won, and huffs the gods. In the second, he decides to violate "a married beauty of untainted virtue," and singles out Tamira for his purpose. In the third, Tamira's husband Artabanus is caught in an abortive rebellion and Tamira herself is tortured and "brought in all bloody." In the fifth, Tamira enters "plundered, her hair and clothes disordered; the rabble with her child, she striving to recover it." "They drag her by the hair" until help arrives, when "they set down the child, which runs into her arms." [41] In the last scene blood flows freely; Xerxes and Artabanus kill one another and Tamira stabs herself with her husband's sword. The author of *The Laureat* reports —and one can well believe him—that the play was rejected by Cibber's

---

[40] *Prompter,* November 19, 1734.
[41] Quotations from Cibber, *Xerxes* (1699), II, i; III, iii; V, iii.

fellow actors at Drury Lane. It was then taken to Lincoln's Inn Fields, Cibber pawning "his credit for money to answer the charges if it should not succeed and be able to answer its own expenses at that theatre." [42] It was damned on the first night and never revived.[43]

- 4 -

For several reasons—among which one must include the failure of *Xerxes* and *Woman's Wit,* and the attack on the dramatists which followed the publication of Collier's *Short View of the Immorality and Profaneness of the English Stage*—Cibber stopped doing original work and in 1700 tried his hand at adaptation. He says in a famous passage in the *Apology:*

It may be observable too that my muse and my spouse were equally prolific, that the one was seldom the mother of a child but in the same year the other made me the father of a play. I think we had a dozen of each sort between us; of both which kinds some died in their infancy and near an equal number of each were alive when I quitted the theatre. But it is no wonder when a muse is only called upon by family duty she should not always rejoice in the fruit of her labor. To this necessity of writing, then, I attribute the defects of my second play, which coming out too hastily the year after my first turned to very little account. But having got as much by my first as I ought to have expected from the success of them both, I had no great reason to complain. Not but I confess so bad was my second that I do not choose to tell you the name of it, and that it might be peaceably forgotten I have not given it a place in the two volumes of those I published in quarto in the year 1721. And whenever I took upon me to make some dormant play of an old author to the best of my judgment fitter for the stage, it was honestly not to be idle that set me to work, as a good housewife will mend old linen when she has not better employment.[44]

This desire to be useful need not be regretted in Cibber, for under its influence he produced in 1700 two excellent acting plays—*The Tragical History of Richard III* and *Love Makes a Man.*

The famous adaptation of *Richard III* has been so frequently and so competently discussed by historians of the drama that a brief description of it here should suffice.[45] Cibber is principally interested in

[42] *The Laureat,* p. 102.   [43] *Tatler,* ed. George A. Aitken (1899), I, 346.
[44] *Apology,* I, 264-65.
[45] See John Genest, *Some Account of the English Stage from the Restoration in 1660 to 1830* (Bath, 1832), II, 195-219; George C. D. Odell, *Shakespeare from Betterton to Irving* (New York, 1920), I, 75-76; A. I. P. Wood, *The Stage History of Shake-*

tightening up the structure of the play. He leaves out purely lyrical passages, and—in order to focus attention on Richard—leaves out such characters as Margaret, Edward IV, Clarence, and Hastings. At the same time he clarifies the action by introducing asides, soliloquies, and expository passages. His workmanship is by no means flawless, but on the whole he undoubtedly succeeds in making the play simpler, clearer, and "fitter" for the stage.

His method is in general one of omission, but he occasionally permits himself to add new scenes to the play. Thus in the first act he gives us, instead of the death of Edward IV and the murder of Clarence, the murder of Henry VI, taken of course from the last of the Henry VI plays. The substitution is appropriate enough, for the new material is even more sensational than the material which it replaces and furthermore it helps to explain much that would otherwise be unintelligible in a play which, in its original form, is not quite self-contained. Again in the fourth act he heightens the melodrama by having the princes smothered on the stage. The horror is certainly somewhat dreary, but one hesitates to say that it is out of place in this rather dreary play.[46] And finally Cibber adds a scene for which there is no authority in Shakespeare—a scene in which Richard brutally dismisses his wife and announces that he is in love with the "fair Elizabeth." Throughout the play he is at pains to make the character of Richard as ogreish as possible, and here he goes out of his way to add lust to Richard's other vices. "Ha!" says the villain aside, when he finds Lady Anne weeping,

> Ha! still in tears; let 'em flow on; they're signs
> Of a substantial grief.—Why don't she die?
> She must: my interest will not let her live.
> The fair Elizabeth has caught my eye,
> My heart's vacant; and she shall fill her place.—
> They say that women have but tender hearts:
> 'Tis a mistake, I doubt; I've found 'em tough:
> They'll bend, indeed: but he must strain that cracks 'em.
> All I can hope's to throw her into sickness:
> Then I may send her a physician's help.

speare's *Richard III* (New York, 1909), pp. 77-91; Hazelton Spencer, *Shakespeare Improved* (Cambridge, U. S. A., 1927), pp. 335-38.

[46] The passage was later rewritten; see Arthur Colby Sprague, "A New Scene in Colley Cibber's *Richard III,*" *Modern Language Notes,* XLII (1927), 29-32.

So, madam. What, you still take care I see
To let the world believe I love you not;
This outward mourning now has malice in't;
So have these sullen disobedient tears:
I'll have you tell the world I dote on you.
LADY ANNE. I wish I could, but 'twill not be believed:
Have I deserved this usage?
RICHARD. You have: you do not please me as at first.
LADY ANNE. What have I done? What horrid crime committed?
RICHARD. To me the worst of crimes—outlived my liking.
LADY ANNE. If that be criminal, just heaven be kind,
And take me while my penitence is warm:
O sir, forgive, and kill me.
RICHARD. Umh! No—the meddling world will call it murder,
And I would have 'em think me pitiful . . .
LADY ANNE. Thy vows of love to me were all dissembled.
RICHARD. Not one: for when I told thee so, I loved:
Thou art the only soul I never yet deceived:
And 'tis my honesty that tells thee now
With all my heart, I hate thee.—
If this have no effect, she is immortal.   [*Aside*.] [47]

The dialogue of the play—which is not unfairly represented by this scene—is of course wretchedly poor. Cibber has no ear for verse, no sense of character, and when he attempts a figure of speech he nearly always falls into deplorable absurdities. Consider, for example, the passage—singled out for ridicule by Genest—in which spiders are represented crawling upon hopes:

> I tell thee, cuz, I've lately had two spiders
> Crawling upon my startled hopes: now though
> Thy friendly hand has brushed 'em from me,
> Yet still they crawl offensive to my eyes;
> I would have some friend to tread upon 'em.[48]

How incredible! but how characteristically Cibberian! Cibber has often been censured for introducing into the play lines from *Henry IV* and *Henry V,* but when one remembers the horrors of his own lines, one is almost thankful for the interpolations. In the first edition he prints Shakespeare's lines in italics, and marks thoughts which he has paraphrased from Shakespeare with inverted commas. He does not—

[47] Cibber, *The Tragical History of King Richard III* (n. d.), III, i.
[48] *Ibid.,* IV, ii.

one is surprised to notice—claim originality for his most famous contribution to the play, "Off with his head! So much for Buckingham." [49]

It is well known that Cibber's adaptation had an extremely long life on the stage, but for one reason or another it was not very successful when it first appeared.[50] *"Richard III,* which I altered from Shakespeare," Cibber himself says in the preface to *Ximena,* "did not raise me £5 on the third day," [51] and in a later work he attributes its failure to the officious interference of the Master of the Revels, who "expunged the whole first act without sparing a line of it. This extraordinary stroke of a *sic volo* occasioned my applying to him for the small indulgence of a speech or two, that the other four acts might limp on with a little less absurdity. No! he had not leisure to consider what might be separately inoffensive. He had an objection to the whole act, and the reason he gave for it was that the distresses of King Henry VI, who is killed by Richard in the first act, would put weak people too much in mind of King James, then living in France; a notable proof of his zeal for the government! Those who have read either the play or the history, I dare say will think he strained hard for the parallel. In a word, we were forced for some few years to let the play take its fate with only four acts divided into five." [52]

But even the four acts might perhaps have been more favorably received, had not Cibber ill-advisedly chosen to play the title-part himself. In the *Apology* he tells us that he took particular pains to imitate the manner of the distinguished actor Sandford, and he goes on to say that Vanbrugh found the imitation perfect in look, gesture, gait, and speech.[53] But less charitable critics assure us that there was considerably more of Lord Foppington than of Sandford in the performance. Thus the author of the *Laureat* says:

He screamed through four acts without dignity or decency. The audience, ill-pleased with the farce, accompanied him with a smile of contempt; but in the fifth act he degenerated all at once into Sir Novelty; and when in the heat of the battle at Bosworth Field the King is dismounted, our comic-tragedian came on the stage, really breathless, and in a seeming panic screaming out this line thus—"A harse, a harse, my kingdom for a harse."

[49] See Spencer, *Shakespeare Improved,* p. 337.
[50] For the stage history of Cibber's adaptation, see Wood, *Stage History of Richard III.*
[51] Cibber, *Ximena, or the Heroic Daughter* (1719), preface "To the Reader."
[52] *Apology,* I, 275-76.   [53] *Ibid.,* I, 139-40.

This highly delighted some and disgusted others of his auditors; and when he was killed by Richmond, one might plainly perceive that the good people were not better pleased that so *execrable a tyrant* was destroyed than that so *execrable an actor* was silent.[54]

This somewhat malicious account is confirmed by Aaron Hill, who at a later period speaks of "the comic shruggings," "the unseasonable grimaces," the "low, mincing curtails of magnanimity," and "the distorted heavings of an unjointed caterpillar" in Cibber's Richard; [55] and by a writer in the *Grub Street Journal,* who says:

When [Cibber] makes love to Lady Anne, he looks like a pickpocket, with his shrugs and grimaces, that has more a design on her purse than her heart; and his utterance is in the same cast with his action. In Bosworth Field he appears no more like King Richard than King Richard was like Falstaff: he foams, struts, and bellows with the voice and cadence of a watchman rather than a hero and a prince.[56]

But though *Richard III* failed on its first appearance, Cibber was not discouraged, and during the next ten years he made repeated attempts to get the play upon the stage. As early as 1702 he persuaded the patentees to offer the suppressed act as part of a "medley," which was also to include *The School-Boy* and select scenes from *Aesop.* The performance is advertised in the *Daily Courant* of October 21:

For the benefit of Will. Penke[th]man.
On Saturday the 24th instant will be acted several new dramatic entertainments called *The Medley;* the first being a tragical interlude of one act only called *The Death of King Henry VI.* The second several select scenes in the comedy of *Aesop;* and the last is a short comedy of two acts called *The School-Boy, or the Comical Rivals:* in all which the several parts of Crookbacked Richard, the Beau, and the Schoolboy will be performed by Mr Cibber; and the Genealogist and the Country Gentleman with his hounds, and Major Rakish, one of the rivals, by William Penke[th]man.

But the Master of the Revels seems to have reiterated his objections to the Henry VI scene, for on Friday, October 23, the medley performance was canceled, and *Love Makes a Man* announced for Penkethman's benefit. The *Daily Courant* notes:

The tickets which were given out for his benefit on Saturday will be received for this play on Monday, both day and play that was put in

[54] *The Laureat,* p. 35.   [55] *Prompter,* November 19, 1734.
[56] *Grub Street Journal,* October 31, 1734.

Wednesday's *Courant* being altered, at the desire of several persons of quality.

The next season Cibber offered *Richard III* for his own benefit, April 4, 1704, but whether the first act was included or not, it is impossible to say. Successful and apparently complete performances were, however, given in 1710, and in 1713 the play proved so popular that it earned a permanent place in the repertory of Drury Lane. It held the stage without much alteration until the middle of the nineteenth century, and even in our own time parts of it, particularly the first act, have been incorporated in performances of Shakespeare's play.

Love Makes a Man, or the Fop's Fortune also owes its material to the Elizabethans, the first two acts coming from Fletcher's *Elder Brother* and the last three from the same author's *Custom of the Country*.[57] *The Elder Brother* tells the story of a bookish young man who is at first insensible to the charms of love but who is finally awakened from his academic slumber in time to claim and prove himself worthy of a mistress. Cibber drops the play at this point and takes up *The Custom of the Country,* where lovers are escaping (in Fletcher from a very real evil sufficiently indicated in the title of the play). The lovers are separated, a typical Fletcher virago appears, and everyone is in imminent danger until of course in the last act the virago reforms. Cibber joins the two sets of scenes satisfactorily enough, at the same time excising the ribaldry, toning down the romance, and providing more opportunities for farcical business on the stage. But his most important change is to shape the characters to the abilities of particular actors in his company and incidentally to add a good many lines in the style of the comedy of manners. He is notably successful with Don Lewis, perhaps the best of many parts written for the farcical actor Will Penkethman, and with the fop Clodio, written of course for himself. Clodio wears swordknots and a fashionable sword, uses pulvillio and essence on his peruke, and boasts of his distinguished acquaintances in Paris. But he has also been in London and in one

[57] See Genest, *Some Account of the English Stage,* II, 229-32; Croissant, *Studies in the Work of Colley Cibber,* pp. 18-19, 48-49; Ashley H. Thorndike, *English Comedy* (New York, 1929), pp. 353-54.

scene—the topical allusions are characteristic—he describes his experiences in the greenrooms.

DON DUART. I find, sir, you know England then.

CLODIO. Ay, sir, and every woman there that's worth knowing, from honest Betty Sands to the Countess of Ogletown. Yes, sir, I do know London pretty well, and the side-box, sir, and behind the scenes, ay, and the greenroom too, and all the girls and women-actresses there, sir.—Sir, I was a whole winter there the particular favorite of the giggling party.— Come, sir, if you please, here's Miss Riggle's health to you.

DON DUART. Pray, sir, how came you so well acquainted there?

CLODIO. Why, sir, I first introduced myself with a single pinch of bergamot; the next night I presented 'em a boxful; next day came to rehearsal: in a week I desired 'em to use my name whenever they pleased for what the chocolate house afforded. Upon this I was chosen Valentine, if I don't mistake, to about eleven of 'em, and in three days more I think it cost me fifty guineas in gloves, knots, heads, fans, muffs, coffee, tea, snuffboxes, orangerie, and chocolate.

DON DUART. But, pray, sir, were you as intimate at both playhouses?

CLODIO. No, stretch 'em! at the new house they are so used to be queens and princesses, and are so often in their airs-royal, forsooth, that, egad! there's no reaching one of their coppertails there without a long pole or a settlement, split me! [58]

Such scenes as this perfectly illustrate Congreve's dictum on *Love's Last Shift*. The dialogue is not perhaps genuinely witty, but it is somewhat like wit. It is pert, lively, vivacious, and one realizes that, despite its shortcomings in the library, it must have been remarkably effective on the stage.

Love Makes a Man was produced on or about December 9, 1700.[59] It ran well for three nights, "lagged" on the fourth, and revived on the fifth only when it was supported by French tumblers, who, Cibber says, "forced the town to see it till it laughed itself into their good graces." [60] Cibber might have added that on the fifth night the tumblers themselves encountered some opposition. As they were giving a scaramouch dance between the second and third acts, "a certain person went in a frolic, incognito, up into the upper gallery, and so pelted [them] with oranges that they were forced to quit the stage." The playhouse was in an uproar; "but some of the auditory perceiving

[58] Cibber, *Love Makes a Man, or the Fop's Fortune* (1701), IV, iv.
[59] Hotson, *Commonwealth and Restoration Stage,* p. 378.
[60] Cibber, *Ximena,* preface.

who threw [the oranges] cried out, 'Fling him into the pit,' which so startled him that he was forced to make the best of his way downstairs; however, a constable having been sent for in the meantime, he was secured and ... sent to the Gatehouse." [61]

This disturbance apparently caused a good deal of comment, for it occurred at a time when feeling against the theatre was running high—occurred, in fact, just after the infamous murder of Sir Andrew Slanning.

Sir Andrew is described by the newspapers as a gentleman of £1,500 a year in Devonshire. On November 18, 1700, he was witnessing a performance at Drury Lane, when he had "some words" with a certain John Cowland. The two men went to the Rose Tavern, apparently to settle their dispute in a private room, but as they were ascending the stairs Cowland drew his sword and ran Sir Andrew through the body. The wound proved mortal, and Cowland was seized, tried, and convicted of willful murder. The verdict was an unusually popular one, and as a special concession to the mob Cowland was brought to Tyburn two hours before the other criminals sentenced for the same day and executed by himself.[62]

Respectable citizens were naturally horrified by the Slanning murder, but their animosity, unlike the mob's, was directed less at Cowland than at the theatre. The case, they knew, was not an isolated one, and they felt that similar cases would continue to arise as long as the more disreputable elements of the town were permitted to gather daily at various places of amusement. They therefore brought the matter to the attention of the Grand Jury of Middlesex, apparently recommending that both theatres, as well as the Bear Garden, be permanently closed. The jurymen had no sooner met and begun their deliberations than reports reached them of the riot at *Love Makes a Man*. If before they had doubted the wisdom of suppressing plays, they could doubt it no longer, and they at once drafted a sweeping presentment of Drury Lane, Lincoln's Inn Fields, and Hockley-in-the-Hole, later published in two London newspapers—the *Post Man* and the *Flying Post* of December 17-19, 1700:

---

[61] *London Post*, December 13-16, 1700; also *English Post* of the same date.

[62] *Post Boy*, November 19-21, 1700, November 21-23, etc. There are many references to the case in the newspapers of the Burney Collection.

We the Grand Jury of the County of Middlesex do present that the plays which are frequently acted in the playhouses in Drury Lane and Lincoln's Inn Fields in this county are full of profane, irreverent, lewd, indecent, and immoral expressions, and tend to the great displeasure of Almighty God, and to the corruption of the auditory both in their principles and practices. We also present that the common acting of plays in the said playhouses very much tend to the debauching and ruining the youth resorting thereto, and to the breach of the peace, and are the occasions of many riots, routs, and disorderly assemblies, whereby many murders and other misdemeanors have been frequently done, and particularly the barbarous murder of Sir Andrew Slanning, which was very lately committed as he came out of one of the said playhouses; and further that the common acting of plays at the said playhouses is a public nuisance. As also the Bear Garden in Hockley-in-the-Hole, in the Parish of St John's Clerkenwell, in the said county, to be of the like nuisance. We hope this honorable court will use the most effectual and speedy means for the suppressing thereof.[63]

The history of legal attacks upon the London stage is of course a long one, and this presentment is not even the first attack of the sort during the period which immediately followed the Collier controversy. For two years—ever since the appearance of Collier's *Short View,* in fact—the Court of King's Bench had made a practice of fining actors "for using profanely and jestingly the name of God upon the stage." Krutch records several such cases,[64] and at least two others are mentioned in the *Flying Post* (June 13-15 and November 28-30, 1700). The grand jury had also taken action before: a presentment in 1698 is recorded by Krutch,[65] and a second presentment is thus described in the *Flying Post* of May 18-21, 1700:

The Grand Jury of London made a presentation last sessions against frequenting playhouses, as a public nuisance and a dangerous and growing evil, corrupting the morals and principles of the youth, and desired that playhouse bills might not be henceforth posted up in the City. Several persons [the *Flying Post* adds] were fined last week for selling bawdy pictures and boxes.

But the presentment of December, 1700, seems to have been more telling than any previous blow directed at the stage, partly because

[63] This presentment, as well as other material from the newspapers, has recently been reprinted in Alfred Jackson, "The Stage and the Authorities, 1700-1714 (as revealed in the Newspapers)," *Review of English Studies,* XIV (1938), 53-62.

[64] Joseph Wood Krutch, *Comedy and Conscience after the Restoration* (New York, 1924), pp. 167-76.

[65] *Ibid.,* p. 169.

it appeared immediately after the Slanning case and partly because it recommended the complete suppression of the theatre. It fanned into flame for several weeks the dying embers of the Collier controversy and evoked an angry reply from Cibber, who, voicing the opinions of his fellow actors, attacked citizens in general and grand juries in particular. In the dedication to *Love Makes a Man* (published January 22, 1701) he contemptuously referred to the "formidable zeal of a presenting Middlesex jury," and went on to say (the violence of his language was perhaps under the circumstances excusable):

Avarice, Hypocrisy, and Ignorance have thrown off their short cloaks, spit in their paws, and are everyone resolved to have a blow at the root of the bay tree, and when it's down, like brethren, they are to share it among 'em. . . . But this we are not to wonder at; for there are among us a sort of gentlemen that have been used to *lopping,* that know how to handle an *axe,* and I think the last time they pulled down the *stage* in the city, they set up a *scaffold* at court; perhaps they are not now the less our enemies because the King's authority supports us. . . . It has been always observable that they who can't endure a prince on the theatre have not been very apt to like him on the throne. So that at worst our comfort is that when we can't be quietly players, we still dare, (as some of our predecessors did) stir and be loyal.

Cibber had, as far as I am aware, the last word in the controversy. The citizens neglected to press their attack on the theatres, and the presentment, though "very favorably" received by the court, was quickly forgotten.

– 5 –

The success of *Love Makes a Man* apparently encouraged Cibber to return to original composition, for in 1702 and 1704 he produced two of his best original plays, *She Would and She Would Not* and *The Careless Husband*.

She Would and She Would Not is a comedy of intrigue, possibly derived from a Spanish source.[66] The chief characters are Don Philip and his mistress Hypolita, Octavio and *his* mistress Rosara, Trappanti

---

[66] The plot may have been taken from John Leanerd, *The Counterfeits* (1679). Croissant, however, suggests (*Studies in the Work of Colley Cibber*, p. 19) that the two plays had a common source—"The Trepanner Trepanned" in John Davies, *La Picara, or the Triumphs of Female Subtilty* (1665). It is also possible that the version of the story used by Cibber has not yet been identified.

(a roguish servant), and Don Manuel (Rosara's father). Don Philip proposes marriage to Hypolita, but—feeling that he presumes too much on his rank and fortune—she rejects him. Nevertheless she loves him, and when he goes to Madrid to marry Rosara, she follows him disguised as a man, steals his portmanteau and credentials, hires his former servant Trappanti, and impersonates him before Rosara and Don Manuel. Octavio also goes to Madrid, to break off Don Philip's marriage and, if possible, to arrange an elopement with Rosara.

Out of this situation many amusing and surprising complications develop. Octavio disguises himself as a friar and interviews his mistress, but he is discovered by Don Manuel and ejected from the house. In the street outside he meets Hypolita dressed as a young gallant. He draws his sword and forces her into a duel, but she is almost immediately rescued by an alguazile. Don Philip introduces himself at the house and claims Rosara, but he is coldly received by Don Manuel, who has been warned against an impostor. The young man then forces Trappanti to confess his rogueries, but when an officer of the law appears, Trappanti recants and supports the story of his new employer Hypolita. Later Don Philip wrings a confession from Hypolita herself, but in company she too recants and Don Philip is thrust into the cellar. Finally Hypolita marries Rosara, admits that she is not the true Don Philip, and offers to have the marriage annulled if Don Manuel will give the bride to Octavio. Don Manuel is only too glad to make the promise, and Hypolita, revealing her identity, throws herself into Don Philip's arms.

The material, as one can see from this brief summary, is thoroughly conventional, but it is used in the play with remarkable effectiveness. The construction could scarcely be better. Each character—as Cibber himself points out in the prologue—each character plays a part in unfolding the story, each incident develops naturally out of the situation outlined in the first act. The dialogue is adequate if not witty ("No scenes of talk for talking's sake are shown"), and the characters are in each case carefully prepared for particular members of Cibber's company. Trappanti, written for Penkethman, is an excellent acting part, and so too is Don Manuel, written for Cibber himself. But the best of all the parts in the play, and perhaps the best Cibber ever wrote, is Hypolita, acted by the versatile Mrs Verbruggen. In scene after scene

Hypolita displays her coquetry, her daring, her timidity, her quick-wittedness, and finally, in the big scene of the fourth act, she runs through her whole gamut of emotions, changing from one to another with almost bewildering rapidity. "I shall expect to see you early to-morrow near the Prado with your sword in your hand," she says to Don Philip when she finds herself alone with him. But to her consternation he locks the door and insists on fighting at once. At first she tries to excuse herself on the ground that the time and place are inappropriate, but when he seizes her and holds his sword at her breast, she can only confess that she dare not fight him. "Have pity on my youth, have pity on my love!" she cries, and she proceeds to tell him an artful story of "the pangs and torments of a successless passion"—the story of a passion not unlike his own. As he listens, as he hears her describe the cold relentless disdain of her proud mistress, his anger disappears and he raises her from the ground. But he still insists that she reveal her plot, and when she hesitates, he again threatens her with his sword. This time, however, she does not yield, for she has heard sounds at the door. She breaks from him, draws, and pretends to fight, while Don Manuel and his servants rush in to protect her.

DON MANUEL. Nay, dear son, hold; we'll find a better way to punish him.
HYPOLITA. Pray, sir, give me way—a villain, to assault me in the very moment of my happiness! [*Struggling.*]
DON PHILIP. By heaven, sir, he this moment has confessed his villainy and begged my pardon upon his knees.
HYPOLITA. D'ye hear him, sir? I beg you let me go, this is beyond bearing.
DON PHILIP. Thou liest, villain; 'tis thy fear that holds thee.
HYPOLITA. Ha! Let me go, I say.
DON MANUEL. Force him out of the room there; call an officer; in the meantime secure him in the cellar.... Stop his mouth—out with him.
[*They hurry him off.*] [67]

And so Hypolita escapes and Don Philip is sent to the cellar. The scene develops a striking situation and at the same time exploits, with a good deal of technical virtuosity, the talent of the most gifted comic actress in Cibber's company.

One of the early scenes—that in which Hypolita orders a dinner at the inn—is apparently borrowed from Fletcher's *Love's Pilgrimage*. Cibber's version reads:

[67] Cibber, *She Would and She Would Not, or the Kind Impostor* (1703), IV, ii.

Host. Did you call, gentlemen?

Trappanti. Yes and bawl too, sir. Here, the gentlemen are almost famished, and nobody comes near 'em. What have you in the house now that will be ready presently?

Host. You may have what you please, sir.

Hypolita. Can you get us a partridge?

Host. Sir, we have no partridges. But we'll get you what you please in a moment. We have a very good neck of mutton, sir; if you please it shall be clapped down in a moment.

Hypolita. Have you no pigeons or chickens?

Host. Truly, sir, we have no fowl in the house at present. If you please, you may have anything else in a moment.

Hypolita. Then prithee get us some young rabbits.

Host. Upon my word, sir, rabbits are so scarce they are not to be had for money.

Flora. Have you any fish?

Host. Fish! Sir, I dressed only yesterday the finest dish that ever came upon a table; I am sorry we have none left, sir; but, if you please, you may have anything else in a moment.

Trappanti. Pox on thee, hast thou nothing but anything elses in the house?

Host. Very good mutton, sir.

Hypolita. Prithee get us a breast then.

Host. Breast! Don't you love the neck, sir?

Hypolita. Have you nothing in the house but the neck?

Host. Really, sir, we don't use to be so unprovided, but at present we have nothing else left.[68]

With a few changes and improvements the scene was later used by Farquhar in the first act of his masterpiece, *The Beaux' Stratagem.*

In the dedication to *She Would and She Would Not* Cibber tells us that the play had a favorable reception, and from the author of *Visits from the Shades* we learn that one of the songs became extremely popular. "Of late," says this malicious critic addressing Cibber, "we have been disturbed by a shoal of seamstresses, whores, and shoplifts, with a gang of highwaymen, pickpockets, and footboys a-humming your *Caelia my Heart.*" [69] But the play's reception was not, it seems, too favorable, for Cibber elsewhere says that the sixth (and probably the last) performance was so poorly attended that he was unable to pay the charges of the house.[70] Like *Richard III,* how-

[68] *Ibid.,* I, i.   [69] *Visits from the Shades,* p. 24.
[70] Cibber, *Ximena,* preface.

ever, the play was successfully revived a decade later, and from this time until the middle of the nineteenth century it enjoyed distinguished popularity at both the London theatres. It was a favorite piece with the Daly company in New York as late as 1886; John Drew acted Don Philip and Ada Rehan, Hypolita.

If *She Would and She Would Not* is on the whole the best of the Cibber plays, *The Careless Husband* is the most original and the most interesting from the historical point of view. It played an important part in the development of sentimental comedy, adumbrated in Cibber's own *Love's Last Shift* and taken up by Steele in *The Lying Lover,* and it helped to fix standards of gentility and politeness which were profoundly to influence comic writing throughout most of the eighteenth century.[71]

Superficially at least the play is a reworking of *Love's Last Shift.* The subject is again infidelity and reconciliation, and the chief characters are a rake, a faithful wife, a fop, and a coquette. But the general atmosphere is much more sentimental, the moral point of view more consistently maintained; there is no jarring contrast between the naughtiness of the first acts and the tearfulness of the last. When Sir Charles Easy first appears on the stage, we see at once that he is not fundamentally a rake. He is bored and from sheer boredom he has drifted into an intrigue with Lady Graveairs. But he soon breaks with this importunate mistress only to fall from grace with Edging, his wife's maid. This painfully low connection, however, is even more disturbing to a man of his sensibilities, and when his wife finds him (without his periwig!) asleep near Edging and lays a steinkirk upon his head to protect him from the "unwholesome air," he realizes that she is aware of his infidelities. "It must be so!" he exclaims when he awakens. "She certainly has seen me here sleeping with her woman.— If so, how low an hypocrite to her must that sight have proved me! The thought has made me despicable even to myself.—How mean a vice is lying and how often have these empty pleasures lulled my honor and my conscience to a lethargy!"[72] A reconciliation scene naturally

[71] Excellent discussions of this play and its importance in the development of sentimental comedy are found in Croissant, *Studies in the Work of Colley Cibber,* pp. 19-20, 49-52; Bernbaum, *Drama of Sensibility,* pp. 91-94; Thorndike, *English Comedy,* pp. 354-56; Bateson, *English Comic Drama, 1700-1750,* pp. 26-31.
[72] Cibber, *The Careless Husband* (1705), V, v.

follows (if anything is natural in sentimental comedy) and Sir Charles
realizes at last that his deepest feelings find expression only in love
for his wife.

The other characters receive similar treatment; all help to illustrate
the moral point of view, all are pretty definitely labeled as good or bad.
Lord Foppington, for example, comes close to being a villain. His
principles are shocking, his conduct is often entirely odious. He brutally
mistreats his wife, who happens to be a "well-bred" and "very prudent"
woman, and carries on a series of shamelessly cold-blooded amours.
When he is asked why he married, he replies: "To pay my debts at
play and disinherit my younger brother." In the Restoration the remark would have called for laughter, but in Cibber we are immediately
reminded that it is not a nice thing to deceive a woman. "Death!"
exclaims the priggish Lord Morelove, and the reprimand clearly re-
flects the author. "My lord, but since you are thus indifferent, why
would you needs marry a woman of so much merit? Could not you
have laid out your spleen upon some ill-natured shrew that wanted
the plague of an ill husband and have let her alone to some plain,
honest man of quality that would have deserved her?" [73] But on the
whole, no doubt, Lord Foppington is a ridiculous coxcomb, related—
though rather distantly related—to many characters in Restoration
comedy. He affects French phrases, he carries himself with too much
of an air, he is entirely too vain to be either discerning or successful
in his amours. Once, he tells us, he was making advances to a man of
quality's wife, but when he suggested an appointment she immediately
forbade him the house.

LORD MORELOVE. But how did her answer agree with you?
LORD FOPPINGTON. Passionately well! For I stared full in her face and
busted out a-laughing; at which she turned upon her heel, gave a crack
with her fan like a coachwhip, and bridled out of the room with the air
and complexion of an incensed turkey-cock.
LORD MORELOVE. What did you then?
LORD FOPPINGTON. I—looked after, gaped, threw up the sash, and fell
a-singing out of the window; so that you see, my lord, while a man is not
in love, there's no great affliction in missing one's way to a woman.[74]

One disapproves perhaps but at the same time one laughs, for one
realizes that after all coxcombs are never very dangerous.

[73] *Ibid.,* II, ii.   [74] *Ibid.*

More amusing than Lord Foppington and at times reminiscent of Congreve's Millamant is the charming Lady Betty Modish. She is, or appears to be, an extremely giddy creature intoxicated by her own beauty, the very last word in fashionable affectation. "Oh, my dear," she says to Lady Easy, who has just come to call on her, "I am over-joyed to see you! I am strangely happy today; I have just received my new scarf from London. . . . 'Tis all extravagance both in mode and fancy; my dear, I believe there's six thousand yards of edging in it.— Then such an enchanting slope from the elbow—something so new, so lively, so noble, so coquette and charming—but you shall see it, my dear—" "Indeed I won't, my dear," Lady Easy replies; "I am resolved to mortify you for being so wrongfully fond of a trifle." [75] From the author's point of view, the rebuke is fully justified, for Lady Betty is entirely too frivolous. She even professes to believe that sincerity in love is as much out of fashion as sweet snuff, and she accordingly neglects Lord Morelove, whose intentions are honorable, and flirts with the infamous Lord Foppington. Morelove and Sir Charles try to arouse her jealousy and thus force her to reveal her true feelings (for like Sir Charles himself, she is really in love). But she discovers their plots and—in a series of amusing scenes—turns the tables so completely upon them that Sir Charles is finally obliged to take her severely to task:

How often [he says] to piece up a quarrel have you appointed [Lord Morelove] to visit you alone; and though you have promised to see no other company the whole day, when he has come, he has found you among the laugh of noisy fops, coquettes, and coxcombs, dissolutely gay, while your full eyes ran o'er with transport of their flattery, and your own vain power of pleasing? How often, I say, have you been known to throw away at least four hours of your good humor upon such wretches? and the minute they were gone, grew only dull to him, sunk into a distasteful spleen, complained you had talked yourself into the headache, and then indulged upon the dear delight of seeing him in pain? and by that time you stretched and gaped him heartily out of patience, of a sudden most impor-tantly remember you had outsat your appointment with my Lady Fiddle-Faddle, and immediately order your coach to the Park? [76]

Reproaches succeed where tricks have failed, and Lady Betty at last realizes how thoughtless she has been. She bursts into tears, renounces

[75] *Ibid.*, II, i.   [76] *Ibid.*, V, vii.

Lord Foppington, and promises never to give her lover another anxious moment.

The coquettes in *Love's Last Shift* experience no such conversion; but the pervasive sentimentality is not the only striking difference between *The Careless Husband* and the earlier play. Cibber is here considerably more attentive to the manners of his fine ladies and gentlemen. He heavily underscores their gentility and good breeding, he assures us again and again that they are not ordinary human beings but persons of quality. In fact, his purpose in writing the play was—as he insists in his dedication to the Duke of Argyle—to establish a new tradition in comedy. He points out that the plays of his time were too coarse to entertain the polite world, that since no one had come forward to reform the taste of the town he himself had decided to do so, that his model in dialogue had been his grace's own manner of conversing.

Dedications are notoriously untrustworthy, but in this case the remark about the Duke's conversation may easily be more than flattery. Cibber was, and had been for some time, trying to get into society, assiduously cultivating the acquaintance of the fine gentlemen who came to the theatre; and in his play, as he suggests, he had probably tried to portray their behavior. But it cannot be said that he is really successful; he writes as an outsider; his gentility, like Pinero's, is tawdry and affected. To understand the manners and the ethics of the aristocracy we go to Congreve and Lord Chesterfield: Cibber gives us only the point of view of the social climber. In the first act—one can choose illustrations at random because they appear on every page—Sir Charles Easy thus greets his wife, who has just entered the room:

Sir Charles. My dear, how do you do? You are dressed very early today; are you going out?

Lady Easy. Only to church, my dear.

Sir Charles. Is it so late then?

Lady Easy. The bell has just rung.

Sir Charles. Well, child, how does Windsor air agree with you? Do you find yourself any better yet? or have you a mind to go to London again?

Lady Easy. No indeed, my dear; the air's so very pleasant that if it were a place of less company I could be content to end my days here.

Sir Charles. Prithee, my dear, what sort of company would most please you?

LADY EASY. When business would permit it, yours; and in your absence a sincere friend that were truly happy in an honest husband to sit a cheerful hour and talk in mutual praise of our condition.[77]

How perfectly polite! but how offensive! One feels stifled in this atmosphere of well-bred chitchat, one longs for a little coarse and unrefined humanity. In saying this I am aware that Cibber's dialogue passed as the real thing throughout the eighteenth century and was accepted even by so good a judge as Horace Walpole.

The play is in many respects an admirable piece of work. The exposition is easy and natural, the construction is excellent, the characters make capital acting parts. But as a whole, it remains a museum piece, a tarnished example of stuffy morality and snobbish manners. It is a forgotten hit and not much more.

In the *Apology* Cibber tells us something about the composition of *The Careless Husband*. He began it apparently in the summer of 1702, preparing the principal parts—Lord Foppington, Sir Charles Easy, and Lady Betty—for himself, Wilks, and Mrs Verbruggen. But when he reached the middle of the play, Mrs Verbruggen left the stage, and he felt obliged to lay aside his unfinished manuscript—"in despair," he says, "of having justice done to the character of Lady Betty Modish by any one woman then among us." [78] A few months later, however, he realized that he had abandoned his play too hastily, for he discovered that there was another actress in the company who was admirably fitted for the part—the young and hitherto neglected Mrs Oldfield.

During the summer of 1703 the company acted at Bath, and Cibber, as he himself admits, had so low an opinion of Mrs Oldfield's ability that he could scarcely be persuaded to rehearse with her the scenes in *Sir Courtly Nice* in which they had the principal parts. But when the play was given she amazed him by "her unexpected performance." "So forward and sudden a step into nature," he says, "I had never seen, and what made her performance more valuable was that I knew it all proceeded from her own understanding, untaught and unassisted by any one more experienced actor....Upon this unexpected sally, then, of the power and disposition of so unforeseen an actress it was that I again took up the two first acts of *The Careless Husband*...

[77] *Ibid.*, I, i.   [78] *Apology*, I, 308.

[which] took its fate upon the stage the winter following, in 1704. Whatever favorable reception this comedy has met with from the public, it would be unjust in me not to place a large share of it to the account of Mrs Oldfield, not only from the uncommon excellence of her action, but even from her personal manner of conversing. There are many sentiments in the character of Lady Betty Modish that I may almost say were originally her own, or only dressed with a little more care than when they negligently fell from her lively humor. Had her birth placed her in a higher rank of life, she had certainly appeared in reality what in this play she only excellently acted, an agreeably gay woman of quality, a little too conscious of her natural attractions. I have often seen her in private societies where women of the best rank might have borrowed some part of her behavior without the least diminution of their sense or dignity." [79]

The play was, as Cibber suggests, unusually successful. Produced on December 7, 1704, it was given nine times during the first fortnight and six times later in the season. It immediately found a place in the repertory of Drury Lane, and for nearly a century remained one of the most popular of English comedies.

Critical opinions about the play are particularly instructive, for by following them throughout the eighteenth century one gets a rough outline of the history of comedy. Two nights after the first performance Congreve wrote to his friend Keally sneering at the gentility of the characters. "Cibber," he says, "has produced a play consisting of fine gentlemen and fine conversation altogether; which the ridiculous town for the most part likes, but there are some that know better." [80] Six years later Steele discussed the play in the *Tatler*.[81] He praised it, but not extravagantly; he dwelt chiefly upon Cibber's craftsmanship. By the middle of the century, however, the play was felt to be a masterpiece, and Pope, Smollett—almost all critics, in fact—spoke of it in the very highest terms. "Comedy," says Samuel Derrick in 1759, "comedy may be divided into two species, genteel and low: the first speaks the language of polite life, of which Cibber's *Careless Husband*

[79] *Ibid.*, I, 307-9.

[80] Congreve, *The Mourning Bride, Poems, and Miscellanies,* ed. Bonamy Dobrée, World's Classics (Oxford, 1928), pp. 496-97.

[81] *Tatler,* III, 356-57. Steele was advertising a particular performance; hence perhaps his emphasis on Cibber's acting parts.

is a very fine specimen, and were it curtailed of one scene which to me is vicious and indelicate, I should not fail to pronounce it not only the best comedy in the English but in any other language." [82] Horace Walpole, writing in 1785, is even more enthusiastic. "Who upon earth has written such perfect comedies [as Molière]?" he asks. *"The Careless Husband* is but one—*The Non-Juror* was built on the *Tartuffe."* [83] But the most unqualified praise comes from David Erskine Baker, whose comments—originally published in *The Companion to the Playhouse* (1764)—were reproduced in the *New Theatrical Dictionary* (1792), as well as in the two editions of *Biographia Dramatica.* Cibber's play, Baker says, contains "the most elegant dialogue and the most perfect knowledge of the manners of persons in real high life extant in any dramatic piece that has yet appeared in any language whatever." This judgment is no doubt absurdly extravagant, but it serves to remind us that, despite the protests of such men as Fielding and Goldsmith, Cibber's work remained the touchstone of genteel comedy for more than a hundred years.

[82] Thomas Wilkes [pseudonym for Samuel Derrick], *A General View of the Stage* (1759), pp. 39-40.

[83] Walpole, *Letters,* ed. Mrs Paget Toynbee (Oxford, 1903-5), XIII, 315.

III. CHRISTOPHER RICH

BETWEEN 1704 and 1709 Cibber produced two original plays—*Perolla and Izadora* and *The Lady's Last Stake*—and three adaptations—*The Comical Lovers, The Double Gallant,* and *The Rival Fools;* but during this period he was chiefly occupied with the management of the theatre. He acted as confidential adviser to Rich, Swiney, and Brett; he played an important part in the managerial intrigues of 1706 and 1708; and finally, just at the end of the period, he became one of the four licensed managers of the Haymarket company. His progress during these troubled years is not easy to follow, but by piecing together odd bits of information and by making frequent excursions into theatrical history, we can perhaps give the reader some notion of its general outline.

− I −

In 1695-96, the season in which Cibber's first play appeared, there were two companies in London, one occupying the theatre in Lincoln's Inn Fields, and the other the theatres in Drury Lane and Dorset Garden. The Lincoln's Inn Fields company was directed by the old Restoration actor Betterton; the Drury Lane company, by the patentees—the shareholders in the theatrical patents which, in the reign of Charles II, had been granted to Davenant and Killigrew. Of these patentees the most important were Sir Thomas Skipwith and Christopher Rich; Sir Thomas, however, seems to have taken little interest in the stage, and the actual management of the company was left entirely in the hands of his more enterprising colleague.[1]

Rich was a lawyer—a pettifogging lawyer, his enemies said—who a few years before had invested money in the patent. He knew little and cared less about the drama: he was interested only in profits. He "had no conception himself of theatrical merit either in authors or

---

[1] For the early careers of Skipwith and Rich at Drury Lane and the litigation among the patentees, see Hotson, *Commonwealth and Restoration Stage,* pp. 284 ff.

actors," Cibber tells us; "yet his judgment was governed by a saving rule in both: he looked into his receipts for the value of a play, and from common fame he judged of his actors." [2] Discovering early in his career that opera and *entr'acte* entertainments paid better than plays, he devoted his repertory as far as possible to performances of this sort. He showed ingenuity if not taste in preparing them, and soon his theatre was distinctly more successful than the rival theatre in Lincoln's Inn Fields. But Rich never shared the money he made with his fellow patentees, possibly because he wanted to reinvest it in his enterprise. He was a projector whose ambition was to dispense with plays entirely and produce a series of spectacular musical shows which would fill the theatre night after night. The scheme was never completely realized, but he established an important tradition in theatrical management, carried on by his son John Rich until after the middle of the eighteenth century.

Between 1695 and 1706 Rich frequently revived such popular operas as *The Tempest, The Prophetess, Psyche,* and *King Arthur;* and at the same time he produced many new operas specially written for his theatre—Settle's *The World in the Moon,* for example, which is thus announced in the *Post Boy* of June 12-15, 1697:

Great preparations are making for a new opera in the playhouse in Dorset Garden, of which there is great expectation, the scenes being several new sets and of a model different from all that have been used in any theatre whatever, being twice as high as any of their former scenes; and the whole decorations of the stage not only infinitely beyond all the operas ever yet performed in England, but also, by the acknowledgment of several gentlemen that have traveled abroad, much exceeding all that has been seen on any of the foreign stages.

These remarkable new sets are fully described in Settle's stage directions. In Act I, for example:

The flat scene draws and discovers three grand arches of clouds extending to the roof of the house, terminated with a prospect of cloud-work, all filled with the figures of fames and Cupids; a circular part of the back clouds rolls softly away and gradually discovers a silver moon, near fourteen foot diameter; after which the silver moon wanes off by degrees and discovers the world within, consisting of four grand circles of clouds, illustrated with Cupids, etc. Twelve golden chariots are seen riding in the

[2] *Apology,* I, 262.

clouds, filled with twelve children, representing the twelve celestial signs. The third arch entirely rolling away, leaves the full prospect terminating with a large lanschape of woods, waters, towns, etc.[3]

Cynthia's train enters: there is

A dance of four swans. To them enter five green men, upon which the swans take wing and fly up into the heavens. The green men dance.[4]

And so on—one spectacular stage effect after another. But "infinitely beyond" all previous operas though it was, *The World in the Moon* soon yielded to *The Island Princess*, to *Arsinoe*, and to other spectacular shows produced at Drury Lane.

Entr'acte entertainments had of course been common enough on the Elizabethan and Restoration stages, but as used by Rich they were more elaborate and more exotic than they had ever been before. He seems to have been the first manager to make a practice of getting his entertainers from the capitals of Europe as well as from the London fairs. In 1699, for example, he brought Clementine to England. "We are now assured," says the *Post Boy*, "that the masters of the Theatre Royal have engaged Signor Clementine, the famous eunuch, servant to the Elector of Bavaria, to sing on their public stage for the short time of his stay in England. There is very great expectation of his performance, as being a person of that extraordinary desert in singing that his yearly salary on that account is £500 a year."[5]

The great expectations were not disappointed; "the ladies paid more for his caponship than they would ha' done for his virility";[6] and Rich soon hired other entertainers from abroad. They were a strange lot—eunuchs, contortionists, rope dancers, harlequins, ventriloquists— anyone, in fact, who could please for a few days an audience that had grown weary of legitimate drama. There was "the famous Mr Evans, lately come into England, vaulter of the managed horse, where he lies with his body extended on one hand, in which posture he drinks several glasses of wine with the other, and from that throws himself a somerset over the horse's head, to the admiration of all that see him."[7] There were "the two famous French girls, lately arrived from the Emperor's court. They will perform several dances on the rope upon

[3] Elkanah Settle, *The World in the Moon* (1697), I, ii.   [4] *Ibid.*
[5] *Post Boy*, April 13-15, 1699.   [6] *Comparison between the Two Stages*, p. 49.
[7] *Daily Courant*, April 23, 1703.

the stage, being improved to that degree far exceeding all others in that art. And their father presents you with the newest humors of Harlequin, as performed by him before the Grand Signior at Constantinople." [8] There was Clinch of Barnett, thus advertised in the *Daily Courant,* June 18, 1703:

At the Theatre Royal in Drury Lane this present Friday, being the 18th of June, will be presented a comedy called *Love's Last Shift, or the Fool in Fashion,* being the last time of acting it this season. With an entertainment of flute music by Mr Bannister and his son. And also a new piece of instrumental music on the stage by the best hands. And the famous Mr Claxton and his son will perform "The Highland" and "The Whip of Dunboyne." And the famous Mr Clinch, being now in town, will for this once, at the desire of several persons of quality, perform his imitation of an organ with three voices, the double curtel, and the bells, the huntsman with his horn and pack of dogs; all which he performs with his mouth on the open stage, being what no man besides himself could ever yet attain to.

The operas and entertainments of the company were probably under the personal direction of Rich himself, but in giving plays Rich was compelled to rely upon advisers and assistants. Thus between 1695 and 1699 he employed Captain Griffin as general manager and Powell as director of rehearsals. But toward the end of the century he began to turn over at least some of the duties of these men to young Cibber, whom he liked personally and whom for some time he had included in his "parties of pleasure—very often *tête-à-tête* and sometimes in a *partie carrée.*" [9]

The exact date of the alliance between Cibber and Rich is uncertain, but a document preserved among the Lord Chamberlain's papers indicates that 1700 cannot be far wrong.[10] The document, probably drafted in the spring of that year, is a protest by the principal actors of the company, who had recently contracted with Rich to rent the theatre and the patent. They charged that Rich had violated the contract by interfering in the management. He had hired singers and

[8] *Ibid.,* April 29, 1703.   [9] *Apology,* I, 254.
[10] L.C. 7/3. The document is undated, but another document apparently written in the same year—a contract with the scene-painter Robinson—is dated March 18, 1699. The contract is signed not by Rich but by the actors, and concerns scenes for a new opera by Settle, presumably *The Virgin Prophetess,* given, according to Nicoll, in 1701. I suppose therefore that 1699 means 1699/1700. See Nicoll, *Restoration Drama,* p. 344, where the contract is printed. A new opera with scenes by Robinson is announced in the *Post Boy* of May 14-16, 1700.

dancers, he had issued pass tickets which his friends had sold, he had "impropriated to his own use" certain scenes and costumes; and they therefore asked that the Lord Chamberlain hold him to his agreement. The document is signed by Wilks, Penkethman, Mills, Bullock, Swiney, Powell—by all the actors of the company, in short, with the single exception of Cibber. The inference is that during the quarrel Cibber had remained faithful to Rich, whose servant he now felt himself to be.

During the next five years Cibber's influence with Rich rapidly increased, and in contemporary pamphlets he is several times referred to as a person of considerable importance at Drury Lane. Thus in *Visits from the Shades* (1704) the following dialogue occurs "between Nat Lee, the tragedian, and Colly C—r, the plagiary":

CIBBER. The town has a [good] opinion of my parts, and my plays have raised me to a sort of viceroy in the theatres; for I try, acquit, or condemn; and there's nought to be represented but what is stamped by my approbation and tried by the touchstone of my own sense.

NAT LEE. Why the truth on't is, you are a very pretty deputy under Apollo, and the poets must need have a fine time on't, to be governed by such a quack of Parnassus, a stage tartar, that graze for your dialogues from the poets of the last age (for thank Heaven the ancients are far enough out of reach of your plagiarism). In short, your plays and your judgment are monstrous and defective.

CIBBER. Mr R[ic]h and Mr S[kipwi]t[h] think otherwise, and I value no one's opinion beside.

NAT LEE. I think it's almost upon the same footing of policy to make a militia captain a general, or give the Britannia to the care of a monkey, as to set you up for a theatric dictator. To be silent of how many better plays you have refused than you ever writ, and how many promising young authors your ignorance or malice have nipped in the bud; your absolute denial of *The Ambitious Stepmother* is an admirable test of your foresight and penetration, and shows how proper a person you are for that employ. Mr R[ic]h, no question, has given you thanks for it; and the town is satisfied just how much your judgment is good for. . . . Jonson, Shakespeare, Dryden, and some others of us not long since were discoursing of the poor estate of your theatre, and after several causes assigned, they all agreed the chief was owing to your mismanagement.[11]

The references here to "mismanagement" and "the poor estate of the theatre" need not, of course, be taken too seriously. If Cibber refused

[11] *Visits from the Shades,* pp. 24-26.

The Ambitious Stepmother—which, after all, was not a promising play—he must have accepted, at about the same time, the first comedies of Steele, Farquhar, and Burnaby, and there is no reason to believe that Rich was dissatisfied with his deputy's conduct of the theatre.

Brief accounts of Cibber's position at Drury Lane are also given in Mrs Manley's *The New Atlantis,* published in 1709 but obviously written several years earlier, and in Dennis's *The Characters and Conduct of Sir John Edgar* (1720). Mrs Manley says:

The favorite poet (in concert with the master) has of course the reading of all new pieces brought to him for his approbation, which he is sure never to give to what seems more meritorious than his own, lest he should put their reputations upon a level. Hence the poor poet is forced with infinite patience and humility (though he be doomed in the beginning) to dance attendance for two or three years together; they refer him to one, then to another, so to a third, till they have run the whole round with him, and then dismiss him with an "It won't do," when they have already plundered it of all that was either new or well expressed, to dress up their own collections; you may judge there's no appearing for him, if they would permit it, when his market has been so forestalled.[12]

The Dennis reference is more casual, for Dennis aims primarily to illustrate Cibber's insolence:

I remember the time in a former reign when three peers of England, a duke and two earls, both the one and the other some of the most illustrious of their respective benches, wanted power to get one poor comedy acted; a certain insolent, impertinent actor, who has lately revived his insolence with large additions, had (through old Rich's weakness, whom he led by the nose) power to withstand them all.[13]

A longer, though in some ways a less accurate, account is to be found in Cibber's own *Apology,* in the section dealing with Wilks and Powell. Cibber describes the rivalry between the two actors for the position of director of rehearsals, and then tells how he persuaded Rich to decide in Wilks's favor. As the story progresses, it becomes apparent that Cibber was very close to the patentee; indeed he himself remarks that he had more of his "master's personal inclination than any actor of the male sex." [14] The passage is worth summarizing because it helps to explain subsequent developments in the theatre.

---

[12] Mrs Manley, *The New Atlantis* (1709), I, 209.
[13] Steele, *Theatre,* ed. John Nichols (1791), II, 351.   [14] *Apology,* I, 254.

Powell was the leading actor of the company from 1695 to about 1700. He was a hot-headed drunkard, the worst person in the world to be responsible for discipline, but from Rich's point of view he had one excellent quality—he knew how to keep the other actors quiet with very little pay. For Rich was never happy when the profits of the company were fairly distributed, he always shrank from fixed salaries and regular payments. Says Cibber:

He gave the actors more liberty, and fewer days' pay than any of his predecessors. He would laugh with them over a bottle and bite them in their bargains. He kept them poor that they might not be able to rebel, and sometimes merry that they might not think of it. All their articles of agreement had a clause in them that he was sure to creep out at, viz. their respective salaries were to be paid in such manner and proportion as others of the same company were paid; which in effect made them all, when he pleased, but limited sharers of loss and himself sole proprietor of profits; and this loss or profit they only had such verbal accounts of as he thought proper to give them. 'Tis true, he would sometimes advance them money (but not more than he knew at most could be due to them) upon their bonds; upon which, whenever they were mutinous, he would threaten to sue them.[15]

Such was Rich's system, which Powell helped to maintain. But in 1698 an even more gifted actor joined the company—Robert Wilks. Within a year or two he was extremely popular and about 1702 Rich allowed him to replace the undependable Powell as director of rehearsals. Wilks, however, could not tolerate the financial uncertainty and he soon insisted on a fair contract and regular payments for himself. The patentee was puzzled; he was reluctant to bring back Powell, who would certainly injure the company, even more reluctant to abandon the disorder of which he was so fond; and as he considered the alternatives, he turned for advice to his other assistant, Cibber. The matter was frequently discussed during their evenings together, and Cibber always showed a distinct preference for Wilks. But the master himself leaned toward Powell. "For you see," he said, "Wilks will never be easy unless I give him his whole pay when others have it not; and what an injustice would that be to the rest if I were to comply with him! How do I know but then they may be all in a mutiny, and mayhap with Powell at the head of 'em?" Finally, how-

15 *Ibid.*, I, 252-53.

ever, Cibber's opinion prevailed, and Wilks got a new contract entitling him to his full pay of £4 a week without any conditional deductions.[16]

The contract was drawn up on October 9, 1704, and exactly a month later Cibber himself received a similar contract. He was engaged for five years at a salary slightly lower than that of Wilks—£3 10 shillings a week—but by a "separate verbal agreement" he was allowed two additional sums—10 shillings a week for casting parts, reading plays, and "other services," and 20 shillings a week for assisting in the management. He thus became—if, indeed, he was not already—the most influential and the highest paid actor in the company.[17]

– 2 –

In 1695 Betterton's theatre in Lincoln's Inn Fields was far more popular than Drury Lane. But Betterton's capital was limited, his stage small and ill-equipped, and when the vogue of operas and entertainments began, he found himself severely handicapped. He hired singers and dancers, it is true, but they proved "exorbitantly expensive, produced small profit to him and his company, but vast gain to themselves." [18] His audiences grew smaller, his profits dwindled away, his actors lost faith in themselves and gave dull and spiritless performances. In 1700—the case was probably not an isolated one—they agreed to produce Crauford's *Courtship a la Mode,* but they made so little effort to study their parts that Crauford finally transferred his play to the rival theatre. In his preface he says:

Mr Betterton did me all the justice I could indeed reasonably hope for. But that example he gave was not, it seems, to be followed by the whole company, since 'tis known that Mr Bowman (I mention his name to keep the reflection from other sharers) kept the first character of my play six weeks and then could hardly read six lines on't. How far that way of management makes of late for the interest and honor of that house, is easy to be judged. Some who valued their reputations more were indeed rarely or never absent. To these I gave my thanks; but finding that six or seven people could not perform what was designed for fifteen, I was obliged

[16] *Ibid.,* I, 238-56.
[17] Public Record Office, C. 10 537/22. Hotson, *Commonwealth and Restoration Stage,* pp. 325-26, lists two other lawsuits which contain information about contracts made at this time: C. 9 464/126 (Wilks v. Rich) and C. 10 528/33 (Johnson v. Rich). C. 9 464/32 (Vanbrugh v. Rich) summarizes the contracts of Bullock and Norris.
[18] John Downes, *Roscius Anglicanus,* ed. Montague Summers (n. d.), p. 46.

to remove it after so many sham rehearsals, and in two days it got footing upon the other stage, where 'twas immediately cast to the best advantage and played in less than twenty days. How far it answered their labors, I leave to be judged by themselves. Their care and readiness is confessed by every man, though, at the same time, 'tis not to be supposed that they act any plays without a prospect of pleasing the town, of whose favor they justly stand possessed. What justice I had done me in the public performance is very well demonstrated by my success.

Too old to struggle indefinitely against overwhelming odds, Betterton at last retired from the management, assigning his license, his actors, and his theatre to the two young playwrights, Congreve and Vanbrugh. Congreve soon withdrew, but the future architect of Blenheim threw himself into the work with quixotic enthusiasm. His plan was to beat Rich on his own ground—to produce a series of spectacular musical shows which would lure the town away from Drury Lane. Accordingly he built a splendid new theatre in the Haymarket, hired a troupe of singers from Italy, and introduced them in *The Loves of Ergasto,* a pastoral opera "all sung after the Italian manner." But unfortunately the singers were poor; they were the worst, the old prompter tells us, who ever came from abroad, and "they in a little time marched back to their own country." [19] The theatre was even poorer, for its acoustics had been ruined by Vanbrugh's architectural flourishes—by the high ceiling and the handsome semi-oval arch above the orchestra. "This extraordinary and superfluous space," says Cibber, "occasioned such an undulation from the voice of every actor that generally what they said sounded like the gabbling of so many people in the lofty aisles in a cathedral. The tone of a trumpet or the swell of an eunuch's holding note, 'tis true, might be sweetened by it, but the articulate sounds of a speaking voice were drowned by the hollow reverberations of one word upon another." [20] The handicap was too much for Vanbrugh, and at the end of three months he petitioned the Lord Chamberlain (as indeed Betterton had done before) to put an end to the theatrical war by uniting the two companies of actors.[21]

[19] *Ibid.,* p. 48. See also Lawrence Whistler, *Sir John Vanbrugh, Architect and Dramatist, 1664-1726* (1938), pp. 104-12.

[20] *Apology,* I, 321-22.

[21] L.C. 7/3; Charles Gildon, *The Post Boy Robbed of His Mail* (2d ed., 1706), pp. 344-45.

The Lord Chamberlain listened sympathetically, but Rich would not consider the proposal. He could do nothing, he evasively explained, without the consent of his fellow patentees; and besides, he objected to "undoing" himself in order "to raise great estates to Mr Vanbrugh and a few others." He persuaded his actors to say that they were content with their salaries at Drury Lane, and that they were "apprehensive of great hardships, if not utter ruin, which they conclude will be brought upon them by such a union." [22] And when the negotiations finally broke down, he publicly announced his satisfaction in the epilogue to the opera *Camilla* (1706):

> Our neighbors lately, with an ill design,
> Strove the contending playhouses to join. . . .
> But this we know, had that dire union been,
> You ne'er in England had *Camilla* seen.
> They would some masque have shown, or country farce,
> *Paris's Judgment* or *The Loves of Mars*.
> But since the stage's freedom you restore,
> And we no more dread arbitrary power,
> To please this audience we'll no charges spare,
> But cheerfully maintain a vigorous war.
> New funds we'll raise, and heavy taxes lay,
> Dancers and singers (dear allies) to pay.

But it soon appeared that Rich was not really hostile to a union, he merely wanted to make his own terms. He wanted two theatres, one for opera and one for plays, and he wanted to exercise a loose control over both.

While the negotiations with Vanbrugh were still in progress, Rich sent for Owen Swiney, a former assistant of his at Drury Lane, through whom he now proposed to get control of the Haymarket. Swiney came to London and on August 14, 1706, arranged to rent Vanbrugh's theatre and take over his lease.[23] It was apparently understood that Rich was to share the profits of the new Haymarket company, which was to give only plays, and that Swiney was to have as

[22] Gildon, *The Post Boy Robbed of His Mail,* pp. 345-47. The petition of the actors printed in Percy Fitzgerald, *A New History of the English Stage* (1882), I, 259-60, is probably the one mentioned by Rich. Fitzgerald is obviously wrong in dating the petition 1707-8.

[23] Grove, *Dictionary of Music and Musicians,* article Swiney; L.C. 7/2; *Apology,* I, 329-32. Swiney's account is not easily reconciled with Cibber's, but the whole episode is obscure.

many of the Drury Lane actors as he wanted. Ultimately no doubt he was to have them all, but for the time being Rich needed a few, as he said, to set his other machines going, and he specifically mentioned the name of Cibber.[24] Swiney agreed or seemed to agree, but almost immediately differences of opinion developed. "Mr Rich complains and rails like Volpone when counterplotted by Mosca," wrote Congreve on September 10;[25] and in October, when the acting season began, the two men seem to have been definitely hostile to one another. Swiney opened the Haymarket with *The Spanish Friar,* and in his playbills pointedly called attention to the fact that it was to be given "without singing or dancing." Rich replied, advertising *The Recruiting Officer* "by the *deserted company* of comedians of the Theatre Royal. ... In which *they pray* there may be *singing by Mrs Tofts* in English and Italian. *And some dancing."*[26] But despite these indications of ill-feeling the two men seem to have remained partners until November, when a further difference of opinion arose over the special status of Cibber.

During the summer in which these events were taking place Cibber was in Gloucestershire, at the home of his friend Colonel Brett. He knew nothing of the new Haymarket company until, on October 5, 1706, he received a letter from Swiney—a letter once in the possession of Grove, in whose *Dictionary of Music and Musicians* its contents are summarized. Swiney addresses Cibber—somewhat ambiguously perhaps—as "puppy," "his angel" (twice), "his dear," and finally "unbeliever;" and while employing these affectionate terms whimsically tells the story of his relations with Rich. He had "quitted his post in the army" to manage the Haymarket, he says, for Rich had promised him "100 guineas per annum salary, a place at court, and the devil and all." But when he had come up to London he had found that Rich was not to be trusted. The actors, however, were generally discontented under Rich, and for this reason Swiney had himself been able to form a company at the Haymarket. He had leased the theatre for seven years at £5 a day, though the patentees might have had it at £3 or £3 10 shillings.[27]

---

[24] *Apology,* I, 332.
[25] Congreve, *Mourning Bride, Poems, and Miscellanies,* ed. Dobrée (1928), p. 499.
[26] *Daily Courant,* October 23, 1706.
[27] Grove, *Dictionary of Music and Musicians,* article Swiney.

Swiney probably added—though the remark is not mentioned by Grove—that Cibber should himself feel free to join the Haymarket company. But Cibber somewhat reluctantly refused. His relations with Swiney were obviously very warm, but he was perhaps on even warmer terms with Rich. Furthermore he was not optimistic about the new company's prospects: he knew that they lacked capital and equipment, knew also that the acoustics of the theatre were poor and that in any case it was on the outskirts of London.

Upon these considerations I was only thankful for the offers made me from the Haymarket, without accepting them, and soon after came to town towards the usual time of their beginning to act, to offer my service to our old master. But I found our company so thinned that it was almost impracticable to bring any one tolerable play upon the stage. When I asked him where were his actors and in what manner he intended to proceed, he replied, "Don't you trouble yourself, come along, and I'll show you." He then led me about all the by-places in the house and showed me fifty little back doors, dark closets, and narrow passages; in alterations and contrivances of which kind he had busied his head most part of the vacation; for he was scarce ever without some notable joiner or a bricklayer extraordinary in pay for twenty years. And there are so many odd obscure places about a theatre that his genius in nook-building was never out of employment; nor could the most vain-headed author be more deaf to an interruption in reciting his works than our wise master was while entertaining me with the improvements he had made in his invisible architecture; all which, without thinking any one part of it necessary, though I seemed to approve, I could not help now and then breaking in upon his delight with the impertinent question of, "But, master, where are your actors?" But it seems I had taken a wrong time for this sort of inquiry; his head was full of matters of more moment . . . his notion was that singing and dancing or any sort of exotic entertainments would make an ordinary company of actors too hard for the best set who had only plain plays to subsist on.[28]

Cibber could scarcely help agreeing, but since plays were now to be almost negligible at Drury Lane, he insisted that his salary should not suffer. He demanded either an advance in his weekly salary or a guarantee that his income for the year should not fall below a specified amount. Rich hesitated for several days, and while he was trying to make up his mind the matter was settled in the course of an interview with Swiney about affairs at the Haymarket. Swiney too wanted a contract, a definite written assurance that he could have all the actors

[28] *Apology*, I, 333-35.

he wanted from Drury Lane and half of whatever profits his company might make. But written contracts were odious to Rich, who had never been accustomed to such methods; he needed time for consideration. Swiney, however, insisted, and to make his partner even more uncomfortable urged his right to add Cibber to the Haymarket company if Cibber was now willing to join it. This Rich absolutely refused; the argument grew heated; and finally the partnership was definitely dissolved.[29] "Before it was publicly known," Cibber says, "Swiney, by fairly letting me into the whole transaction, took effectual means to secure me in his interest. When the mystery of the patentee's indifference to me was unfolded, and that his slighting me was owing to the security he relied on of Swiney's not daring to engage me, I could have no further debate with myself which side of the question I should adhere to. To conclude, I agreed in two words to act with Swiney." [30]

Norris, Bullock, and Johnson soon followed Cibber's example, and by December Drury Lane was indeed a deserted company.

Rich was at first inclined to annoy his rivals by suing them, individually, for breach of contract. He sued Wilks and Cibber, for example, on the basis of the agreements of 1704—Cibber for acting in *Love's Last Shift* at the Haymarket, and Wilks for acting in plays at Oxford during the summer and at the new theatre during the regular season. He was especially vindictive against Wilks, for he started—or threatened to start—a separate action for each time Wilks had violated his contract. But he did not ignore the managers of the Haymarket company and he soon found a way of annoying both Vanbrugh and Swiney. He sued Norris and Bullock for breach of contract, and having obtained judgment against them, persuaded them to put in writs of error, for which Vanbrugh and Swiney furnished bail. He then promised not to demand damages from them if they would agree not to prosecute the writs. They accepted the conditions, and he was thus able to sue Vanbrugh and Swiney for the bail. But these tricks were merely a lawyer's diversion, for the old patentee got his real revenge in the theatre itself.[31]

---

[29] *Ibid.*, I, 335-36. [30] *Ibid.*, I, 336-37.
[31] C. 9 464/126 and 464/32; C. 10 528/33 and 537/22; Chancery Decrees and Orders, 1708 B, p. 175.

- 3 -

Rich's first performance in the autumn of 1706 was, as we have seen, *The Recruiting Officer*, but when the alterations at Drury Lane were finished, he turned his attention almost exclusively to music and spectacle. He revived *Pastor Fido, Camilla, The Island Princess, The Tempest, The Sea Voyage,* and *Macbeth,* and at the same time he produced two new operas, *Rosamund* and *Thomyris. Camilla* had some twenty performances during the season, and *Thomyris* was even more successful—it received, says the *Muses Mercury,* as much encouragement "as would have furnished the town for a whole winter with as good tragedies and comedies as they have seen these twenty years." [32] The journal adds: "The opera has been always crowded since it has been under the present management, and is now in a fairer way to live than ever." [33] Rich, indeed, had never been more prosperous, his policies as a manager never more completely vindicated.

In the meantime Swiney and his friends at the Haymarket were encountering repeated misfortunes. Their repertory was excellent, their casts were perhaps the best that had ever been seen at a London theatre. They gave *She Would and She Would Not* with Norris, Underhill, Wilks, Mills, Mrs Barry, Mrs Bracegirdle, and Mrs Lee; *Hamlet* with Keen, Betterton, Verbruggen, Booth, Johnson, Bowen, and Mrs Bracegirdle; *Henry VIII* with Betterton, Mills, Booth, Verbruggen, Cibber, and Mrs Barry. But good acting and good plays were no match for the operas of Rich, and in January, 1707, Swiney was forced to begin a series of subscription performances, "for the encouragement of the comedians acting in the Haymarket, and to enable them to keep the diversion of plays under a separate interest from operas." [34] Three plays were given and for each a guinea was charged. The plays were *Julius Caesar, King and No King,* and *The Comical Lovers,* Cibber's reworking of *The Maiden Queen* and *Marriage a la Mode.* But though the subscription was successful, the relief it afforded was only temporary, and Swiney was soon compelled to

[32] *Muses Mercury, or Monthly Miscellany,* March, 1707.   [33] *Ibid.,* December, 1707.
[34] *Daily Courant,* January 14, 1707. "I labor under the disadvantage of Mr Rich's being suffered to act plays," Swiney wrote to the Lord Chamberlain on January 27, "notwithstanding the extraordinary encouragement the town has given the opera" (L.C. 7/3).

encroach upon the domain of his rival. In March he produced *The British Enchanters,* "lately revised and altered by the author. With all the original scenes, machines, and decorations. To which will be added several new ones, particularly the entire front prospect of Blenheim Castle. And another piece alluding to the late glorious successes of Her Majesty's arms, etc." [35] But the scenes were apparently less glorious than the triumphs to which they made reference, for *The British Enchanters* was acted only three times. Swiney did not—possibly could not—try a second opera, and even the *Muses Mercury* now admitted that the outlook for his company was dark. "Indeed 'tis necessary," says the journal, "those who have served the stage should do their utmost to support her, for there's little hopes of her maintaining herself by credit and character of her new servants.... We don't hear of any other play of note that will be represented this season, and cannot hope for many more the next, unless the poets are encouraged a little as well as the singers, dancers, etc." [36]

The journal seems scarcely to have exaggerated, the drama was in a desperate condition: even new plays failed at the Haymarket with distressing and ominous regularity. Mrs Centlivre's *The Platonic Lady* was acted only four nights, Mrs Manley's *Almyna* only three; Farquhar's *The Beaux' Stratagem* and Smith's *Phaedra and Hippolitus* had longer runs but neither was very successful.[37] Cibber tried to help Swiney with *The Double Gallant* (November 1, 1707) and *The Lady's Last Stake* (December 13), but his plays too failed, the former running only three nights, the latter only five.

The Double Gallant is pieced together out of three contemporary comedies—Burnaby's *The Reformed Wife* and *The Lady's Visiting Day,* and Mrs Centlivre's *Love at a Venture.*[38] The chief characters are Atall, Lady Dainty, and Lady Sadlife. Atall (from Mrs Centlivre) makes love to three women at once and involves himself in conventional difficulties. Lady Dainty combines the affectations of two Burnaby characters: she is always fashionably ill and she is passion-

[35] *Daily Courant,* March 19, 1707.   [36] *Muses Mercury,* May and March, 1707.

[37] For *Phaedra and Hippolitus,* see the *Muses Mercury* for May, 1707. *The Beaux' Stratagem* was used as a benefit play on the eighth night (March 31, 1707).

[38] For the indebtedness of this play to earlier works, see Genest, *Some Account of the English Stage,* II, 388-91; Croissant, *Studies in the Work of Colley Cibber,* pp. 20-22, 52-53.

ately fond of everything foreign. Her diseases and those of her friends, she assures us, are rarely or never profaned by the crowd. "The apoplexy, the gout, and vapors are all peculiar to the nobility.—Huh! huh! and I could almost wish that colds were only ours; there's something in 'em so genteel—so agreeably disordering—Huh! huh!" [39] The character, one need scarcely say, was written for Mrs Oldfield. Lady Sadlife comes, through Burnaby, from the Restoration. She is a lecherous intriguer who hides gallants in the closet and writes her amorous letters under the very nose of her citizen-husband Sir Solomon. The wit in these scenes is brilliantly incisive, reminiscent at its best of *The Plain Dealer* and *The Country Wife.* "But hark you, hussy," says Sir Solomon to Wishwell, his wife's woman. "Suppose now you should be a little scornful and insolent to show your breeding, and a little ill-natured . . . to show your wit."

WISHWELL. Ay, sir, that is if I designed him for my gallant. But since he is to be but my husband, I must be very good-natured and civil before I have him, and huff him and show my wit after.

SIR SOLOMON. Here's a jade for you! [*Aside.*] But why must you huff your husband, hussy?

WISHWELL. Oh, sir, that's to give him a good opinion of my virtue; for you know, sir, a husband can't think one could be so very domineering if one were not very honest.

SIR SOLOMON. 'Sbud! this fool on my conscience speaks the sense of the whole sex. [*Aside.*]

WISHWELL. Then, sir, I have been told that a husband loves one the better the more one hectors him, as a spaniel does the more one beats him. [40]

Other scenes are equally good, and indeed the whole play is capital entertainment. But the audience refused to like it, largely no doubt because Cibber's indebtedness had just been pointed out to them by Rich, who had maliciously revived *The Reformed Wife* at the theatre in Drury Lane.

In publishing *The Double Gallant* Cibber felt obliged to explain his borrowings at considerable length. "When I undertook to make the following sheets into a play," he says, "I only proposed to call it a revised one; but some who had read it were of opinion that the additions in it were of consequence enough to call it a new one; and the

---

[39] Cibber, *The Double Gallant, or the Sick Lady's Cure* (n. d.), III, i.

[40] *Ibid.,* III, iii. The passage comes almost verbatim from *The Lady's Visiting Day;* see Burnaby, *Dramatic Works,* ed. F. E. Budd (1931), p. 223.

actors proposing an advantage by it, the little concern I had for it made
me comply with their desires; notwithstanding, I thought myself
obliged in the prologue to own how far other authors had a claim to
it." [41] But since in the prologue in question he grossly understates his
indebtedness—

> For though from former scenes some hints he draws,
> The ground-plot's wholly changed from what it was—

one cannot take his explanation too seriously. It should be added that
The Double Gallant had successful revivals in 1712 and 1714, and
remained a stock play at the London theatres until after the end of
the eighteenth century.

The Lady's Last Stake, or the Wife's Resentment is a companion
piece to *The Careless Husband,* a second and more mature exercise in
genteel-sentimental comedy.[42] Lord Wronglove, the husband in the
play, resembles Sir Charles Easy in that he is unfaithful to his wife;
but with this difference, that Lord Wronglove has definite grievances.
He resents his wife's reserve; he feels that she deliberately keeps him at
a distance, that she is not, in fact, a wife at all in the full sense of the
word or even a friend and companion. But when he raises the issue
she puts him off by blaming nature. Hence his flirtations and infidelities; for, he argues, "Am I bound to fast because her ladyship has
no appetite?" [43] Later in the play he states his grievances even more
clearly. "I could never sleep with her," he says. "For though she loves
late hours, yet when she has seen me gape for bed like a waiter at the
Groom Porter's in a morning, she would still reserve to herself the
tedious decorum of being first solicited for her company; so that she
usually contrived to let me be three-quarters asleep before she would
do me the honor to disturb me." [44] The problem is a real one (more
generally appreciated perhaps in our own time than in the eighteenth
century), and though it would be useless to maintain that Cibber treats
it with profound psychological insight, he is interesting and—up to a
point at least—realistic. The ending, however, is deplorably super-

[41] Cibber, *Double Gallant,* preface "To the Reader."
[42] Discussions of *The Lady's Last Stake* may be found in Croissant, *Studies in the
Work of Colley Cibber,* pp. 53-55; Bernbaum, *Drama of Sensibility,* pp. 103-7; Bateson,
English Comic Drama, 1700-1750, pp. 31-35.
[43] Cibber, *The Lady's Last Stake, or the Wife's Resentment* (n. d.), I, i.
[44] *Ibid.,* IV, i.

ficial. For after several scenes of domestic bickering, Lady Wronglove
—who is no Griselda, who in fact is "furious, proud, and insolently
chaste" [45]—reaches the point of proposing a separation. Her husband is
about to grant it, when suddenly a new character appears on the
stage, the *raisonneur,* Sir Friendly Moral; and through the efforts of
this somewhat tedious person a complete and highly emotional reconciliation is finally brought about.

The parts of the play which concern Lady Gentle, Mrs Conquest,
and Sir George Brilliant are wholly conventional. Lady Gentle is a
strictly virtuous woman who has only one fault—she is fond of
gambling. She loses £2,000 to the unscrupulous Sir George and almost
loses her virtue as well; but at the last moment she is saved by a
mysterious stranger, who gives her bank bills to the exact amount of
her debt. "A play without a just moral," Cibber says in the dedication, "is a poor and mercenary undertaking." Possibly so, but in this
case a sermon against gambling can scarcely justify the use of the
stereotyped characters and hackneyed incidents. Mrs Conquest is a
part (though a rather inferior one) for the talented Mrs Oldfield.
Throughout the play she pursues Sir George Brilliant, who avoids her
because her fortune is small. Finally she puts on breeches, challenges
him to a duel, receives a mortal wound in the course of a robbery in
the park, and marries him on her deathbed. Later, of course, it
transpires that the robbery and the wound were part of a trick designed to expose Sir George's inconstancy.

Flagrant improbability of this sort is clearly out of place in domestic
drama, and were it not for the early Wronglove scenes, one might
dismiss the play as a distinctly inferior work. Its stage history is
unimpressive, for though, like *The Double Gallant,* it was later revived, it never had much success.

Two failures in one season were very disconcerting, but Cibber was
to some extent consoled by his personal triumph in the epilogue to
The Lady's Last Stake, which ran for two weeks after the play itself
had been discontinued. It is a particularly good specimen of his work
in this genre, and incidentally gives information about the desperate
plight of the actors at the Haymarket and the popularity of the singers
at Drury Lane:

[45] *Ibid.,* prologue.

I'm thinking, when poor plays are quite cried down,
(As nothing's strange in this revolving town,
Though what the latter age had thought amazing)
What we poor slaves shall do when turned a-grazing.
Perhaps great Caesar, who the world commanded,
May snuff the opera candles, when disbanded;
And proud Roxana, from her high disdain,
Most vilely stoop to spread Toftissa's train....
But I, whose beauty only is grimace,
Have no such prospects from this hatchet face;
All I can do must be—
With humble ale and toast, round sea-coal fire,
At nights my pensive spouse and brats to inspire
With tags of crambo rimes, and tack 'em to the Italian lyre.
Nay, e'en when hunger prompts 'em for relief,
I'll make 'em ask for food in recitative;
As thus: [*Sings in recitative.*] "Mamma!"—"Well, what, what is't
   you mutter?"
"Pray cut me a great piece of bread and butter."
"There's all you're like to have,
   Nor can you ask for supper;
'Tis cut quite round the loaf
   'Tis under side and upper."
Who knows in time but this in bills inserted
May crowd a house when Shakespeare is deserted.
Or say that I myself—
Since painted nature no recruits will bring in,
Should e'en, in spite of nature, stick to singing.
My voice, 'tis true, the gipsy's but unkind to,
Though that's a fault you every day are blind to.
But if I change my name, that half will win ye;
Oh soft the name of Signor Cibberini!
Imagine, then, that thus with amorous air
I give you raptures while I squall despair.   [*Sings Italian.*]
If this won't do, I'll try another touch,
Half French, some English, and a spice of Dutch.
                         [*Sings in broken English.*]
Now, sirs, you've seen the utmost I can do,
As poet, player, and as songster too;
But if you can't allow my voice inviting,
E'en let me live by acting and by writing.

- 4 -

The failure of *The Lady's Last Stake* completed the ruin of the
Haymarket Company, and Swiney was on the point of yielding to
Rich, when suddenly relief came from an unexpected quarter—from
Drury Lane itself. The theatrical war ceased, the policies of Rich
were abandoned, and Swiney was invited by the Lord Chamberlain
to take part in still another reorganization of the theatres, the purpose
of which was to insure the success of legitimate entertainments.

The conciliatory attitude of the older theatre was of course made
possible by changes in the management—changes for which, curiously
enough, Cibber and his friend Colonel Brett were largely responsible.
Brett was well acquainted with Sir Thomas Skipwith, who owned a
controlling interest in the patent of Drury Lane, and in the summer
of 1707 he happened to entertain him at Sandywell Park. The visit
was a long one, and the two friends had ample opportunity to discuss
the theatre. Skipwith complained of heavy losses—as indeed he had
complained many times before—and finally he offered to give Brett
his share in the patent if Brett could find a way of making it profitable.
Brett hesitated, Skipwith repeated his offer, and at last "after a great
deal of raillery on both sides, of what Sir Thomas had *not* made of
[the patent] and the particular advantages the colonel was likely to
make of it," [46] the bargain was struck. A lawyer who happened to be
visiting at the house prepared a deed of conveyance, and for the
ridiculous sum of ten shillings the patent was formally "sold." Skipwith and Brett then left for London, the one to enjoy the pleasures
of the metropolis, the other to effect the downfall of Rich and the
rescue of the distressed company in the Haymarket.[47]

Brett's first step after his arrival was to find Cibber and to tell him
the strange story of the purchase. "Notwithstanding he knew I was
then engaged in another interest at the Haymarket," Cibber says, "he
desired we might consider together of the best use he could make of
[his interest in the patent], assuring me at the same time he should
think it of none to himself unless it could in some shape be turned

[46] *Apology*, II, 33.
[47] *Ibid.*; Hotson, *Commonwealth and Restoration Stage*, pp. 386-97; Fitzgerald, *New History of the English Stage*, I, 252-57.

to my advantage. This friendly declaration, though it might be generous in him to make, was not needful to incline me in whatever might be honestly in my power, whether by interest or negotiation, to serve him. My first advice, therefore, was that he should produce his deed to the other managing patentee of Drury Lane, and demand immediate entrance to a joint possession of all effects and powers to which that deed had given him an equal title. After which, if he met with no opposition to this demand (as upon sight of it he did not) that he should be watchful against any contradiction from his colleague in whatever he might propose in carrying on the affair, but to let him see that he was determined in all his measures. . . ." [48]

So Cibber advised, and Brett went quickly to work. He presented his deed to Rich, took over the management of Drury Lane, and persuaded the Lord Chamberlain to unite the two companies of actors. The details were quickly settled, and in January, 1708, the union took place. The actors of the Haymarket company and the few actors who had remained with Rich were brought together at Drury Lane under the management of the patentees, and the singers and dancers that Rich had collected were sent to Swiney, who now became manager of the opera. The separation between the two forms of entertainment was strictly enforced, the Lord Chamberlain forbidding Swiney to give plays, and threatening to "silence" the patent if singers appeared on the stage at Drury Lane. The wisdom of the Lord Chamberlain's injunctions—and indeed of the whole plan—became immediately apparent. Both theatres prospered, and for the first time in years the drama vied with the opera in popularity. [49]

But though the new arrangements were satisfactory to the town, to the actors, and to Swiney, it soon appeared that they were definitely unsatisfactory to Rich. The old patentee had not changed his views: he still believed in the theatre of opera and entertainments, still distrusted legitimate performances; and furthermore he was still a power at Drury Lane. He had been taken by surprise but he had not been beaten, and he was ready to make serious trouble for Brett and his friends as soon as a favorable opportunity should present itself.

His opportunity came in March, 1708, when Brett, who had grown

---

[48] *Apology,* II, 42-43.
[49] *Ibid.,* II, 46-49; British Museum, Add. MSS. 12, 201 and 20, 726.

weary of playing the part of reformer, retired from the management and delegated his power to three of the principal actors of the company—Wilks, Cibber, and Estcourt.[50] For Rich the actors had no terrors, and he at once made plans to reduce their salaries and deprive them of their power. Fortified with the authority of Brett, they resisted and made plans of their own, and before a year had elapsed the theatre was again drifting toward anarchy—drifting, in fact, toward the theatrical revolution of June, 1709, which finally destroyed the power of Rich and laid the foundations for the theatre of the actor-managers.

The plans that Rich made to humble the deputies of Brett were characteristically complicated and devious. He began by attempting to propitiate the minor patentees of the theatre, whom for years he had systematically cheated. He recommended himself to them, Cibber says, by admitting them for the first time to the councils of the management, and by "proposing to make some small dividend of the profits (though he did not design that jest should be repeated)."[51] When by this means he had made them his allies, he proposed changes which, he knew, would be vexatious to the hired actors of the company as well as to the actor-managers. He reduced some salaries and threatened to reduce others, and he took "for the use of the patent" a third of the profits of each benefit play. The actors bitterly resented the indulto—as the charge on benefits was called—but Rich forced them to sign a paper accepting it before their benefit dates could be fixed. Several actors, Cibber says, "at first refused to sign this paper; upon which the next in rank were offered on the same conditions to come before the refusers; this smart expedient got some few of the fearful the preference to their seniors; who, at last seeing the time was too short for a present remedy and that they must either come into the boat or lose their tide, were forced to comply with what they as yet silently resented as the severest injury."[52]

Thus Rich triumphed and the indulto was levied, but in the meantime the actors had not been idle. They had met secretly to discuss their grievances, they had consulted Swiney, they had appealed to the Lord Chamberlain, and finally they had formed an ingenious plan to

[50] Fitzgerald, *New History of the English Stage*, I, 263; II, 443-46.
[51] *Apology*, II, 58.   [52] *Ibid.*, II, 68.

humble Rich and destroy the authority of the patent. They had arranged—this was their first step—to enter into a partnership with Swiney and to return to the Haymarket in the autumn of 1709. Then they had persuaded the Lord Chamberlain to warn Rich to pay them the full profits of their benefit plays. When Rich should refuse—and they had good reason to suppose that he would—the Lord Chamberlain was to silence the patent, Drury Lane was to be closed, and the Haymarket was to become the only theatre in London.[53]

The actors who were at first chosen to become partners of Swiney were Wilks, Cibber, Doggett, and Mrs Oldfield, but before the discussions came to an end Mrs Oldfield was dropped. "Doggett," says Cibber, "who had no objection to her merit, insisted that our affairs could never be upon a secure foundation if there was more than one sex admitted to the management of them. He therefore hoped that if we offered Mrs Oldfield a *carte blanche* instead of a share she would not think herself slighted. This was instantly agreed to, and Mrs Oldfield received it rather as a favor than a disobligation. Her demands therefore were £200 a year certain and a benefit clear of all charges; which were readily signed to." [54]

The four men then drew up the following articles of agreement: The partnership was to last fourteen years—that is, until the expiration of Swiney's lease of the Haymarket Theatre—and during this period the profit and loss of the company were to be shared. Each of the partners was to have a voice in determining the policies of the company, and each was to help "oversee, govern, and manage the affairs and business"; but Wilks alone was to direct rehearsals. The profits were to be used, first of all, to pay the rent of the building and the salaries of the hired actors. The net profits were to be divided as follows: Swiney was to get £300 a year, and Wilks, Cibber, and Doggett £200 each. Wilks was to get an additional £50 for directing rehearsals. In March each of the actors was to have a benefit play clear of all charges. If after these payments any money remained in the treasury, half of it was to go to Swiney and the other half was to be divided equally among the three actors.[55]

The articles were signed March 10, 1709, and from this time until

[53] *Ibid.*, II, 68-69.   [54] *Ibid.*, II, 70-71.
[55] C. 7 299/10 and 668/31; Add. Ms. 38, 607.

the end of the season the conspirators could only wait in silence and hope that their plan would not miscarry. Fortunately it did not. When the time for action came, the Lord Chamberlain did not fail them, and the power of Rich at Drury Lane was finally and completely destroyed.

Early in March Mrs Oldfield, who had been chosen to represent the actors, formally called the Lord Chamberlain's attention to the unusual procedure with regard to her benefit. She pointed out that £71 had been deducted from her profits—£31 more than the charges of the house. The reply of Rich was, as the conspirators had anticipated, evasive and unsatisfactory. He had agreed to pay Mrs Oldfield fifty shillings a week, he said, but he was actually paying her £4; he could, therefore, hardly be accused of treating her unjustly.[56] The Lord Chamberlain ignored the evasion and peremptorily ordered Rich to pay the benefit in full, deducting only £40 for the charges of the house.[57] Rich hesitated, and before he could make up his mind what to do, the blow was struck—the order of silence was issued.[58]

A rehearsal was in progress at the theatre and the actor who had been principally responsible for the negotiations with the Lord Chamberlain was at first absent. When he appeared Rich began a reprimand by asking him how he dared neglect his business. But the actor insolently answered that he had no business there at all—no more business in fact than Rich himself. Puzzled and even alarmed by this mysterious remark, Rich had just time to change his tone when a messenger entered with the order of silence in his hand. The actor was now no longer obliged to conceal the conspiracy, and somewhat melodramatically quoting *Henry VIII* he said to Rich: "Read o'er this; and then to breakfast with what appetite you have." The incident —which comes from Cibber's *Apology*—gains point when one realizes that Cibber himself was almost certainly the actor in question.[59]

Some time apparently elapsed before Rich fully realized the significance of the order. In June he did nothing to contest its legality, though he made several half-hearted attempts to annoy the managers of the new Haymarket company. In the name of his treasurer, Zachary Baggs, he issued a statement defending the indulto,[60] and at the same

[56] L.C. 7/3.   [57] L.C. 5/154.
[58] *Ibid.*; also *Apology*, II, 73, note.   [59] *Apology*, II, 72-73.
[60] Fitzgerald, *New History of the English Stage*, I, 267-69.

time he revived old breach-of-contract suits against several of the deserting actors.[61] But during the summer he made plans to reopen Drury Lane; indeed he actually went so far as to advertise *The Recruiting Officer* for September 6, when he was peremptorily told by the Lord Chamberlain that he must not presume to act until he had further orders from the Queen. Realizing by this time that he would have to go to law, he appealed to Her Majesty in Council, contending that the Lord Chamberlain had no authority over the patent theatre. But before his appeal could be heard, Drury Lane was taken from him by Collier, and he was compelled to build a new theatre, the completion of which he did not live to see.[62]

[61] C. 10 528/33 and 537/22; Add. MS. 38, 607.
[62] Add. MS. 20, 726; Fitzgerald, *New History of the English Stage,* I, 271-80.

IV. THE RISE OF THE
ACTOR-MANAGERS

- I -

THE LORD CHAMBERLAIN's order of silence fulfilled its purpose—it destroyed the power of Rich—but it left the theatre in a sad state of confusion. For again it separated the actors of the town into two hostile groups—those who had remained faithful to Rich and those who had gone over to Swiney. Rich's actors gave performances at Drury Lane under the direction of William Collier, one of the minor patentees; but after producing one successful play, *The Fair Quaker of Deal,* they quarreled with Collier, revolted, and compelled him to solicit the intervention of the Lord Chamberlain. The actors at the Haymarket had similar experiences. They, too, had trouble with their employer, and at the end of the season they, too, were involved in an appeal to the Lord Chamberlain's office. In order to understand these two appeals and the settlement which was ultimately effected, we must briefly consider the fortunes of the two companies during this singularly perplexing season.

The articles of agreement between Swiney and the new actor-managers—Wilks, Cibber, and Doggett—were signed on March 10, 1709, and during the spring and summer of the same year the new Haymarket company was organized. In view of the order of silence, Swiney felt that he need fear no competition from Rich, and accordingly he made elaborate preparations for the season's campaign. He hired actors and singers at absurdly high salaries, and made plans to take over both the theatres of the town, for he felt that he could reserve the Haymarket for opera and use Drury Lane for plays. On August 11, therefore, he put the following notice in the *Daily Courant:*

All persons who have any concern or property in the shares of rent of Drury Lane Playhouse are desired to meet Mr Swiney at Nando's Coffeehouse within Temple Bar (upon Tuesday next the 16th instant, at 3 o'clock in the afternoon), who will make 'em very advantageous proposals relating to the said house.

But the negotiations at Nando's apparently broke down, for Swiney was obliged to prepare the Haymarket for both forms of entertainment. He bought the scenes and costumes his partners thought necessary and materially improved the building's acoustics: he lowered the ceiling, filled in the arch over the orchestra, and constructed three tiers of boxes on either side of the pit. His expenses were of course high, but at the time neither he nor his partners expressed any uneasiness. They all believed that they were about to make profits far greater than any managers had ever made before.[1]

But soon after the acting season began they discovered that they were wrong, for they encountered one difficulty after another. As early as the autumn they had trouble with their operas, which proved "a constant drawback upon their gains." [2] They gave old favorites like *Camilla* and *Thomyr*is; they revived *Macbeth* with "several new decorations or scenes and machines never shown before"; they produced two new operas, *Almahide* and *Hydaspes*. But none of their offerings were really successful, and when in December Drury Lane reopened and they had to meet unexpected competition with their plays, their position became extremely difficult. With the Lord Chamberlain's consent they reduced salaries throughout the company, but even so they were soon obliged to ape the methods of their old employer, Rich.[3] They prepared entertainments, brought out Italian "night-scenes," imported a new actor from Dublin, even experimented with a Dutch contortionist, "the famous Mr Higgins." Higgins, the playbills announced, "turns himself into such variety of amazing shapes and figures that the particulars would be incredible to all persons who have not seen him." [4] Addison visited the theatre during Higgins' stay and was profoundly shocked. He wrote in the *Tatler:*

I found the audience hushed in a very deep attention and did not question but some noble tragedy was just then in its crisis, or that an incident was to be unraveled which would determine the fate of a hero. While I was in this suspense, expecting every moment to see my old friend Mr Betterton appear in all the majesty of distress, to my unspeakable amazement there

---

[1] *Apology*, I, 321, II, 79-87; C. 8 621/30 and 493/77.
[2] *Apology*, II, 87.   [3] *Ibid.*, II, 87-91; Add. MS. 38, 607.
[4] *Daily Courant,* December 7, 1709; also December 27, etc.

came up a monster with a face between his feet; and as I was looking on, he raised himself on one leg in such a perpendicular posture that the other grew in a direct line above his head. It afterwards twisted itself into the motions and wreathings of several different animals, and after great variety of shapes and transformations, went off the stage in the figure of a human creature. The admiration, the applause, the satisfaction of the audience during this strange entertainment is not to be expressed.[5]

Higgins, in short, was a happy discovery and the company apparently prospered during his stay in London. But there was another run of poor audiences later during the trial of Dr Sacheverel, and the season ended with a loss of £206.[6]

For the three actor-managers the loss was a serious matter, and they at once took unprecedented steps to provide themselves with money. On June 10 the theatre officially closed, and on the 13th (after Swiney had left for Ireland) they reopened it to give benefit plays for themselves—*The Careless Husband* for Wilks, *Othello* for Cibber, and *The Old Bachelor* for Doggett. In *Othello* Wilks took the title part for the first time in London, and Cibber "writ and spoke ... a new epilogue (intended to be humorous) ... upon all mankind's being actors on the stage of the world." [7] The three plays were generously advertised by Steele, who was apparently in the confidence of the partners. Benefits were subsequently given for Mrs Oldfield, Estcourt, Bowen, Mrs Rogers, and Mills. But—possibly because the benefit profits were small—the partners further reimbursed themselves by drawing £350 from the treasury—£150 for Wilks and £100 each for Doggett and Cibber.[8]

As early as the spring of 1710 the three actors had become very suspicious of Swiney. They knew that his bookkeeping was bad, and they were inclined to think that he had mismanaged the finances of the company and possibly overcharged them for costumes and scenes. They felt, therefore, that the £350 which they took during the summer was only their due. But Swiney had maintained from the beginning that his accounts were accurate, and when he returned from Ireland he insisted that, in view of the £206 loss, his partners had no

[5] *Tatler,* ed. Aitken, II, 389.   [6] *Apology,* II, 91, 94-96; C. 7 668/31.
[7] *Daily Courant,* June 22, 1710. The epilogue was repeated March 12, 15, and 19, 1711, at the benefits of Cibber, Wilks, and Doggett.
[8] C. 8 621/30, C. 7 668/31.

right to borrow money from the treasury. He probably laid his grievances before the Lord Chamberlain, and in any case by September,
1710, negotiations were under way for a new settlement of theatrical
affairs. On October 4 Swiney opened the Haymarket, but because the
elections were coming on and because he felt unable to pay the salaries
of his singers, he closed it again on October 7. It remained closed until
November 4, when the two companies of actors were again united.[9]

In the meantime Collier had taken over Drury Lane, quarreled with
his actors, lost his theatre, and finally appealed to the Lord Chamberlain much as Swiney had done. These events, which occurred between
the winter of 1709 and the autumn of 1710, form an almost exact
parallel to the events which were taking place at the Haymarket.

Collier is described by Cibber as "a lawyer of an enterprising head
and a jovial heart." [10] He was a Tory Member of Parliament, had
some influence at court, and owned a small share in the patent of
Drury Lane. After the order of silence he began taking an active
interest in the theatre; he contributed £25 a week toward the support of the unemployed actors and helped prepare the patentees' appeal to Her Majesty in Council. But soon realizing that the appeal was
hopeless, he urged his colleagues to compromise—to give up the patent
and accept in its place a license, which he was assured that they
could have for the asking. They refused, and after some deliberation
he decided to make the attempt alone. In the autumn of 1709 he formally resigned his share in the patent to the Attorney and Solicitor
General and applied for permission to give performances at Drury
Lane. His application was granted on November 19, and he at once set
about getting control of the theatre and the stock which it contained.[11]

The theatre was owned by the Duke of Bedford and leased to a
group of "renters," who in their turn leased it to the patentees. By
offering the renters £4 instead of £3 a day, Collier persuaded them
to accept him as a tenant, and he got the stock by simply taking it
and forcing Rich out of the house. On November 22, 1709, he built a
bonfire before the doors of the theatre, assembled his actors about it,
and gave them money to drink the healths of the Queen and the Lord

[9] C. 7 299/10, C. 8 621/30 and 493/77. Nicolini alone got a salary of £860.
[10] Apology, II, 92.
[11] Ibid., II, 91-93; Add. MS. 20, 726; C. 11 1175/59; L.C. 7/3.

Chamberlain. When the liquor had taken effect, he summoned a corporal and some soldiers, described his negotiations with the Lord Chamberlain's office, and announced that acting could begin at once. His followers were naturally in high spirits, and after a short siege they broke into the theatre and ejected the employees of Rich. But when they had a chance to examine the building, their enthusiasm cooled, for they discovered that Rich had anticipated them. During the previous night he had ransacked the store-rooms and carried off "everything that was worth moving except a great number of old scenes." [12]

These scenes—later the subject of a lawsuit between John Rich and the actor-managers—are thus described in the records of the Court of Chancery:

A scene of Naples, a scene of Venice, a scene of Richmond, a scene of two chambers, a scene of Don Carlos' chambers, a scene of two churches, a scene of a temple, a scene of a Turkish Army, a scene of Bosworth Field, a scene of a multitude, a scene of Morocco, a scene of the Temple walks, a scene of Epsom town, a scene of Epsom Wells, a scene of Covent Garden, a scene of St James's Street, a scene of Moor Fields, a scene of Eagle Palace, a figure scene, a tapestry scene, the *Alchemist* scene, a prison scene, a scene of Timon's Gates, a scene of shipping, a scene of St James's Park or torture scene, a scene of Westm[inster] Hall, a bawdy-house scene, a scene of Alexander's throne, two side scenes of shipping, six side scenes of tents, twelve side scenes of a palace, twelve scenes of Cupids' wings, twelve mirtle-side scenes, twelve scenes of frost wings, twelve scenes of orange wings, and twelve other change wing scenes, and several scene frames and other goods and things commonly made use of in the acting of plays there.[13]

On the night after his occupation of Drury Lane, Collier advertised a performance of *Aureng-Zebe* with Booth, Powell, Keen, Mrs Bradshaw, and Mrs Knight in the principal parts.[14] On December 3 he gave *Love for Love,* with the dancer Mrs Santlow as Prue, it "being the first time of her acting;" and on the 27th of the same month he revived *The Emperor of the Moon.* But his audiences were small, and soon convinced that he would make no money, he turned over the management of the company to seven of his principal actors.[15] The actors, too, did badly—in fact, they were scarcely able to buy the

[12] *Apology,* II, 92-93; also Add. MS. 20, 726.   [13] C. 11 225/50.
[14] *Aureng-Zebe* was advertised but another play was given (Add. MS. 20, 726).
[15] C. 11 1175/59; Add. MS. 38, 607.

costumes that they so sorely needed—until, at the end of February, they had the good luck to produce *The Fair Quaker of Deal*. The work of Charles Shadwell, this comedy had been passed about in manuscript for several years, and had once—probably in 1707—been offered to Cibber, who was then reader for Swiney's first Haymarket company. Cibber, Shadwell says, "took care to beat down the value of it so much as to offer the author to alter it, fit to appear on the stage, on condition he might have half the profits of the third day and the dedication entire, that is as much as to say that it might pass for one of his, according to custom. The author not agreeing to this reasonable proposal, it lay in his hands till the beginning of this winter, when Mr Booth read it and liked it, and persuaded the author that with a little alteration 'twould please the town." [16] Booth proved to be right, for *The Fair Quaker*—attractively portrayed by the beautiful Mrs Santlow—had so long and successful a run that it caused acute distress at the Haymarket and remarkable, if only temporary, prosperity at Drury Lane.

But Collier was apparently unwilling to allow the actors to enjoy the profits of the play, for he suddenly dismissed them from the management and farmed out the theatre to the dramatist Aaron Hill. From every point of view the change was ill-advised. The actors grew negligent, quarreled with the hot-headed Hill, and finally transferred their allegiance from Collier to Rich. On May 31 they broke down the great doors of the theatre, stabbed Hill's brother, forced Hill to run for his life, and discharged the doorkeepers and assistants whom Hill had appointed. Then, seeing Rich in the playhouse passage, they rushed out to cheer him and kiss his hands. "God bless you, master!" cried Leigh. "See, here we are at work for you." Collier was helpless— he had no lease, no contracts with the actors—and he was only too glad to join Swiney in a general conference at the Lord Chamberlain's office. [17]

Negotiations began, as we have seen, in September, 1710, and each of the participants stated his demands. Collier wanted actors and a theatre—a company whose profits he could share. Swiney wanted the

---

[16] Charles Shadwell, *The Fair Quaker of Deal, or the Humors of the Navy* (1710), preface.

[17] Add. MS. 38, 607; L.C. 5/155, printed in Nicoll, *A History of Early Eighteenth Century Drama, 1700-1750* (Cambridge, England, 1925), p. 292.

financial affairs of the Haymarket settled—wanted his partners to acknowledge responsibility for the deficit of 1709-10; and he was also anxious to have something done for the opera, which seemed no longer able to support itself. He suggested a subsidy—of, say, £500—to be paid by the manager responsible for plays. The three actors—Wilks, Cibber, and Doggett—wanted a license in their own names and complete control of the drama; and they wanted to return to Drury Lane, if a lease of that theatre could possibly be secured.[18]

Each of the demands was discussed, proposals and counter-proposals were made, and on November 4 a tentative agreement was reached.

(1) The two companies of actors were united at the Haymarket, and a new license for comedy was issued, in which the names of Wilks, Cibber, and Doggett were included. In exchange for this concession, the three actor-managers promised to share the theatre with the opera. They were to give plays only on Mondays, Tuesdays, Thursdays, and Fridays, leaving the house free for Collier and his singers on Wednesdays and Saturdays.[19] That they accepted this compromise with considerable reluctance is indicated by a letter which they wrote to the Vice-Chamberlain during the course of the negotiations:

We are willing to accept of Her Majesty's license and to act on such days in the Haymarket as his grace the Lord Chamberlain shall appoint. We hope our ready submission will entitle us to his grace's favor, in case we are not able to support the company under the loss of Saturday. We are, sir, etc.[20]

(2) The singers remained at the Haymarket under the direction of Collier, who, of course, was to give performances only on Wednesdays and Saturdays.

Further changes were made November 20, after Collier had secured a three-year lease of Drury Lane. It was arranged that he and the singers should remain at the Haymarket, while the actors moved to the older theatre, taking the Haymarket comedy stock with them. The actors were to pay the rent of their theatre, even though Collier still held the lease, and they were also to contribute £200 a year toward the rent of the Haymarket. Swiney and Vanbrugh held that this additional payment was rent for the scenes and costumes which had been moved to Drury Lane. The actors, on the other hand, felt

[18] Add. MS. 38, 607.   [19] *Ibid.*; C. 8 621/30.   [20] Add. MS. 38, 607.

that it was really a subsidy to the opera—a subsidy such as Swiney had suggested—and they were naturally reluctant to give money to what was now a rival company.[21]

There were two hard articles in this treaty [says Cibber, who deeply resented the favoritism which was shown to the opera], which, though it might be policy in the actors to comply with, yet the imposition of them seemed little less despotic than a tax upon the poor when a government did not want it. The first of these articles was, that whereas the sole license for acting plays was presumed to be a more profitable authority than that for acting operas only, that therefore £200 a year should be paid to Collier, while master of the opera, by the comedians; to whom a verbal assurance was given by the plenipos on the court side, that while such payment subsisted no other company should be permitted to act plays against them within the liberties, etc. The other article was, that on every Wednesday whereon an opera could be performed, the plays should, *toties quoties,* be silent at Drury Lane, to give the opera a fairer chance for a full house.[22]

But despite the two hard articles, it cannot be said that the actor-managers fared badly. They got the license, the theatre, and the actors that they wanted, and—what was perhaps even more important—they freed themselves completely from the domination of Swiney.

Shortly after the new settlement, indeed, they made sweeping changes in the organization of the company. They ordered their treasurer to keep systematic accounts; they divided their profits, not once a year, but once a week; they reduced Swiney's salary, paying him only a fourth of their net receipts. They still refused to help pay off the debts of the preceding season—in fact, they made it quite clear that they were starting afresh—and to prevent Swiney from interfering with them in any way, they instructed their treasurer not to make any payments unless he had a written order signed by at least three of the managers.[23]

Swiney was now definitely alarmed, particularly in view of the fact that his partners were drawing large sums of money from the treasury. "These proceedings, if not immediately stopped, must prove of the worst consequence to me," he wrote to the Lord Chamberlain, "and

[21] Add. MS. 20, 726; L.C. 7/3; C. 8 621/30.

[22] *Apology,* II, 102-3. The company moved to Drury Lane on November 20, and thereafter they were permitted to act on Saturdays. Actually they gave performances on Wednesdays and Saturdays at the Haymarket November 4-18 because the opera was not yet ready to begin.

[23] C. 7 668/31.

I hope I shan't be thought ill of for preventing my ruin." [24] But the actors also communicated with the Lord Chamberlain, urging him formally to cancel the articles of 1709, and suggesting that Swiney be allowed a fixed annual income, so that "for the future [he] might not have any pretense to perplex them in their endeavors to carry on the business of the theatre." [25] On the whole they seem to have come off rather well in the conferences that followed, for on January 12, 1711, Swiney took his case to the Court of Chancery. The suit went on until May 19, when the litigants finally reached a tentative settlement out of court. They delivered up and canceled the articles of 1709, fixed Swiney's stipend at £600 a year, and agreed to submit their financial differences to arbitration. The arbiters worked for many months, and by the spring of 1712 they seem at last to have settled—though in what way we have no means of knowing—the accounts of the disastrous season at the Haymarket.[26]

Soon after the decision of the arbiters was made, Swiney approached Collier, and holding out the £600 a year as an inducement, suggested a second exchange of theatres. Collier liked the terms but before definitely accepting made inquiries of Doggett. The information he received was reassuring, for Doggett explained that Swiney had no connection with the management, though he was paid a flat sum of £600 a year. Doggett added that the managers would welcome the change because Swiney was a "troublesome person" and one "that they did not care to be concerned with." With this encouragement Collier hesitated no longer, and in April, 1712, the exchange took place. Swiney got a license for opera, and Collier, Wilks, Cibber, and Doggett a license for comedy. Collier bargained to reduce the rent of the Haymarket comedy stock from £200 to £100, and being successful, kept the extra £100 for himself.[27]

Swiney took over the opera shortly after the advent of Handel, and in 1712-13 he was able to produce two new Handel operas, *Pastor Fido* and *Teseo*. But even so his company was unsuccessful, and before the

[24] Add. MS. 38, 607.   [25] C. 8 621/30.

[26] Masters' Reports, Vol. 317 (1711). When Swiney returned to the Haymarket in April, 1712, the managers paid him £350 for his interest in the stock of Drury Lane (C. 11 6/44 and 2342/26). But this payment probably had no connection with the decision of the arbiters.

[27] C. 11 1175/59. A different account is given in the *Apology*, II, 107-9.

end of the season he was obliged to escape his creditors by retiring to the Continent. "Mr Swiney breaks and runs away," says a newspaper advertisement, "and leaves the singers unpaid, and the scenes and habits (of a new opera) also unpaid for. The singers were in some confusion, but at last concluded to go on on their own account." [28] Swiney remained abroad for twenty years, became (according to Cibber) a well-known figure in the capitals of Europe, and experienced many vicissitudes of fortune. But at last he returned to England, a middle-aged man with "milk-white" hair. He had with him a remarkable collection of pictures, "fit for the gallery of a man of taste," which "with much labor and expense" he had completed. The subjects were "his own invention and elegantly executed by the pencils of the most celebrated painters in Italy." [29] But the collection was not, it seems, immediately profitable, for on February 26, 1735, Swiney had a benefit performance at Drury Lane, at which Cibber, now about to retire from the stage, played the part of Fondlewife in *The Old Bachelor*. The benefit led the two men to renew their former intimacy. They went to balls and assemblies together, and they engaged in a friendly rivalry for the affections of Mrs Woffington. Swiney came off victorious—though he was over sixty, he passed a summer in Paris with the actress—and when he died he is said to have left her an estate in Ireland of £200 a year.[30]

– 2 –

As soon as the lawsuit with Swiney was over, the managers undertook to prevent disputes among themselves by drawing up a set of rules for the regulation of the company. Each of the three pledged himself not to pay any bill, or to make any purchase exceeding forty shillings, or to hire or discharge any actor or other employee without the consent of his partners.[31] In short, they were now prepared to

---

[28] Fitzgerald, *New History of the English Stage*, I, 283.

[29] Advertisement headed: "To the Ladies and Gentlemen of Taste in Great Britain and Ireland, Owen Swiney, etc."

[30] *Apology*, I, 330; II, 108; The Earl of March, *A Duke and His Friends. The Life and Letters of the Second Duke of Richmond* (1911), II, 650; Benjamin Victor, *The History of the Theatres of London and Dublin from the Year 1730 to the Present Time* (1761), I, 157.

[31] The agreement is summarized by Doggett in C. 11 6/44. It is similar to the "Rules and Regulations for the Management of the Theatres," L.C. 7/3, printed in Nicoll,

make all their decisions unanimous. But unanimity is often difficult to secure, especially when men do not agree on fundamental principles; and the actors agreed on nothing. Fire, air, and water, Cibber says, could not be more "vexatiously opposite" than their different tempers.[32]

Doggett's passion was economy; he was continually trying to save pennies and continually quarreling with Wilks, who refused to follow his example. He was a humorist in the eighteenth-century sense of the word who clung to his whimsical notions with sullen tenacity. "In all matters that concerned our common weal and interest," says Cibber, "[Doggett] little regarded our opinion and even to obstinacy walked by his own."[33] Wilks was as extravagant as Doggett was niggardly. The stage was the passion of his life, and he did what he could to improve and embellish it. He directed the company's rehearsals, acted in nearly every play that was given, and did more than his share of the work of management. Though a stern disciplinarian, he liberally rewarded the hired actors of the company, and there was scarcely an author of any importance between 1710 and 1732 who was not indebted to him for help and encouragement. He was the most popular of the managers, and the one to whom the success of the theatre was usually attributed. He often deferred to Cibber, whose judgment he respected, but he never hesitated to join issue with Doggett. Cibber speaks bitterly of Wilks's violent temper. He was the "Achilles of our confederacy," Cibber remarks, "who, I may be bold to say, came very little short of the spirit Horace gives to that hero of his—

> Impiger, iracundus, inexorabilis, acer."[34]

In *Tom Jones* Fielding represents him thundering out, "Where are the carpenters to walk on before King Pyrrhus?" while Pyrrhus – the stolid Booth—sat at an ale-house near the theatre, quietly eating his mutton.[35] The action was typical: Wilks was continually thundering at his partners, who, he felt, slighted their work and were indifferent

Early Eighteenth Century Drama, pp. 280-81, and probably drawn up by the Lord Chamberlain during the dispute between Doggett and his partners (see Add. MS. 38, 607).

[32] *Apology,* II, 121.   [33] *Ibid.,* II, 143.   [34] *Ibid.,* II, 127.
[35] Fielding, *Works,* ed. James P. Browne (1871), VI, 155.

to the glory of the stage. Cibber was of course the most influential
manager when plays were to be accepted or rejected, and he usually
handled the company's correspondence and legal work. Like Doggett
he favored the strictest economy, but he seldom dared to stand by
his opinions, partly because he feared the hot-tempered Wilks and
partly because he realized that compromise was imperative.[36]

The history of the management from the retirement of Swiney
to the admission of Booth is the history of petty differences between
Doggett and Wilks which Cibber tried, though not always successfully, to reconcile. The two men quarreled about everything; about
the signed notes or complimentary tickets which the managers issued,
about the purchase of costumes and the hiring of actors, about the
production of new plays. Once, for example, Wilks hired a certain
Knapton, a relation of his, to estimate the attendance at the theatre
each night and thus prevent fraud in the doorkeepers. For this work
he paid Knapton eighteen shillings a week. Doggett objected to the
expenditure, but his protests were ignored. Early in 1713 Wilks—
probably with Cibber's consent—accepted Gay's *Wife of Bath* and
Taverner's *Female Advocates*. When both plays failed, Wilks gave
Gay the profits of the second night of his play and Taverner the
profits of *The Humors of the Army*. Doggett found the arrangements
irregular, but in spite of his objections they were allowed to stand.
In the *Apology* Cibber relates several other incidents of the kind,
which, though equally trivial in themselves, help to explain Doggett's
stubborn opposition to the admission of Booth.[37]

But Booth was almost certain to enter the partnership; he was
fully the equal of the three actor-managers, in some respects even
their superior. In the first place, he was a scholar and a gentleman;
he appreciated Horace, memorized passages from *Paradise Lost,* and
boasted an education at Westminster School—facts of considerable
importance where negotiations with the Lord Chamberlain were
concerned. Furthermore he was the only great tragic actor of the
company in an age when tragedy stood high in critical estimation.

[36] W. R. Chetwood, *A General History of the Stage* (1749), p. 235; *The Laureat*,
pp. 39-40; Davies, *Dramatic Miscellanies* (1783-84), III, 456-60; *Apology*, II, 111-12.
[37] C. 11 6/44 and 2342/26; *Apology*, II, 111, 121-27.

He was the successor of Betterton, he carried on the most highly prized traditions of the English stage.[38]

Contemporary accounts of Booth as he appeared between 1711 and 1713 are unfortunately not available, but accounts published after his death and based upon somewhat later observation can scarcely flatter the young man, for he was not lazy, as he afterwards became, and he was already—by 1712 at least—an actor of consummate skill. He was not tall, we are told, but so dignified in appearance that on the stage no one seemed taller. He could not even enter the Bedford Coffeehouse, Delane told Davies, without attracting the eyes of everybody because of "the benevolence of his aspect, the grandeur of his step, and the dignity of his demeanor." [39] His voice was particularly rich, and he had trained it to a fine point of perfection. "No one ever heard a dissonant note come from him. He was not only harmonious, but properly so." [40] The high point of his performances, however, was not infrequently his pantomime—the "attitudes" which contemporary critics discuss with such obvious enthusiasm. In the fifth act of Othello, for example, he listened while Emilia addressed her dying mistress—listened in so striking a pose and with such appropriate gestures that the audience seemed pleased that poor Desdemona had been strangled out of the way.[41]

Othello became in later years his masterpiece, but the parts which established his reputation and encouraged him to apply for a share in the license of Drury Lane were Pyrrhus in The Distressed Mother (produced in March, 1712) and Cato in Addison's tragedy of that name (produced almost exactly a year later). "Pyrrhus," says the prompter Chetwood, "... placed him in the seat of tragedy and Cato fixed him there." [42]

Shortly after his success in the first of these plays, Booth wrote a long letter to his friend Lord Lansdowne, describing the misfortunes of his career and suggesting that application be made to the Lord

---

[38] For Booth, see Benjamin Victor, Memoirs of the Life of Barton Booth (1733); Theophilus Cibber, The Lives and Characters of the Most Eminent Actors and Actresses (1753).

[39] Thomas Davies, Memoirs of the Life of David Garrick (1780), II, 351.

[40] Theophilus Cibber, Lives of the Actors, p. 44.

[41] Chetwood, General History of the Stage, p. 30.   [42] Ibid., p. 92.

Chamberlain. The letter is one of the only surviving examples of Booth's prose style and it shows him a master of simple eloquence and striking phrase.

After having been six years at Westminster School, instead of going to either university to pursue my studies, my folly led me to the profession I now must stick to while I live: as the world goes, actors are very rarely preferred to any other employment. I blush to own my indiscretion: I was very young; but since I have brought myself to a bad market, I must make the best of it. I have been thirteen years an actor—five years in Lincoln's Inn Fields under Mr Betterton and during that time I did not receive *communibus annis* £30 by my salary; from thence I removed under Mr Vanbrugh and Mr Congreve to the playhouse in the Haymarket, where for four years I fared not much better than before; these misfortunes threw me naturally behindhand in the world and had I not married a gentle-woman of some fortune I must have perished. For the four remaining years I received my full pay, which amounted to £110 per annum or thereabout; I have had success in my benefit plays for four years past, but never yet was able to retrieve my losses. . . . Thus, my lord, if I am not redressed, I must be a sacrifice to my equals; Mr Wilks, Mr Cibber, and Mr Doggett must raise fortunes to themselves and families while I starve.[43]

The letter ultimately found its way into the Lord Chamberlain's office and while his application was being considered Booth materially strengthened his position by his astonishing performance in Cato. He became the actor of the hour; he received a public present of 50 guineas from the Tories, and another present of the same amount from the managers themselves, who were craftily trying to buy him off. But Booth was not so naïve. Under the patronage of Bolingbroke he went to court to urge his claims, and though opposed by Cibber—sent to court by the management—he so persuasively stated his case that on November 11, 1713, a new license was issued. The Lord Chamberlain notified the managers that Booth was now their partner and asked them to sell him, as soon as they could, an interest in their stock.[44]

The managers met and terms were discussed, but as usual Wilks and Doggett failed to agree. Wilks wanted to set a high price upon the stock in order to make up for the loss they would sustain in giving a fourth of their profits to Booth. But Doggett would set no

[43] Add. MS. 38, 607.
[44] *Apology*, II, 130-33, 140-41; Chetwood, *General History of the Stage*, pp. 92-93; Theophilus Cibber, *Lives of the Actors*, pp. 6-8.

price at all; for, he said, the stock was—in part, at least—his property, and he had no mind to dispose of it, to Booth or anyone else. Cibber argued that, under the circumstances, neither course of action was practicable; that the first step was to negotiate with Booth at once and then perhaps to hold out for as good a bargain as possible. To this Wilks whole-heartedly agreed. "For my part," he said, "I do not care what we do as long as the business of acting is not interrupted." And he suggested that, if Cibber was willing, Doggett should conduct the negotiations. But Doggett sullenly refused, saying that he would not be concerned in anything of the sort. Cibber then proposed Wilks as negotiator, but Wilks answered that, as he was not good at making bargains, Cibber himself would be the better person. At this point Doggett ominously rose from his seat. "You may do as you please," he said, "but nothing but the law will make me part with my property." And he turned and left the room.[45]

Doggett's unreasonable attitude put the two other managers in an extremely embarrassing position. On the one hand, they were reluctant to come to terms with Booth, for they knew that they could not legally sell their stock, of which Doggett was part owner, without Doggett's consent. On the other hand, they were reluctant to antagonize the Lord Chamberlain by refusing to offer any terms at all. Booth was impatient, they had to do something; and in their perplexity they finally decided to revert to the original suggestion of Wilks, hoping perhaps that they could either prolong the negotiations or get so much money that Doggett would be reconciled to Booth's admission. They therefore drew up "An Humble Remonstrance" to the Lord Chamberlain in which they valued their stock at £5,350 (£3,600 for the stock of Drury Lane, £1,400 for the opera stock at the Haymarket, and £350 which they had paid to Swiney); obviously hinting that Booth would have to pay some £1,200 or £1,300.[46]

The Lord Chamberlain was extremely angry, and ignoring the humble remonstrance, immediately made terms of his own. He appraised the stock, fixed the value of a fourth share at £600, and told the managers that if they did not admit Booth without further delay, he would inform the Queen of their disobedience and have their names struck from the license. Wilks and Cibber acquiesced—indeed

[45] *Apology*, II, 141-44.   [46] C. 11 6/44.

they could do nothing else—and Booth paid the £600 and entered the partnership.[47]

But though they had failed completely in these negotiations, the managers still hoped to strike some sort of bargain with the Lord Chamberlain. They refused to believe that he would insist on their giving up a clear fourth of their profits, and it now occurred to them that he might allow them to compensate themselves by reducing, or even stopping altogether, the two permanent payments of the company—the £700 due to Collier, and the £100 due originally to Swiney and now to Vanbrugh as rent for the comedy stock of the Haymarket Theatre. Accordingly, late in November, 1713, Cibber wrote to Collier announcing that the £700 payment would be discontinued. The new license had made all previous agreements void, he said, and since Collier had no share in the stock of the theatre, he was not entitled to any part of the £600 paid by Booth. But Collier immediately appealed to the Lord Chamberlain, and before his next payment fell due he was assured that he would get exactly as much as he had got before. Vanbrugh, however, was less fortunate. For though he, too, appealed to the Lord Chamberlain when his payment was stopped, and though he forced the managers to prepare an inventory of the Haymarket comedy stock which they still had at Drury Lane, he was not able to get a warrant until January, 1715; but by this time, as we shall see, it was too late—the managers had replaced their license with a patent and no longer felt obliged to obey the Lord Chamberlain's commands.[48]

In the meantime Doggett's attitude remained unchanged. He was a party neither to the humble remonstrance nor to the negotiations with Vanbrugh and Collier, and when the new license was brought to the theatre by Wilks, he refused to admit its authority. "I know there is such a license," he said, "but I will not look at it, or acknowledge it, or act under it, or have anything directly or indirectly to do with it." In fact—after instructing the treasurer not to pay any bills without his consent—he dropped out of the company and announced that he would henceforth live on his investment. Wilks and Cibber wrote the Lord Chamberlain stating their grievances; Doggett did

[47] *Ibid.;* L.C. 7/3.
[48] L.C. 7/3 and 5/156; Vanbrugh, *Works,* ed. Dobrée and Webb, IV, 57-58.

likewise; and soon there were discussions, meetings between legal advisers, and humble remonstrances enough to stagger the whole force of the Royal Household. The Lord Chamberlain was completely bewildered. He ordered Wilks and Cibber to pay Doggett his share of the profits, ordered Doggett to return to the theatre, ordered the managers to meet and draw up a new set of rules and regulations. But in each case his orders were ignored, and in each case one party or the other drafted a humble remonstrance.[49]

Quarrels in the theatre nearly always ended in the Court of Chancery, and the Doggett quarrel was no exception. On December 17, 1714, Doggett started an action; on March 5, 1715, his partners started a cross-action; and for two years the complicated case dragged on, principally, it seems, because Cibber, conducting the defense, arranged to protract it as long as possible. I knew, he says in the Apology, "we had at our first setting out this advantage of Doggett, that we had three pockets to support our expense where he had but one. My first direction to our solicitor was to use all possible delay that the law would admit of—a direction lawyers seldom neglect; by this means we hung up our plaintiff about two years in Chancery till we were at full leisure to come to a hearing before the Lord Chancellor Cooper; which did not happen till after the accession of his late Majesty." [50]

At the hearing the Lord Chancellor decided that Doggett was entitled to a share of the profits; but clearly the theatre had suffered by his absence and the other managers were also entitled to a special allowance for doing his share of the work. Figures were therefore compiled and computations made, and it was finally discovered, rather surprisingly, that Doggett was actually in debt to the company. The whole account was then for obvious reasons set aside and the other questions at issue were settled as simply as possible. The managers were to pay Doggett one third of the £600 given by Booth for the stock, less two thirds of the £233 which still remained in his possession. At the same time the Master in Chancery was to draw up articles of agreement for the regulation of the company—similar to the articles of March 10, 1709—and was to insert a special clause

49 C. 11 6/44 and 2342/26; L.C. 7/3; Add. MS. 38, 607; Apology, II, 144-48.
50 Apology, II, 149.

freeing Doggett from the obligation to act tragic parts. Within fourteen days Doggett was to sign the articles and return to the theatre. But if he refused to sign he was to be paid £600 for his interest in the stock and permanently excluded from the management.[51]

Doggett apparently found the decision acceptable, for he returned to the stage on March 18, 1717, as Barnaby Brittle in *The Amorous Widow,* and later acted Ben in *Love for Love* and Hob in *The Country Wake.* But—possibly when the articles were drafted—he changed his mind: accepted the £600 and severed all connection with Drury Lane.[52]

The outcome of the lawsuit was a severe blow to Doggett's pride, and for a long time he could scarcely bear the sight of his former partners. But unfortunately he was compelled to meet them almost every day at Button's Coffeehouse, where he came to enjoy the conversation of Addison, Steele, Pope, and other distinguished men of letters. He never spoke to them and he never returned their greetings, though for more than a year Cibber ceremoniously lifted his hat and said "Your servant" whenever Doggett appeared. This awkward relationship between men who had formerly been so intimate caused considerable amusement in the coffeehouse, and once, when Cibber was out of town, a common friend tried to play a practical joke upon him by sending him a formal letter announcing Doggett's death. Cibber was not deceived, but realizing that his answer (if he sent one) would probably be shown to Doggett, he undertook to write in such a way as to make possible a reconciliation. He drew a favorable picture of Doggett's character, dwelling at length upon his virtues and excusing his faults. The lawsuit, for example, he attributed entirely to Doggett's having deceived himself in the justice of his case. But at the end he pointedly complained of Doggett's churlish

[51] Chancery Decrees and Orders, 1715 A, pp. 180, 212; 1716 A, p. 226; Masters' Reports, Vol. 335 (1716).

[52] *Apology,* II, 149-50. In another passage (II, 157-58) Cibber says: "To show the town at least that he had not forsworn the stage, [Doggett] one day condescended to play for the benefit of Mrs Porter in *The Wanton Wife,* at which he knew his late Majesty was to be present. . . . But as he acted only to do a particular favor, the managers owed him no compliment for it beyond common civilities." Victor says (*Memoirs of the Life of Barton Booth,* p. 8: "[Doggett] left the stage forthwith and played but twice some years after at the particular command of the late King." But the Chancery records suggest that there was a connection between the court decision and Doggett's return to the stage.

reluctance to forgive so close a friend as he had once been, especially after he had shown on so many occasions how eager he was to renew their former intimacy.[53]

A month later he returned to town, and going one day to Button's, found himself seated exactly opposite Doggett at the same table. To his surprise—for he had not heard from his friend in the meantime— Doggett suddenly stretched out his hand for a pinch of snuff. Encouraged by this friendly gesture, Cibber asked him how he liked it. "Umh!" Doggett hesitantly replied, "the best—umh!—I have tasted a great while." These few words led to others, and within a day or two Doggett had become so friendly that Cibber ventured to ask him what his real motive was for leaving the theatre. "For," Cibber said, "though our income might not have been quite so large as it was before the admission of Booth, it was certainly too large to be quarreled with without very good reasons." And to encourage Doggett to be frank, Cibber added that if he himself had done anything to disoblige him, he would gladly make any amends within his power, but first he wanted to hear the whole truth without reserve. Doggett, however, was naturally reserved and try as he would he could not at once clearly say that he had been offended by the overbearing behavior of Wilks. "No," he began, "I did not take anything particularly ill—for my part I am very easy as I am; but where others were to dispose of my property as they pleased—if you had stood it out as I did, Booth might have paid a better price for it.—You were too much afraid of the court—but that's all over. There were other things in the playhouse.—No man of spirit.—In short, to be always pestered and provoked by a trifling wasp—a—vain—shallow.—A man would sooner beg his bread than bear it."

At this point Cibber, who had clearly understood the allusion to Wilks, interrupted. "What," he asked, "had you to bear that I had not my share of?" "No," Doggett continued, "it was not the same thing. You can play with a bear or let him alone and do what he would; but I could not let him lay his paws upon me without being hurt; you did not feel him as I did.—And for a man to be cutting of throats upon every trifle at every time of day!—If I had been as

[53] This paragraph and the remaining paragraphs in the chapter are based on *Apology*, II, 150-55.

covetous as he thought me, maybe I might have borne it as well as you—but I would not be a lord of the treasury if such a temper as Wilks's were to be at the head of it."

The name of Wilks having once been mentioned, the two men conversed more freely, and gradually, as they enlarged upon their common grievances against the intolerable Wilks, their coolness disappeared.

V. THE STRUGGLE WITH LINCOLN'S INN FIELDS

DESPITE their quarrels, their lawsuits, and their bickerings with Vanbrugh and Collier, the actor-managers had found time for much valuable work during their first four seasons at Drury Lane. They had reorganized the financial system of the company, they had trained young actors and actresses, they had worked out a routine for the production of new plays and revivals; and the results of their efforts had been reflected not only in the performances of the company, which had been smoother and more exact, but in the profits, which had far exceeded the profits made by the companies of the previous decade. In 1712-13, for example, the managers had made (according to Cibber) £4,000;[1] in 1713-14 they had made only slightly less, £3,600; and between September 21 and December 17, 1714, they had made £1,700, without doubt the largest sum that any English managers had ever received during the autumn.[2] But in the winter of 1714-15 Lincoln's Inn Fields reopened, and the managers saw their enormous profits suddenly dwindle to nothing. Deserted by many of their younger actors and faced with the revival of opera and *entr'acte* entertainments, they were compelled completely to change their policies and to reorganize their company for the second time. It was a difficult undertaking, and some two years seem to have passed before they began to recover their prosperity.

The theatre in Lincoln's Inn Fields had a rather curious history. Abandoned by Betterton and his company when they moved to the Haymarket in 1705, it remained vacant until 1708, when it was offered for rent as a tennis court. On September 7 the *Daily Courant* notes:

The playhouse in Little Lincoln's Inn Fields is to be let for a tennis court or any other use (except a playhouse). Inquire of Mr John Hall next door

---

[1] *Apology*, II, 139.
[2] Masters' Reports, Vol. 335 (1716). It is scarcely necessary to add here that the value of money was much greater in the eighteenth century than it is today.

to the sign of the Angel in Little Russell Street, between Drury Lane and the Rose Tavern near Covent Garden, and you may be further informed.

Inquiries, however, seem not to have been received, for a year later the proprietors of the theatre again advertised in the *Courant*.

Any persons who have a mind to be concerned in or to rent the playhouse in Little Lincoln's Inn Fields are desired to meet Mr Porcino and Mr Sniff at Nando's Coffeehouse within Temple Bar, upon Tuesday next the 16th instant, at 4 o'clock in the afternoon; who will be there to make very reasonable proposals relating to the said house, which may be seen in the meantime. Inquire of Mr Colley, next door to the Scowrers under the said house, or at the Magpy.[3]

This second advertisement was obviously intended to attract the attention of Swiney, who had arranged to meet the proprietors of Drury Lane at Nando's at three o'clock on the same afternoon.[4] But Swiney was not interested in Lincoln's Inn Fields, and Porcino and Sniff were ultimately compelled to lease their theatre, "at a low rent," to Christopher Rich, who had recently been silenced by the Lord Chamberlain.[5] At the time Rich seems to have had no intention of using his new acquisition, for he still held the lease of a better theatre—Drury Lane. But in November, 1709, Drury Lane was taken from him by Collier, and he immediately conceived the idea of rebuilding the old tennis court and turning it into a modern theatre. The reconstruction was slow because the old man's resources were limited, but he took a natural delight in the work, which for several years went steadily forward.[6]

In 1714 Rich died, leaving his theatre, his hopes, and his debts to his two sons, John Rich and Christopher Mosier Rich. John, the elder of the two, immediately took over the work and applied for permission to form a company. The permission was granted by the King himself, and during the autumn the company was assembled and the building hastily completed.[7]

The young man at once showed that he intended to walk in his father's footsteps. He hired actors, it is true—he got some from the strolling companies and some from Drury Lane—but he prepared to

[3] *Daily Courant*, August 12, 1709.

[4] *Ibid.*, August 11, 1709.

[5] According to Cibber, Rich took a lease of Lincoln's Inn Fields as early as 1705 (*Apology*, II, 100); but this seems improbable.

[6] *Apology*, II, 100-101.

[7] *Ibid.*, II, 165-66; C. 11 2346/4.

rely principally upon singers and dancers. He built a stage far larger than that of Drury Lane and consequently more suitable for spectacular performances, and he took particular pains to make the decorations of the theatre elaborate and impressive. On either side of the stage there were mirrors,[8] and above it there was a painting of Apollo and the muses. Over the pit there was a "magnificent piece of architecture" upon which was represented a group of figures leaning over a long gallery—Shakespeare, Jonson, and others, who seemed in conference with Betterton.[9] On the opening night, Saturday, December 18, 1714, Rich gave his father's favorite comedy, *The Recruiting Officer,* and with it offered a full bill of *entr'acte* entertainments. *The Confederacy* and *The Fair Quaker of Deal,* also with entertainments, followed, and on January 25, 1715, he brought out that monument of Richian stage-craft, *The Island Princess.* The description in the playbill is significant: "With all new clothes, scenes, and decorations proper to the play. To which will be added the Frost Music out of *King Arthur,* composed by the late Mr Henry Purcell, and performed by Mr Leveridge, Mr Pack, Mr Cook, Mr Jones, Mr Reading, Mrs Cross, and Mrs Cook. With several new entertainments of dancing by Monsieur de la Garde, Monsieur Moreau, Mr Bovill, Mr Sandham, Miss Russell, and Miss Scholding." [10] How clearly the spectators must have realized on that night that the four-year interregnum of the legitimate drama was over, and that the reign of opera and entertainments had begun again!

To meet the challenge of the new theatre the managers of Drury Lane had to make their own repertory more popular. They had to get up musical shows and revive farces, build machines, buy costumes, and hire singers and dancers; they had to replace the younger members of the company, who almost without exception had gone over to Rich; and they had to make new arrangements with their colleague, for they saw clearly that they would no longer be able to pay him a flat sum of £700 a year.

The question of the £700 was a particularly difficult one and, as a matter of fact, had already involved the managers in fresh legal squabbles. In the autumn of 1714 they had taken the opportunity offered by

[8] Davies, *Dramatic Miscellanies* (1783-84), I, 247-48.
[9] Fitzgerald, *New History of the English Stage,* I, 387-88.
[10] *Daily Courant,* January 25, 1715.

the Queen's death and the fall of the Tory Ministry to get rid of
Collier. They had gone to Richard Steele and offered him Collier's
stipend and place in the management if he could persuade the government to issue a new license in which their names as well as his would
be included. Steele had done so, the new license had been issued, and
Collier had been dismissed.[11] But Collier was not entirely defenseless,
for he held the lease of Drury Lane, and though he had twice promised to assign it to the actors, he had done so with the understanding
that he would continue to get his £700. When, therefore, his payments
were stopped he immediately sued for a writ of ejectment, and the
managers were obliged to start a counter-suit for an injunction in
Chancery. Actually the case never came to trial, probably because Collier was unable to stand the expense of prolonged litigation. But for
the time being the managers were worried, and their tenure of Drury
Lane remained to some extent uncertain.[12]

In December, 1714, therefore, they approached their new colleague
Steele and frankly explained their difficulties. They pointed out that
his position was exactly the same as Collier's and that he was obliged,
now that a second theatre had opened, to give up his fixed stipend and
accept an equal share with them in the profits of the company. Steele
immediately agreed, but when they suggested that he put the agreement into writing, he urged them not to hurry. For, he said, he had
recently learned that he could get the company a patent if they were
willing that it should be granted to him and by him assigned over to
them. This, Cibber tells us, was a prospect beyond their hopes; it offered them an opportunity which they had long sought to free themselves from subservience to the Lord Chamberlain's office; and they
urged Steele to proceed as rapidly as possible with his application.
He did so and on January 19, 1715, the patent was delivered at the
theatre.[13]

The new authority proved immediately useful, for the Lord Chamberlain had just ordered the managers to continue paying Vanbrugh's
rent of £100 for the opera stock taken from the Haymarket to Drury
Lane.[14] On January 22 Cibber bluntly refused to comply with the order

11 *Apology,* II, 161-65.
12 C. 11 1175/59; Chancery Decrees and Orders, 1714 B, p. 258; 1718 B, pp. 292, 347.
13 *Apology,* II, 172-75.
14 L.C. 5/156.

and by implication challenged the Lord Chamberlain's right to exact obedience from a patent theatre.

When we had first the honor of Her Majesty's license [Cibber wrote] Sir John Stanley persuaded us to do something in favor of the opera, in consideration of our being the sole company then permitted to act; and we, hoping it would recommend us to the court, did spontaneously pay several hundred pounds to the opera. But when our license was broke into by the addition of Mr Booth's name, we thought ourselves no longer under that obligation, and have never paid it since nor received any order about it till now, which at this time seems as reasonable to be sent to the other company as ours, especially since the best part of theirs are made up of our actors, whom we cannot get an order to oblige them to return to us. And farther, neither the late license nor His Majesty's letters patents (by virtue of which we now act) nor any agreement whatsoever obliges us to continue such payments. This, sir, is what I am directed to acquaint you with.[15]

The letter accomplished its purpose—Vanbrugh and the Lord Chamberlain acquiesced—but the unnecessary abruptness of Cibber's style may perhaps help to explain the Lord Chamberlain's attack on Cibber and Steele in 1719-20, when he revoked the patent and ultimately forced the managers to swear obedience to himself and two other officers of the Royal Household before they could get it back.

In the meantime the reorganization of the company was proceeding. The managers found and trained young actors, devised entertainments, featured the more farcical members of the company (particularly Will Penkethman, whose name alone frequently appeared in the playbills), revived *The Emperor of the Moon* (November 19, 1714) "with new scenes, machines, and all other original decorations proper to the play," and *The Island Princess* (December 22), anticipating by nearly a month the elaborate production at Lincoln's Inn Fields. But these were only preliminary steps in the managers' campaign to win back their former popularity. On March 12, 1715, they brought out Cibber's *Venus and Adonis,* an Italian opera in English, designed like Addison's *Rosamund* "to give the town a little good music in a language they understand." [16] The scene is pastoral and the classical myth is crudely changed in order to illustrate the triumph of virtue. Venus courts her swain and finally succeeds in "touching" his heart. But then he encounters the jealous

---

[15] L.C. 7/3.
[16] Cibber, *Venus and Adonis* (1715), preface.

Mars, discovers her previous attachment, and decides that in his eyes at least she is no longer fair.

> Thy charms adorned with truth
> Might have subdued my youth,
> But falsehood never shall my heart ensnare.[17]

The verse is not unfairly represented by this specimen, but despite its obvious silliness the piece had a good many performances and apparently helped the managers in their struggle with Lincoln's Inn Fields.

During the summer of 1715 Drury Lane was completely redecorated [18] and before the new season was far advanced the managers began producing more musical afterpieces. The quality of Cibber's *Myrtillo* (November 5), which deals with a coquette and her unhappy lover, is sufficiently indicated by one of the opening stanzas:

> Myrtillo, would you woo me?
> Love less lest I despise you;
> Or I, though 'twould undo me,
> Shall tantalize you.[19]

Hughes's *Apollo and Daphne* and Booth's *Death of Dido* followed, and in the spring of 1716 the managers began experimenting with other types of entertainment, the *commedia dell'arte* and the pantomime. Their first efforts—*The Whimsical Death of Harlequin* and *La Guinguette, or Harlequin turned Tapster*—were, one gathers, moderately successful, but their greatest triumph was Weaver's *The Loves of Mars and Venus* (March 2, 1717) "after the manner of the ancient pantomimes," designed, Cibber says, "to give even dancing . . . some improvement and to make it something more than motion without meaning." The classical myth of the god of war and the goddess of love "was formed into a connected presentation of dances in character, wherein the passions were so happily expressed and the whole story so intelligibly told by a mute narration of gesture only that even thinking spectators allowed it both a pleasing and a rational entertainment; though at the same time, from our distrust of its reception, we durst not venture to decorate it with any extraordinary expense of scenes or habits." [20]

The new pieces at Drury Lane seem on the whole to have been

---

[17] *Ibid.*, p. 20.   [19] Cibber, *Myrtillo* (1716), p. 8.
[18] *Daily Courant,* October 6, 1715.   [20] *Apology,* II, 180.

popular and the managers gradually won back the favor of the town. The story of their varying fortunes between 1714 and 1717—of their hardships during the first season that the new theatre was open and of their gradual recovery two years later—is told with extraordinary vividness in their treasurer's account-book, summaries of which have been preserved in the Chancery records.

The managers were unusually successful throughout the season of 1713-14. Their stock plays ran well and they had good luck with several novelties and revivals, notably *An Evening's Love* (October 14), *Jane Shore* (February 2), and *She Would and She Would Not* (April 10). The average profit was £19 a night. During the autumn of 1714 the coronation helped them and their success was even more sensational. Their four revivals—*A Jovial Crew, Love's Last Shift, The Comical Lovers,* and *Wit Without Money*—ran brilliantly and their average profit rose to £26. But in December, 1714, the new theatre opened and their profits at once began to decline; in January, 1715, they averaged only £16 a night and in March only £7 or £8. The season of 1715-16 was even more trying, for nothing seemed to succeed, not even old favorites like *Philaster, The Maid's Tragedy,* and *The Relapse,* which they now hastened to revive. Their average sank to £5 a night, less than a fifth of what they had made in the period of their prosperity. But during the spring of 1716 there were indications that the worst was over and during the autumn recovery definitely began. The managers took in £200 during the third week in November and £100 during the fourth, and though they had a run of poor audiences early in December, they undoubtedly made further progress in midwinter and early spring.[21]

The most successful of their plays in 1716-17 were *Tamerlane, Henry VIII,* and *The Rehearsal.* Rowe's tragedy, revived November 5 because of its pointed political allusions, had eleven performances. The cast was a brilliant one, including Booth, Mills, Wilks, Quin, Mrs Santlow, and Mrs Oldfield. *Henry VIII* was revived two weeks later and given eight times, a tribute no doubt to the brilliant Henry of Booth and the almost equally brilliant Katharine of Mrs Porter, the gifted tragic actress who in 1714 had taken over the parts of Mrs Rogers. One is reminded that Dr Johnson, in his famous conversa-

[21] Masters' Reports, Vol. 335 (1716).

tion with Mrs Siddons, remarked that he had never seen Mrs Porter equaled in the vehemence of rage. Cibber acted Wolsey in the same revival, but though he was praised by some critics, it seems clear that he was not really suited to the part. The exaggerated gestures and grimaces that he employed belonged to Lord Foppington and his high-pitched voice at once suggested comedy. In delivering the lines,

> This candle burns not clear: 'tis I must snuff it;
> Then out it goes,

he is said to have imitated with his forefinger and thumb the extinguishing of a candle with a pair of snuffers. The mimicry was overdone, Davies tells us, and the speech became almost farcical.[22] *The Rehearsal* (February 7, 1717) offered him of course a more suitable part, but here again he seems to have been guilty of overemphasis. Copying the dress and mannerisms of Tom D'Urfey, "he rather exhibited the laughter at Bayes's extravagances," Davies says, "than the man that was enamored of them."[23] Horace Walpole's punning comparison between Cibber and Garrick in the part is interesting but quite obviously colored by his hostility to the younger actor. Garrick, he says, was inferior to Cibber. "Indeed his Bayes was original but not the true part: Cibber was the burlesque of a great poet, as the part was designed, but Garrick made it a garreteer."[24]

The three happy revivals of 1716-17 were followed, during the next season, by *The Non-Juror,* Cibber's remarkably successful adaptation of *Tartuffe.*[25] The emphasis in the play is on politics, for the chief character is not a hypocrite in general but a member of that group of clergymen of the Church of England who had refused to take the oath of allegiance to the successors of James II. But the diabolical Dr Wolf is surely a nonjuror of a rather unusual type, for he is not only a monster of iniquity but a secret emissary of the Pope as well.

[22] Davies, *Dramatic Miscellanies,* I, 397; also *The Laureat,* p. 41.

[23] Davies, *Dramatic Miscellanies,* III, 303; also Wilkes, *General View of the Stage,* p. 256.

[24] Walpole, *Letters,* ed. Toynbee, VI, 204.

[25] Dudley H. Miles has published three valuable articles on this play: "The Original of *The Non-Juror,*" *P. M. L. A.,* new series, XXIII (1915), 195-214; "The Political Satire of *The Non-Juror,*" *Modern Philology,* XIII (1915-16), 281-304; "A Forgotten Hit: *The Non-Juror,*" *Studies in Philology,* XVI (1919), 67-77. See also Croissant, *Studies in the Work of Colley Cibber,* pp. 23-24, 55; Thorndike, *English Comedy,* p. 361.

During the Jacobite Rebellion he fights for the Pretender, and after its failure he conveys bribes to juries, journalists, and disaffected soldiers. By professing to be an English, not a Roman, Catholic, he gains the confidence of the naïve Sir John Woodvil. He plans to seduce Lady Woodvil, to disinherit Sir John's son, and to make himself master of the Woodvil estate; but in the end of course he is outwitted and unmasked. As in *Tartuffe* the climax comes when Sir John hides under a table and overhears the advances made by the doctor to his wife.

The character of Wolf is so frankly a piece of propaganda that it scarcely deserves serious criticism. It is closer to the forced violence of the satires of Oldham than it is to life. The comedy in the play is furnished by Maria, a coquette of the Lady Betty Modish type, written—one need scarcely say—as a vehicle for Mrs Oldfield. Her antics are perhaps best illustrated by the stage directions in the scenes in which she teases her somewhat obtuse lover, Heartly: "She goes to [him], mimics his posture and uneasiness, then looks seriously in his face and blurts into a laugh"; she glances "gently" at him; she looks at her fan "as not hearing him"; she smiles "in his face"; she speaks "wantonly." [26] Her behavior, in short, verges on rudeness, but she is elsewhere presented as an attractive example of coquetry in high life. For throughout the play Cibber is careful to eliminate the bourgeois atmosphere which he found in Molière and to substitute his own spurious conception of gentility.

The play was produced on December 6, 1717—less than two years after the Rebellion collapsed—and though a few Jacobites came to the theatre to sneer at it, its success was never really in doubt. It was given sixteen times during December and was frequently revived later in the season. Cibber received permission to dedicate it to the King, and on January 1, 1718, he joined the New Year's throng at St James's Palace, presented a copy to His Majesty, and accepted a purse containing £200.[27] The first edition of the play appeared on January 2. Two other editions were published during the same month and two more before the end of the year.

These facts suggest that the play was almost universally admired—

[26] Cibber, *The Non-Juror* (1718), I, i; IV, i.
[27] Applebee's *Original Weekly Journal*, December 28, 1717, and January 4, 1718; Cibber, *A Letter from Mr Cibber to Mr Pope* (1742), p. 24.

by Hanoverians at least—but there was some unfavorable criticism. Pope ridiculed it in a pamphlet called *The Plot Discovered, or a Clue to the Comedy of the Non-Juror,* and Breval in *A Compleat Key to the Non-Juror.* Breval pointed out with complete justice that Cibber had been grossly unfair in suggesting that most nonjurors were like Dr Wolf. Of several other attacks the most interesting is a letter published in Mist's *Weekly Journal* of March 1, 1718, and directed not so much at the play as at Cibber's private life. It was signed, and possibly written, by the Whig playwright Charles Johnson:

BUTTON'S COFFEEHOUSE, FEB. 20

MR MIST,

I can't help desiring you to inform the public of the strange revolution of fortune which the author of a late play called *The N—J—r* hath met with. This *would-be wit (in spite of nature)* having more than once imposed upon the town some good plays for his own, has at last discovered his own stupid barrenness of genius by not making but turning a play to a subject which ought rather to be pitied than ridiculed; in which he has heaped together more malice, nonsense, and obscenity than ever was presented in one dramatic performance before. And as to his character of the parson, there is not one instance (among all those unhappy gentlemen) to be found that can justify the least part of his representation. I will not speak of the want of generosity to insult a fallen people, for the wretch never could have one spark of honor in him.

But to my present purpose. It is believed he got by the profits of this doughty performance above £1,000, which I hear he has been decently stripped of at the Groom Porter's, and I am assured it is truth; as also another piece of barbarous extravagancy: for the other masters of the playhouse, seeing his daughter very bare in clothes, kindly offered him a private benefit for her; and I am credibly informed that it amounted to fourscore pounds, which this inhuman father, rather than let his child have necessaries, made away with it also. Now I will appeal to the town whether their partial kindness is not very worthily bestowed on such a worthless creature, and whether there does not seem to be some justice in fortune in depriving a man of such ill-got pelf as that money which he got for a stolen, malicious, insulting performance, which has nothing but the name to support it, and which hereafter he must have the mortification to see acted gratis. I did not think to have taken up so much room in your diverting paper, but if you like me for a correspondent, I may hereafter furnish you with something more to the purpose. I am

Your constant customer and well-wisher,

CHARLES JOHNSON

Though obviously malicious, the story of the benefit is not improbable, and one can say that Johnson (if he was indeed the author) knew Wilks well enough to be able to report accurately what went on at Drury Lane. On the other hand, the story may have been invented out of whole cloth by the Jacobite publisher Mist, who is never very trustworthy where his political enemies are concerned.

But despite Johnson's letter and the attacks of Breval and Pope, the play continued to be popular—so popular, in fact, that it may almost be said to mark a new epoch in the history of Drury Lane. It climaxed the gradual progress of recovery which had been going on for more than a year, so that Steele was soon able to say that the theatre was flourishing "in all manner of respects to a degree unknown in any former time." [28] Completely deserted, Lincoln's Inn Fields became "the contempt of the town," and its playwrights petulantly urged the "bailiffs and catchpoles" who made up its audience to "restrain the growing power of rival Drury Lane." [29] The prosperity of the managers is perhaps best illustrated by their lavish expenditures, for, no longer uncertain of their profits, they were often able to provide their best plays with new scenes and costumes. One notices, for example, that in 1716 *Tamerlane* and *The Man of Mode* and in 1718 *The Indian Emperor* and *The Way of the World* were advertised as "new dressed"; that in 1717 *The Orphan* was presented with "an entire set of new scenes from the opera, never used here before and proper to this play"; and that in 1718 Cibber's *Ximena* was revived "with new scenes and other decorations." Their most magnificent production, however, was Dryden's *All for Love* (December 3, 1718), which, splendidly cast with Booth, Mills, Wilks, Cibber, Mrs Oldfield, and Mrs Porter, was costumed and decorated at an expense of nearly £600 —"a sum," Cibber says, "unheard of for many years before on the like occasions. But we thought such extraordinary marks of our acknowledgment were due to the favors which the public were now again pouring in upon us." [30]

[28] Steele, *Theatre*, ed. Nichols, I, 64-65.
[29] Corinna, *Critical Remarks on the Four Taking Plays of this Season* (1719), p. 6; Gabriel Rennel, *Tragi-Comical Reflections Occasioned by the Present State of the Two Rival Theatres* (n. d.), p. 8; Aaron Hill, *The Fatal Vision, or the Fall of Siam* (1716), epilogue.
[30] *Apology*, II, 175-76.

To the favors of the public Cibber should perhaps have added the favors of the court, for the prestige of the company was materially increased by the performances which, in the autumn of 1718, they were commanded to give before the King. A stage was equipped for them in the Great Hall of Hampton Court, where Shakespeare and Burbage had once acted, and here they gave seven of their best plays—*Hamlet* (September 23), *Henry VIII* (October 1), *Sir Courtly Nice* (October 6), *The Constant Couple* (October 9), *Love for Money* (October 13), *Volpone* (October 16), and *Rule a Wife and Have a Wife* (October 23).[31] " 'Tis scarce to be imagined what a great deal of company came," says a contemporary newspaper, "... especially ladies." [32] But the actors were more interested in the King than in the ladies of the court. They knew that he was difficult to please, for he scarcely understood their language, but when they observed him closely they noticed —or seemed to notice—a "frequent satisfaction in his looks at particular scenes and passages." [33] After the last performance he graciously paid their expenses, which amounted to £374, and gave them besides a present of £200, "from no other motive," we are told, "than his own bounty." [34]

[31] Daniel Lysons, *Parishes of Middlesex* (1800), p. 67. The *Weekly Journal, or British Gazeteer* of September 20, 1718, announces *The Beaux' Stratagem* for September 23, but newspaper announcements are frequently inaccurate.

[32] *St James's Evening Post,* September 23-25, 1718.

[33] *Apology,* II, 215.

[34] *Ibid.,* II, 219; also L.C. 5/157.

VI. DENNIS AND MIST

- I -

In the *Apology* Cibber recalls with considerable pride the success of his comedy *The Non-Juror*. "But," he adds, "happy was it for this play that the very subject was its own protection"; [1] for the enemies of the government immediately became his enemies and, had they not been afraid of disclosing their identities, they would have attacked him as unscrupulously in 1717 as, in the pages of *Mist's Journal,* they attacked him during the next decade. "How far I may be vain then in supposing," he goes on to say, "that this play brought me into the disfavor of so many wits and valiant auditors as afterwards appeared against me, let those who may think it worth their notice judge. In the meantime, till I can find a better excuse for their sometimes particular treatment of me, I cannot easily give up my suspicion." [2]

Possibly Cibber is right, but there are other (if not better) explanations of his unpopularity during his last years on the stage. In 1720, some time before he became the regular butt on *Mist's Journal,* he was attacked by a staunch Whig, John Dennis, and even before the appearance of the Dennis pamphlet he himself complained that part of his audience was so prejudiced against him that he could no longer get a fair hearing for his plays. The truth seems to be that for a variety of reasons he was personally unpopular, and before taking up the attacks of Dennis and Mist we should perhaps turn aside for a moment and try to determine what some of these reasons were.

In the first place it can safely be said that he was not the sort of person to endear himself to his immediate associates at Drury Lane. He was a snob and a social climber. In his early years he associated with Rich, Skipwith, and Brett, men of considerable influence in the theatre who could be useful to him in his career, and later, when he became a manager in his own right, he kept even better company—

[1] *Apology*, II, 186.   [2] *Ibid.,* II, 189.

the list of his acquaintances, in so far as we know it, is made up very largely of peers. But there is no evidence that he had many intimate friends or that he tried to make himself agreeable to his fellow actors and fellow playwrights. Furthermore he was singularly tactless, capable of deliberately antagonizing men with whom he should never have quarreled. In 1715, for example, he was asked by his fellow managers to write a letter to the Lord Chamberlain refusing to pay Vanbrugh's rent. It was, or should have been, a formal statement, but Cibber adopted so peremptory a tone that the Lord Chamberlain was almost certainly offended. Later no doubt Cibber regretted what he had done, but the damage was irreparable, the background of the theatre controversy in 1719-20 had already been prepared.

Rudeness to an actor or inconsiderate treatment of a playwright was perhaps less serious, but in the small gossipy world of the eighteenth-century theatre it was almost certain to be reported and discussed. And Cibber was frequently the subject of such reports. We are told that he was so cordially disliked by the hired actors of his company that he seldom ventured into the greenroom and that his behavior toward them was often tyrannical and unjust. On one occasion, for example, he arbitrarily reduced the salary of a certain Bickerstaffe from £4 to £2 a week. Bickerstaffe had a family, and feeling that he would no longer be able to support them, he confronted Cibber and challenged him to a duel. The timid Cibber quailed, assured the actor that a mistake had been made, and promised on the Saturday following to rectify it. He did so and Bickerstaffe was henceforth given his £4 a week. But the incident, whatever its outcome, was not very creditable to Cibber and it not unnaturally encouraged the belief that he could be influenced only through his timidity.[3]

His callous treatment of playwrights was even more notorious and playwrights were dangerous men to antagonize. They had friends, they helped to form coffeehouse opinion, they exercised a very considerable influence over what was called "the town." Cibber's position as principal reader for the company was not, to be sure, an easy one. He had to reject bad plays and touch up good ones, to discourage poetasters and sometimes offend the delicate sensibilities of men undeniably talented. He had to make sure that every piece accepted

[3] Davies, *Dramatic Miscellanies* (1783-84), III, 457-58.

for production was "theatrical." The word was ridiculed again and
again in his time,[4] but one can understand what he meant by it—
effective situations, plenty of opportunities for stage business, good
acting parts suitable for Wilks, Booth, Mrs Oldfield, and himself.
If a piece met these requirements he accepted it, if not he either
rejected it completely or demanded alterations—alterations which of
course were to be carried out under his direction. But playwrights
seldom enjoy becoming familiar with their faults, and in many cases
the foppish manager was severely taken to task. In 1704, as we have
seen, he was rebuked because he had dared to reject *The Ambitious
Stepmother,* and in 1710 he was accused of trying to appropriate work
not his own because he had offered—at a price—to improve *The Fair
Quaker of Deal.*

Cibber, however, was not a man to shrink from the unpleasantness
of discouraging his fellow playwrights: he actually liked it, he called
it choking singing birds. During the readings which were always held
when a new play was to be considered, he would frequently interrupt
with frivolous comments, and sometimes before the author had half
finished he would scream, "It is not fit for our stage, sir, it is not
theatrical." [5] But occasionally he was even more captious and unjust.
In 1711-12, it is said, he was handed a manuscript play and asked to
give it his personal attention. He turned over the first leaf, glanced
at a few lines, and dismissed the author with his usual comment,
"Sir, it will not do." Then he hurried to Button's and between con-
vulsions of laughter described the incident to Colonel Brett. His
friend, however, was not amused and after saying frankly what he
thought of the actor's conduct, left the room. Cibber squinted, took
a large pinch of snuff, and covered his confusion by pretending to
read a copy of the *Spectator.*[6]

In 1712—it is perhaps well to assemble the evidence on Cibber's
treatment of playwrights—he expressed approval of *The Perplexed
Lovers,* a comedy by Mrs Centlivre. "The business will support it,"
he said, and though Wilks caustically remarked that there was indeed

[4] See, for example, the *Grub Street Journal,* February 24 and March 16, 1732.
[5] *The Laureat,* p. 121; *An Apology for the Life of Mr T... C..., Comedian.
Supposed to Be Written by Himself* (1740), p. 71; Davies, *Dramatic Miscellanies,* III,
443-46.
[6] *The Laureat,* pp. 66-68.

a great deal of business but not laughing business, Cibber's opinion prevailed and that incredible piece of Spanish intrigue was accepted and produced.[7] Six years later he and his fellow managers took Breval's comedy *The Play Is the Plot,* but it proved only moderately successful and on the fourth night Cibber interrupted its run by announcing a performance of *Cato* with an inferior cast. The result was a disturbance in the playhouse, reported in the *Weekly Journal, or British Gazeteer* of March 1, 1718:

The night before had been the third night of a new comedy written by a young gentleman of good interest and well respected, and the boxes were bespoke for Monday night; but a certain ruler of that house, remarkable for ill-nature and immorality, stopped the run of the play and caused the tragedy of *Cato* to be given out for Monday; and though he was earnestly expostulated with on the injustice of such a proceeding, yet he obstinately persisted in his resolution, which the friends of the author of the new play very much resented. But this was not all, for when *Cato* came to be played, Mr Wilks, Mrs Oldfield, and Mrs Porter, who have principal parts, had given them to some of the inferior players; which was looked on as riding the audience, who would no longer brook what they looked on as an insult, but with their hisses, catcalls, etc., deafened the house and drowned the shrill pipes of the actors; insomuch that the loudest rant in Lee or Shakespeare had been no more to be preferred to it than the noise of a flageolet to the whistling of a tempest; till [in] the end the players were obliged to retreat to their fastnesses, unable any longer to stand their assaults; for they were stormed with orange peels, etc., as well as bombarded with hisses, huzzas, and catcalls. [Nor] would the audience suffer them to capitulate or receive any offers of submission, but calling for a dance, put an end to the play in the middle of the fourth act, to the great scandal of *Vivitur Ingenio.*[8]

Less serious as far as the theatre was concerned but even more damaging to Cibber's reputation was his inconsiderate treatment of John Hughes, whose *Siege of Damascus* was offered to the company in 1719. When the play was read Cibber strongly objected to a scene in the fourth act in which Phocyas was made to turn Mohammedan to save his mistress and his city. "It will not do, sir," he declared. "The audience will never tolerate a hero who changes his religion." And accordingly Hughes was obliged to rewrite the whole passage.

[7] Mrs Centlivre, *The Perplexed Lovers* (1712), preface.
[8] Monday is here an error for Saturday; compare the *Weekly Journal, or Saturday's Post,* March 1, 1718.

When, on his death-bed, he finished it, he sent Wilks the names of the actors he would like to see take the principal parts. But his suggestions were disregarded at the theatre and Hughes lived just long enough to see his tragedy, mutilated and perhaps wilfully mis-interpreted by the managers, become the sensation of the year.[9] Similar differences of opinion seem to have marked the reading of Steele's masterpiece, *The Conscious Lovers*. In his preface, indeed, Steele thanked Cibber for directing the rehearsals and altering the disposi-tion of the scenes at a time when he himself was, through illness, unable to attend to such matters. But he later insisted that Cibber had injured the play,[10] and other authorities point out that the altera-tions were fairly substantial.[11] Thus the authors of the *Lives of the Poets* (1753) report that though on the whole Cibber liked the play he felt that it was too grave for English audiences and demanded that comic characters be added to insure its success. Steele complied by preparing the sub-plot of Tom and Phyllis, but whether willingly or not it is difficult to say. The facts are also rather obscure in the case of Fenton's *Mariamne,* offered at Drury Lane between 1719 and 1723. According to one account, Cibber accepted the play but for three or four years postponed its production.[12] According to another, he rejected it at once and gratuitously insulted the author. "Sir," he said, "will you take the advice of a friend? Apply yourself to some honest and laborious calling; the *belles lettres* and you will never agree; you have no manner of genius for poetry." [13] In any case, Fenton took the play to Lincoln's Inn Fields, where it had a remarkably good run and considerably increased the prestige of Rich's company, which for several years had been a miserable failure. In 1731—to give still an-other example—Cibber touched up Hill's epilogue to the tragedy of *Eurydice,* and Hill complained in an agitated letter of the shameless manager's "indecent, not to say impudent, liberty." [14] But a few

[9] Davies, *Garrick* (1780), I, 209-10; John Hughes, *Correspondence* (2d ed., 1773), I, 248-52.

[10] George A. Aitken, *The Life of Richard Steele* (1889), II, 314.

[11] *Apology,* II, 206; *The Laureat,* pp. 121-22; Theophilus Cibber, *The Lives of the Poets* (1753), IV, 120.

[12] Thomas Whincop, *Scanderbeg, or Love and Liberty. To Which Are Added a List of All the Dramatic Authors, with Some Account of Their Lives, and of All the Dramatic Pieces Ever Published in the English Language to the Year 1747* (1747), p. 231.

[13] *The Laureat,* pp. 120-21.

[14] Aaron Hill, *Works* (1753), I, 47-48.

months later his anger was appeased, for his own tragedy *Athelwold* was accepted and at the reading Cibber made a suggestion of considerable value. "I have added two or three scenes in the third and fifth acts," Hill wrote to Wilks, "which I believe will have a stronger effect on an audience than all the rest of the play; but I cannot allow myself the merit of this improvement without confessing that I owe it to a hint that Mr Cibber gave me, for which I desire you to thank him in my name....I wish him also to know that I now no longer remember with a parent's animosity the murder he committed on my epilogue to *Eurydice*....His service was of so much more importance than his offense was."[15]

But one can perhaps insist too much, for the general character of the evidence is already pretty clear. Cibber was on the whole a sensible and judicious reader, well qualified to gauge the theatrical effectiveness of the plays that were offered at Drury Lane. He made mistakes, sometimes (as in the case of *Mariamne*) bad ones, but he was rarely accused of suggesting alterations that proved unacceptable on the stage. At the same time his limitations were obvious. He was interested in the theatre, not in the drama: he was almost completely indifferent to literary distinction. Furthermore his temper was frequently uncertain when he was called upon to deal with the smaller fry of the literary world. He could be rude, supercilious, even insufferably insolent when a hint, an excuse, or a few words of flattery would have saved a great deal of unpleasantness. In fact, he deliberately made himself enemies and in the long run his reputation was almost certain to suffer, not only with literary men but with the public at large.

– 2 –

Cibber's first important statement about his own unpopularity is associated with his tragedy *Ximena, or the Heroic Daughter,* an ambitious attempt to adapt—and improve—the *Cid* of Corneille. His changes to some extent reflect the canons of pseudo-classical criticism, but few of them are happy. He devotes his first act to the lovers, Rodrigue and Chimène, emphasizing the "dignity" of their passion so that when catastrophe threatens them we may be "more sensible

[15] *Ibid.,* I, 87.

of their distress." [16] He whitewashes the character of the Count (who in Corneille, he feels, "is below the dignity of the subject") and provides a villain interested in obstructing the marriage. And in the last act he resolves Chimène's dilemma by assuring us, just before the final curtain, that the Count was not really killed after all. In short, he turns tragedy into melodrama, as one might expect from the author of *Xerxes* and *Richard III*. But the audience refused to like his play, either in 1712 when it was originally performed or in 1718 when it was revived. In 1719 Cibber belatedly published it with an extravagant dedication to Steele, an elaborate defense of his changes, and a statement of his grievances against the town.

He begins the most interesting part of this prefatory matter by explaining his reasons for keeping the play so long from the press. It was principally idleness or indifference, he says; but also "it was from an observation I had made that most of my plays (except the first, *The Fool in Fashion*) had a better reception from the public when my interest was no longer concerned in them: I therefore supposed this might have a fairer chance for favor when the author had no farther stake upon it, and I hope I may be allowed the honest vanity of this complaint while I have (to my cost) so many facts to support it." By way of illustration he reviews his career as playwright, mentioning the opposition encountered by *Love Makes a Man* and *The Careless Husband,* as well as the early failure and subsequent success of *Richard III* and *She Would and She Would Not.* He attributes the indifferent reception of these works to "a certain low, latent malice" inherent in human nature—malice also responsible for the failure of *The Double Dealer* and *The Tender Husband.* He then describes in detail the reactions of the audience during the first performances of the play at hand, *Ximena.*

When *The Heroic Daughter* was first acted [he says] I had the curiosity (not having then any part in it) sometimes to slip unseen into the side-boxes, where I met with the highest mixture of pleasure and mortification: the pleasure was in observing the generality of the audience in silent, fixed attention, never failing by their looks or gestures to discover those pleasing

[16] Quotations in this paragraph and the next come from Cibber, *Ximena,* preface. For the relation of Cibber's play to Corneille's, see Dorothea Frances Canfield, *Corneille and Racine in England* (New York, 1904), pp. 167-79; Croissant, *Studies in the Work of Colley Cibber,* pp. 11-12.

emotions of the mind which I was always confident would arise from so
elevated a subject: the mortification was from a set of well-dressed merry-
making critics that call themselves the town, whose private wit was continually insulting the public diversion by their waggish endeavors to
burlesque everything that seemed to have a serious effect on their neigh-
bors; and treating the poor rogue the author (who stood with his hat over
his eyes at their elbow) with the utmost insults, scandal, and malevolence:
and when the play was over, some of the same persons (which had like to
have made me laugh) came and wished me joy of its success: but I have
since seen frequent instances that the same sort of auditors, with a little
management, have been made as enterprising friends to other authors as
they were then enemies to me: for with some leading man of the town or
celebrated wit at the head of them, they have been often known, by their
overbearing manner of applause, to make a wretched sickly play stand
stoutly upon its legs for six days together: but (as in mine and most cases)
when they are not so engaged and marshalled, they naturally run riot
into mischief and cruelty. Upon the whole, till this accident convinced me,
I never could believe that to bring a play upon the stage was so invidious
a task: and as it was with great reluctance that I from hence resolved
never to trouble the town with another, so I found it necessary (while I
was a player at least) not to put people of mere pleasure and fortune in
mind that I durst pretend to any talent that their footmen might not be
equally masters of.

Much of what Cibber says in this passage about himself and his
plays can almost certainly be taken at its face value. *Richard III* was
indeed a failure when it first appeared, and *She Would and She
Would Not* was only moderately successful. One can even believe
that the well-dressed merry-making critics were a reality, not a fig-
ment of Cibber's imagination, for malice in the theatre was much
more common in the eighteenth century than it is today. On the
whole, however, one feels that the chief interest of the passage is
psychological. It shows that even before the attacks of Dennis and
Mist, Cibber was aware of his own unpopularity—so acutely aware,
in fact, that he had made up his mind (for the time being at least)
never to write for the stage again.

John Dennis—for his quarrel with Cibber was well under way
when the preface to *Ximena* appeared.—John Dennis was one of the
more distinguished critics of the early eighteenth century. He was
perhaps too passionately devoted to the rules and too fond of insisting
upon the ethical function of literature, but he was learned without

often being pedantic, and his works are full of good sense and acute observation. Many of them—the *Essay on the Genius and Writings of Shakespeare,* for example—may be studied with profit even today, though the modern reader finds himself continually annoyed by the tiresome overemphasis of the style. In his youth Dennis had frequented Will's Coffeehouse and been numbered among the wits, but he was irritable and eccentric—an easy butt for the ridicule of his more malicious contemporaries—and with the appearance of the new generation he had gradually lost his high position in the world of letters. Poverty and almost continuous literary warfare had soured him and by 1719 he was a dangerous friend and an unscrupulous enemy. A slight, a pun, an unfortunate reference to his poverty or his plays was enough to make him lose his temper and produce those fulminations of rage which were at once the delight and terror of the town. A famous and probably unauthentic story is told of a visit to a tavern which he made with Congreve and Purcell. The two friends wanted to get rid of him and accordingly Purcell rang the bell several times and then put his hand under the table, remarking, "I think this table is like the tavern." "God's death, sir," said Dennis, for he was always profane, "how is this table like the tavern?" "Why," answered Purcell, "because there's no drawer in it." Dennis started up. "God's death, sir," he exclaimed, "the man that will make such an execrable pun as that in my company will pick my pocket," and so left the room.[17] The action was thoroughly characteristic: Dennis could neither appreciate frivolity nor control those sudden gusts of passion that swept over him. For this reason he quarreled with Swift, Pope, and Addison; for this reason too he fell foul of the actor-manager of Drury Lane, calling him an atheist, a gambler, and a rake and suggesting that he had been fathered by a cane chair upon a flowerpot.

The cause of the quarrel between Dennis and Cibber was trivial enough, if not quite so trivial as one of Purcell's deplorable puns. In 1718 Dennis offered the managers his adaptation of *Coriolanus, The Invader of His Country,* a play which he had written some years before but which he now considered particularly timely because of the recent Jacobite rebellion. Realizing that it might find favor with the Whigs,

---

[17] H. G. Paul, *John Dennis, His Life and Criticism* (New York, 1911), p. 82, note.

the managers treated Dennis with great courtesy—invited him to give his reading at Steele's house, and finally agreed to produce the play, with a few alterations, at the beginning of the following winter. But circumstances made it impossible for them to keep their promise.[18] In November they were busy with their elaborate production of *All for Love,* and in December, when they had time to consider *The Invader of His Country,* they found that Rich had forestalled them by bringing out *Coriolanus* itself, with new scenes, machines, triumphal arches, "and other decorations after the custom of the Romans." It was apparent that the adaptation could not succeed while the original was being acted, and *The Invader* was therefore postponed until the season of 1719-20.

But the reasons that the managers gave for their delay carried little weight with the impatient critic, who could not forget that his tragedy, with its lofty moral, had been neglected earlier in the autumn for the lascivious tragedy of Cleopatra. "I am almost overwhelmed both with sickness and grief," he wrote to Steele, "yet I cannot forbear making a just complaint to you for your being the occasion of both these, either by actually breaking your word with me, or being perfectly passive while your managers broke it." [19] To postpone *The Invader* was one thing, he said, but to postpone it for *All for Love* was quite another; "for was ever anything so pernicious, so immoral, so criminal as the design of that play? ... Can you believe then, after having recommended virtue and public spirit for so many years to the world, that you can give your subalterns authority to preach up adultery to a town which stands so little in need of their doctrine? ... As I had infinitely the advantage of *All for Love* in the moral of *Coriolanus,* I had it by consequence in the whole tragedy." [20] The argument was perhaps too pedantic to be persuasive, but Dennis was in no mood to weigh his words. In a second letter he reflected bitterly on the present state of the stage, and in a third he attempted to prove that Shakespeare could never have survived in an age of actor-managers. The last two letters were directed, not to Steele, but to Judas Iscariot, Esquire, a name which Dennis seems to have applied to each of the four managers in turn.[21]

[18] Dennis, *Letters,* pp. 103-11.   [20] *Ibid.,* pp. 105-8.
[19] *Ibid.,* p. 103.   [21] *Ibid.,* pp. 61-66, 70-80.

In the meantime autumn came, but though the plans for the production of the play went forward, the old critic still irritably caviled. He found fault with the cast—not, indeed, with Booth as Coriolanus nor with Mrs Porter as Volumnia, but with the actors who took the comic parts. He pointed out that the alterations had seriously affected the play, mutilating beyond recognition two of his best scenes. He objected even to the date fixed for the first performance, November 10, because, he said, the King was not yet in town; and when the play was postponed until the 11th on account of a new play at the other theatre, he again vehemently protested.[22] Pleased by the size of the audience and the competence of the actors on the first night, he was on the point of forgetting his grievances, when suddenly he discovered to his horror that Cibber's epilogue contained frivolous lines that might possibly be a satire on himself and his play. At first he could not be quite sure, for he was a long way from Mrs Oldfield, the speaker, and heard the epilogue "very imperfectly," but when he read it his suspicions were confirmed—it was "a wretched medley of impudence and nonsense." "As I saw [Cibber] had made exceeding bold with me," he wrote later, "so I found that, like a very honest gentleman, he had betrayed the trust reposed in him and endeavored to give the audience an ill impression of the play." [23] He now felt that he was the victim of a carefully planned conspiracy, and subsequent events did little to shake his conviction. The Invader failed on the second night, and after the third it was withdrawn, the managers announcing that a play which brought in less than a hundred pounds a night was not worth their while. They were willing, they said, to give Dennis a benefit play later in the season, but they definitely refused to allow The Invader to continue its run.[24]

The fury of the disappointed critic now knew no bounds, and scornfully rejecting the managers' offer, he demanded justice or nothing—justice for himself and his play, justice for the Whigs and the country, justice for the British drama and the British theatre, for no less was now at stake in this momentous controversy. On November 20, 1719, he published his play with a dedication to the Lord Cham-

[22] Dennis, The Invader of His Country, or the Fatal Resentment (1720), dedication.
[23] Ibid., advertisement before the epilogue.
[24] Ibid., dedication; Paul, Dennis, pp. 76-77.

berlain, the Duke of Newcastle. The Duke, Dennis felt, would obviously be sympathetic, for at the time he himself happened to be involved in a controversy with the managers. He had taken offense at Steele's opposition to the Peerage Bill and at Cibber's refusal to advance the Irish actor Elrington—another significant example of Cibber's lack of diplomacy. For when the Duke had asked him to give Elrington the part of Torrismond in *The Spanish Friar,* he had refused. He had pointed out that the part belonged to Booth and that in any case the managers—as a sort of separate ministry—were unwilling to tolerate interference in their affairs.[25] The rebuke had no doubt been justified, but Newcastle, already anxious to assert his authority, had determined to punish Cibber and henceforth exact obedience from all the managers of the theatre. It was just at this moment that Dennis's dedication appeared.

My lord ... this is a dedication of an extraordinary nature and an application to your grace for justice in a cause that is determinable by your grace alone, by virtue of your office, as all causes of the like nature, ever since I could remember, have been decided in the last appeal by your grace's predecessors. My lord, Coriolanus throws himself at your grace's feet, in order to obtain justice of you after having received as injurious treatment from the petulant deportment of two or three insolent players as ever he formerly did at Rome from the brutal rage of the rabble. ... I am sure all those will be apt to believe me who will reflect with indignation and disdain that that Roman is not the first nobleman whom they have audaciously dared to exclude from thence. And I hope this provoking reflection will oblige your grace to vindicate your own just right and the Crown's undoubted prerogative. If the concern which I have in this cause were the only thing in question, I should make a conscience of giving your grace any trouble about it. But, my lord, 'tis a cause of far more extensive and important consequence. 'Tis the noble cause of your country, in which your grace has been so active and so successful, and in which this play was altered; 'tis the cause of dramatic poetry, the cause of the British Muses and of all those whom they vouchsafe to inspire. 'Tis your grace who is to determine whether these shall flourish for the future and do honor to Great Britain, and consequently to augment in some measure the interest and power of your country, or whether the best professors of the noblest art, and the art itself, must die.

[25] Steele, *Theatre,* ed. Nichols, II, 532-33; *Orphan Revived,* December 26, 1719; *Weekly Journal, or Saturday's Post,* December 26, 1719; *The Laureat,* pp. 78-79; Davies, *Dramatic Miscellanies,* III, 472.

Though perhaps not influenced by this exhortation, the Duke acted as promptly as Dennis could have wished. On December 19, 1719, he suspended Cibber; on January 23, 1720, he closed the theatre and revoked the patent; and on the 27th of the same month he compelled the managers to accept a license in which Steele's name was not included, and to swear obedience to three officers of the Royal Household, the Lord Chamberlain, the Vice-Chamberlain, and the Gentleman Usher in Waiting.[26] The Duke's victory was complete, Drury Lane was at his mercy; and Dennis hastened to express gratitude and pleasure in a second communication to the public, *The Characters and Conduct of Sir John Edgar, Called by Himself Sole Monarch of the Stage in Drury Lane, and His Three Deputy Governors. In Two Letters to Sir John Edgar.*

In his dedication Dennis had been obliged to use restrained language in deference to his noble patron, but in his pamphlet he was under no such necessity. He wrote as he thought, sometimes pedantically, sometimes savagely and vindictively. He discussed articles which Steele, under the name of Sir John Edgar, had published in his journal the *Theatre.* He considered actors in general, warmly defending the popular prejudice against the profession. "Good actors," he said, ". . . ought to be encouraged and esteemed; yet to be encouraged and esteemed as *actors,* not as *gentlemen,* nor as *persons* who have a thousand times their merit: but even the best actors, with the most unblamable conduct, are never to be trusted with power." [27] And finally he sketched the character of Cibber, whom he held principally responsible for the lamentable failure of *The Invader of His Country:*

What Butler tells us of the religion of Hudibras is justly applicable to [Cibber], the deputy governor [of Drury Lane]:

> For his religion, it is fit
> To match his learning and his wit.

For having neither wit by nature nor learning by education, he has religion neither by nature nor education. . . . This irreproachable, inoffensive person has a thousand times denied the very being of a God: he has made his brags and his boasts of that senseless infidelity: he has told all the world that he retained it lately when he believed he was in the article of death.

[26] For details see Aitken, *Steele,* II, 221-36.
[27] Steele, *Theatre,* II, 351.

Oh the manly, the elegant, the generous, the ornamental qualifications of a miscreant who is stupid enough to believe that though there is mind and spirit in his wretched carcass there is none in the Heavens! For the Christian religion, he does not modestly doubt of it nor dispute candidly against it, but attacks it with the most impudent and outrageous insolence. It is credibly reported that he spit on the face of our Savior's picture at the Bath, with words too execrable and too horrible to be repeated. ... He has neither tenderness for his wife nor natural affection for his children nor any sympathizing regard for the rest of men. He has in the compass of two years squandered away £6,000 at the Groom Porter's without making the least provision for either his wife or his children. He has not the least regard for the rest of men and has had the impudence to declare that if he were on one side of the way and some miserable creature were on the other, racked with the most tormenting pain and roaring aloud for succor, he would not cross the channel to give him ease nor to save him from death and damnation.[28]

The whole passage is a typical Dennis fulmination, written in his most explosive style. But it undoubtedly annoyed and injured Cibber, for a few days later he inserted the following advertisement in the *Daily Post:*

Ten pounds will be paid by Mr Cibber of the Theatre Royal to any person who shall (by a legal proof) discover the author of a pamphlet entitled *The Characters and Conduct of Sir John Edgar, etc.*[29]

But naturally the author was not discovered. Steele helped his colleague to the extent of calling Dennis a kite and a polecat,[30] and an anonymous writer took up and denied one by one the scandalous stories in the pamphlet. "You fall foul of Mr Cibber, the deputy governor as you call him, and tell a notorious lie in saying he lost £6,000 one season without providing for his family, when everyone that knows him can tell you that he settled £3,000 that very year upon his children. Again you tax him with blasphemy, hardness of heart, etc., and I have inquired of everybody that has the least acquaintance—nay, even some that hate him without any reason—and all affirm they never heard of the story of the Bath. Therefore it must be concluded that thou hast minted it thyself."[31] But despite the denial the stories gained currency and by some people at least Cibber was probably identified with the monster described in the pamphlet.

[28] *Ibid.*, II, 358-60.
[29] *Ibid.*, II, 401.
[30] *Ibid.*, I, 97.
[31] *Ibid.*, II, 396.

- 3 -

Nathaniel Mist, whose attacks on Cibber immediately followed those of Dennis, is a shadowy figure in early eighteenth-century journalism. It is known that he was a Jacobite who for some twenty years published a paper called the *Weekly Journal,* later *Mist's* or *Fog's Journal* —it twice changed its name during its career. It is also known that he employed a staff of fairly able writers, among whom the most notable was Defoe (acting as a spy for the government!). But it is difficult to determine exactly what share Mist himself had in the paper, whether he was only a publisher with views or whether he actually wrote and edited the leading articles. In any case, the paper is distinguished by remarkable uniformity of style and subject matter. It is frequently unscrupulous, usually very witty, and always abusive of the Whigs, the Ministry, Walpole—and Cibber. For Cibber too plays a prominent part in the pages of this scandalously delightful journal.

Mist's quarrel with Cibber was, quite simply, *The Non-Juror.* Immediately after its appearance he had printed Johnson's malicious letter and from time to time he had himself written squibs about the actor-playwright, whose political opportunism—*The Non-Juror* did not of course appear until the Jacobite rebellion was safely ended —was to him peculiarly offensive. But his notices were neither particularly frequent nor particularly interesting until after the theatre controversy and the Dennis pamphlet—until, in fact, Mist realized that Cibber was not only a flagrant example of Whiggism but also extremely good copy. It was only then that he began devoting so much space to his adversary, ridiculing the man, the manager, the plays and pantomimes accepted by the company—everything, in short, connected with Cibber and Drury Lane. Contemporaries point out that these attacks were widely read and that they were, in part at least, responsible for the difficulties encountered by Cibber's theatre during the 1720s. Thus in 1727 we are told that

whatever the old house undertakes is sure to meet with opposition and derision though in itself ne'er so good.... The same man, the same performance shall have different success, so prevalent is the air of Lincoln's Inn Fields over that of Drury Lane. This shows that the town are not only

very partial but foolish in the bargain to be led by nose by such a lying
fellow as Mist, who is Rich's toad-eater in ordinary and spits his venom on
a set of players that in all probability are the best Britain may ever boast of.
Cibber is his standing jest, and right or wrong he attacks him.... But yet
Rich goes on triumphantly, his house fills, and though there are many dissatisfied, yet there are more fools to be pleased; the old house is empty,
good action and oratory at a stand, and puppet show is the word. For
my part I wish Mist at the devil.[32]

But the shameless publisher was only encouraged by complaints
of this sort and during the next three years he devoted even more
space to Cibber and Drury Lane. In 1728, when he turned over his
paper to "Fog," he charged his successor particularly to keep "Keyber"
under due correction (Keyber being the form of the name habitually
used by Mist, who possibly thought that it was the Danish original
of Cibber): "Have a strict eye over him and call him to order whenever he steals, that is to say whenever he writes." [33] Fog carried out
the charge so well that in the issue of March 1, 1729, it was suggested
that he had left Walpole ("Wolsey") to the mercy of "Caleb d'Anvers"
in the *Craftsman* in order to devote his attention entirely to Cibber:

> Each Saturday by Fog abused,
>   Whilst Keyber mourns his fate,
> Wolsey by Caleb is accused
>   Of crimes against the state.
>
> Corinthians both! alike they stand,
>   In pamphlets both defamed:
> Both on the stage bear high command,
>   Both hated and both damned.

But this is to anticipate. The first play freely ridiculed by Mist was
The Refusal, or the Ladies' Philosophy, an adaptation of *Les Femmes
Savantes* of Molière. It contains a fair part for Mrs Oldfield—the blue-
stocking Sophronia—and a good deal of topical satire at the expense
of South Sea beaux and South Sea directors. But on the whole it is
distinctly inferior to Cibber's best work and one can scarcely regret
the opposition which it encountered both on the stage and in the
press.[34]

[32] *Weekly Journal, or British Gazeteer,* March 11, 1727.
[33] *Fog's Weekly Journal,* September 28, 1728.
[34] See Croissant, *Studies in the Work of Colley Cibber,* pp. 24-25.

About five weeks before the production the company in Lincoln's Inn Fields brought out an older adaptation of the same play by Thomas Wright, *The Female Vertuosoes*. It was acted three times and subsequently published by Curll—with a dedication to Cibber— under the double title: *No Fools like Wits, or the Female Vertuosoes. A comedy as it was acted at the theatre in Lincoln's Inn Fields. Or The Refusal, or the Ladies' Philosophy. As it was acted at the Theatre Royal in Drury Lane.*

Cibber's indebtedness having thus been made plain, his enemies did not hesitate to damn *The Refusal* before they had heard it. On the first night—February 14, 1721—they began hissing as soon as Cibber appeared to speak the prologue and the uproar continued throughout the performance. The play ran six nights in all, but not, says Whincop, without disturbances every one of them.[35] Mist's *Weekly Journal* reported: "On Tuesday night last at the theatre in Drury Lane was acted a comedy called *The Refusal, or the Ladies' Philosophy,* which was stolen from a comedy lately acted in Lincoln's Inn Fields called *No Fools like Wits,* which was stolen from a comedy called *The Female Vertuosoes,* which was stolen from a comedy of Molière called *Les Femmes Savantes.* Such authors as this Mr D——s says are fed like hogs in Westphalia; one is tied to the tail of another and the last feeds only upon the excrements of the rest and therefore is generally when full grown no bigger than a pig." [36]

For several months thereafter Mist's persiflage was not at its best, but early the next year he again found an opportunity for one of his most pointed witticisms. During the winter of 1721-22 it had been rumored—maliciously rumored, we are told—that Drury Lane was in danger of falling. Attendance had apparently dropped off and the managers had finally been compelled to hire Sir Thomas Hewitt to make an official survey of the building. The results of the survey, published in the *Daily Courant,* had plainly shown that there was no danger whatsoever, Hewitt having found "the walls, roofing, stage, pit, boxes, galleries, machinery, scenes, etc. sound and almost as good as when first built." [37] Nevertheless Mist encouraged the rumor. "Has

[35] Whincop, *Scanderbeg*, p. 197.
[36] *Weekly Journal, or Saturday's Post,* February 18, 1721.
[37] *Daily Courant,* January 26, 1722; also L.C. 5/158; *Apology,* II, 177, note.

it not been suggested," he wrote, "that the builders, after a strict
survey of their playhouse, reported that it *might* stand two years
longer? ... Doubtless since their theatre is in so crazy a condition,
the claps of an audience might prove as fatal to it as a battery of
cannon and consequently no plays but Mr C[ibber]'s can safely be
acted." [38]

While the survey of the theatre was being made, Cibber had revived an old play of his which had once before been damned, *The
Rival Fools,* an adaptation—one might almost say a transcript—of
Fletcher's *Wit at Several Weapons.* It had originally been brought
out in 1709 as a vehicle for the two farcical actors of Drury Lane,
Penkethman and Bullock, but—partly no doubt because of the extravagant claims of originality in the prologue—it had "had very bad
success indeed." "I remember," says Whincop, "there was something
in it very ridiculous of a man's coming on the stage with a long
angling rod, going to fish for miller's thumbs, which made the audience afterwards, frequently when the author appeared, call out,
'Miller's thumbs.' " [39]

For the revival in January, 1722, the managers had chosen a second-
rate cast—always a dangerous thing to do because it was generally
felt that each play should contain at least one or two of the best
actors in the company. On the first night the audience silently dis-
approved, but on the second they raised such a clamor and threw so
much fruit at the actors that the performance could not go on. Cibber
came before the curtain and begged for silence, pointing out that the
play had been revived, not to make profit for himself, but to display
the talents of the younger actors of the company. But by this time the
spectators were too angry to weigh arguments, and loudly demanding
the return of their money or another play, they turned their artillery
upon Cibber himself. Oranges, apples, and turnips flew about his
head as he retreated, and among them a stone, a missile that had long
been outlawed in playhouse disturbances. The barrage suddenly
stopped, the house became quiet, and white with rage, Cibber again
came forward, offering two guineas to anyone who would discover

[38] *Weekly Journal, or Saturday's Post,* January 27, 1722.
[39] Whincop, *Scanderbeg,* p. 195. For the relation of Cibber's play to Fletcher's, see
Arthur Colby Sprague, *Beaumont and Fletcher on the Restoration Stage* (Cambridge,
U. S. A., 1926), pp. 257-63.

the author of the barbarity. But as the reward was small no one cared to turn informer, and Cibber was at last compelled to drop the curtain after announcing that *The Rival Fools* would appear at Drury Lane no more.[40]

Mist was delighted and for weeks published squibs and letters alluding to the disturbance. In his issue of January 13, 1722, there was a complaint to Steele, written "at the request of above twenty gentlemen of the Temple."

Dear Chevalier, We choose to address you in this public manner because it is upon a public occasion. You being monarch of the stage (if you are not a king of straw) tell us, we beseech you, why you suffer your ministers to abuse your people? . . . Their behavior in respect of that execrable play on Thursday and Friday in last week looked as if they were setting up for infallibility. They used us as Peter in the *Tale of a Tub* did his two brothers when he would persuade them that a slice of the brown loaf was partridge and venison; and when we discovered our dislike of the play, the speech which its author of most undaunted modesty [made] was a perfect sneer and deserved correction, viz., that this stuff was got up to show the young actors. Then it seems it is their interest to show the young actors in such horrid parts on purpose that they should not be liked. . . . The house no doubt was the first aggressor; their representing a miserable play so stuffed with filth and obscenity that it would have shamed an audience from Billingsgate was an high affront to good manners; they knew well that this play was dismissed with the utmost contempt at its first appearance and they were not content with trying it again but, finding the whole audience discovered a dislike to it, they gave it out in defiance as it were of the whole town. The second night, finding that the company would not suffer them to go on with it, they would neither give them another play nor return their money. Among tradesmen we always suppose when a man grows saucy to his customers it is time he should leave off trade; but this detaining the money is a kind of robbery.

On February 3 Mist printed "The Playhouse Scuffle, being an excellent new ballad to the tune of *London is a Fine Town, etc."* It begins:

> The playhouse is a fine place,
> The finest in the suburbs;
> 'Tis governed by three managers,
> Which causes many hububs.
> The playhouse is a fine place, etc. . . .

[40] *London Journal*, January 13, 1722; *The Laureat*, p. 47.

The first, he is a poet rare
Of wondrous parts and sense,
But all allow his greatest gift's
His stock of impudence.
The playhouse is a fine place, etc.

And in the issue of February 17 there was a letter from a certain J. H., who discussed stones, oranges, and a new invention—wooden balls. He pointed out that he had been shown two of these balls by a nobleman of the first rank. He had been surprised by their appearance, and the nobleman had kindly explained the use for which they were intended. "There was," he had said, "at Rome one Vatinius, whom an ancient author describes to have been *hominem natum et ad risum et ad odium;* his scurrility rendered him so odious to the people that they pelted him with stones in all public assemblies. At last the proper magistrates interposed and confined their fury to the use of apples. Soon after this decree a grave advocate was consulted on the decision of a wager to determine whether the fruit of the pine tree was to be reckoned an apple or a nut. 'Gentlemen,' said he, 'if you intend to throw it at Vatinius it is an apple.' Now, sir, these balls, and some twenty dozen more that I and my friends have provided, being intended solely for the service of Keyber, will not the Inns o' Court to a man allow them to be oranges, very good oranges?"

The next play of Cibber's scheduled for production was *Papal Tyranny in the Reign of King John.* It was, or seems to have been, in rehearsal during the autumn of 1723, for an adaptation of *King John* is announced by Mist on October 12; but at the last minute it was apparently withdrawn.[41] Cibber may have felt that its political lesson was untimely, or, as Victor says, he may have failed to secure the Lord Chamberlain's consent.[42] For during these years the Lord Chamberlain was extremely jealous of his authority and occasionally postponed or suppressed plays chiefly, one gathers, just to show that he could do it.

In the following year, however, Cibber was permitted to bring out another new tragedy, *Caesar in Egypt.*[43] It deals with the historical

[41] *Plain Dealer,* December 25, 1724.
[42] Victor, *History of the Theatres,* II, 49, 162-63.
[43] See Canfield, *Corneille and Racine in England,* pp. 220-23; Croissant, *Studies in the Work of Colley Cibber,* pp. 11-12.

material covered in Fletcher's *False One,* in Corneille's *Pompée,* and more recently in Shaw's *Caesar and Cleopatra.* But Cibber is interested less in history than in good acting parts, the story being clearly arranged so that Booth may be a hero (Caesar), Wilks an unhappy lover (Antony), Mrs Oldfield an impetuous mistress (Cleopatra), and Mrs Porter a Roman matron (Cornelia). Careful attention is also paid to decorum and the rules, but despite, perhaps because of, this fashionable classicism, the play never comes to life; it is as chilly as a tragedy by Thomson and quite as insipid. On the first night a "merry party," of whom Victor was one, laughed at Cibber's "quavering tragedy tones" and at the pasteboard swans which the carpenters drew along the Nile.[44] The play survived five more nights but it was definitely a failure.

Mist's comment appeared on January 2, 1725. Mr Cibber, he says, "seems to have a great aversion to the English tongue and mangles it without the least mercy. We may say of him what Sir John Falstaff did of the Welshman, 'He makes fritters of English.' . . . As for Cleopatra, he has made her a perfect Moll Frisky and I suspect that while he was writing this character he designed it for the farce of *Harlequin Sheppard* in order to help out his brother wit Mr Thurmond [the dancing master at Drury Lane]. These two gentlemen may have parts but it seems to me as if they had misapplied them: to make myself better understood, I would have Cibber *dance* and Thurmond *write,* which may tend much towards improving our public diversions."

Cibber was profoundly discouraged by his three failures, and it is possible that he reaffirmed his resolution, made in the preface to *Ximena,* never to write for the stage again. But two more of his works were still to appear—and both were to suffer indignities at the hands of the malicious Mist—*The Provoked Husband* and *Love in a Riddle.*

[44] Victor, *History of the Theatres,* II, 164.

VII. THE LAST YEARS OF THE ACTOR-MANAGERS

THUS MIST made his influence felt at Drury Lane during the 1720s, but Mist was neither the only nor the most formidable opponent with whom the managers had to contend. Between 1718 and 1722 they had to face companies of French players who specialized in *commedia dell'arte,* and between 1723 and the end of the decade they had to compete with a rejuvenated company in Lincoln's Inn Fields which brought out an amazingly successful series of pantomimes and English operas. At times they were hard pressed, for they were actors by training as well as by inclination and, try as they would, they never seemed quite able to master the new forms of entertainment. At other times they recovered much of their popularity, they gave brilliantly successful plays, like *Henry VIII* in 1727 and *The Provoked Husband* in 1728. But on the whole it was a difficult period; they were never quite out of trouble, never quite so sure of their following as they had been a few years before. They could command modest audiences but they were rarely able to equal the success of *The Necromancer, The Beggar's Opera,* and other pieces produced by the ingenious Lun at Lincoln's Inn Fields.

The French players announced their first visit in the autumn of 1717, and a writer in Mist's *Weekly Journal* at once vehemently protested. Why should we be interested in French plays? he asked. "It is well known that the French theatres never produced one good tragedy well performed; all they have signalized themselves for have been the parts of buffoons, scaramouches, harlequins, etc., which, when we borrowed from them, have been thought by men of sense and taste to tend to our disgrace." [1] The hostility of this sturdy patriot may perhaps have delayed the French company's arrival, but at last in 1718 they came, bringing with them a complete repertory of the entertainments for which, in England at least, they were celebrated. They

[1] *Weekly Journal, or Saturday's Post,* October 5, 1717.

gave *La Foire de St. Germain, Le Maître Étourdi* ("for the benefit of Pierrot, who will leap over a man upon a large coach-horse"),[2] *Arlequin Laron,* and *Columbine Avocat;* in short, they performed, as they boasted in one of their playbills, all the characters of the Italian theatre. One of their entertainments is described for us by Richard Steele, who was deeply shocked—who felt indeed that the obnoxious piece was calculated not so much to instruct as to people the British nation.

Those who did not understand the language were, it seems, informed by the gesture of the actor the main drift of the play, which was no more nor less than to promote (as one of our own prologues of King Charles's reign has it) the hopeful work of propagation. You must know, Harlequin appears as a lady dressing at her looking-glass, and there goes through the beginning, progress, and consummation of a courtship against all sense of decency or so much as cleanliness; and in order to mix with moral turpitude bodily uncleanness, the odious mimic points to all those parts which your imagination may blush to think of and then the *she* is fit for the *he* brute; the sloven is represented by motion with face downwards, the slattern by action of one falling or fallen backwards. To such abandoned and stupid wickedness is the stage already degenerated: there is no hope of amendment but that by the setting out with the utmost baseness it can arrive at it can proceed no further.... To acquaint women of honor with what is more filthy than could be seen at a brothel, to entertain our wives and daughters with what their whole education tended to make them abhor, is something more monstrous than I believed even this age of contradictions could ever produce. All this dishonor is to be purchased also at an higher price than any reasonable entertainment, and you are to pay for this abomination what would lately have been thought the most impudent extortion to have demanded for the decoration of a noble tragedy....

The wench in Petronius [Steele continues sadly] who said she did not remember the time when she was a maid will soon be among us no extraordinary character; if we go on, the very appellations of innocence and words to express inexperience of evil will be lost in our language.[3]

Steele was perhaps right, but despite his passionate strictures French companies frequently appeared in London, acting at Lincoln's Inn

---

[2] *Daily Courant,* February 5, 1719. The play is probably to be identified with *L'Étourdi* of Molière. It is only fair to add that the French companies gave performances of Corneille, Molière, Racine, and Regnard as well as of Italian farce; see Nicoll, *Early Eighteenth Century Drama,* pp. 400-407; Emmett L. Avery, "Foreign Performers in the London Theatres in the Early Eighteenth Century," *Philological Quarterly,* XVI (1937), 105-23.

[3] Steele, *Theatre,* ed. Nichols, I, 164-66.

Fields in 1718 and at the Haymarket between 1719 and 1722.[4] Their season was not long and they seldom gave plays more than two or three nights a week, but even so they occasionally affected attendance at Drury Lane. In March, 1720, Dr Rundle reports that the managers were deeply discouraged and even afraid of starving, and he goes on to say that they were contemplating a sort of reprisal—they planned a trip to Paris during the summer time "to barter our sterling poets for their tumblers and the improving grimaces of Harlequin." [5] But Dr Rundle was certainly an alarmist, for the managers were never seriously injured by the French companies, even though in the spring of 1720 they may have expressed some concern and may have waited, somewhat impatiently perhaps, for the town to change its taste. The change came—the French harlequins departed—but a year later English harlequins appeared and for a time the managers suffered really serious reverses at the hands of their old rivals at the theatre in Lincoln's Inn Fields.

Pantomimes of one sort or another had long been familiar to English audiences. As early as 1702 Christopher Rich had brought out *The Tavern Bilkers,* an Italian pantomime prepared by John Weaver; in 1717 the actor-managers had produced *The Loves of Mars and Venus,* "an attempt in imitation of the ancient pantomimes"; and between 1717 and 1722 the two theatres had vied with each other in preparing works which, according to Weaver, belonged to the same general type —*Orpheus and Eurydice, Harlequin Turned Judge, The Dumb Farce,* and *The Escapes of Harlequin* (at Drury Lane), and *The Jealous Doctor, Harlequin Executed, Amadis,* and *Jupiter and Europa* (at Lincoln's Inn Fields).[6] But the pantomime which made history on the stage and which should perhaps be considered the first English pantomime, was *Harlequin Doctor Faustus* (1723). It was the invention of the dancing-master John Thurmond and was produced, curiously enough, by the actor-managers of Drury Lane, who were soon to regret the experiment. The following quotations from Thurmond's

4 First at the Opera House, later at the Little Theatre in the Haymarket.

5 Thomas Rundle, *Letters to Mrs Barbara Sandys* (1789), pp. 18-22.

6 John Weaver, *The History of the Mimes and Pantomimes* (1728). See also Emmett L. Avery, "Dancing and Pantomime on the English Stage, 1700-1737," *Studies in Philology,* XXXI (1934), 417-52; Mitchell P. Wells, "Some Notes on the Early Eighteenth-Century Pantomime," *Studies in Philology,* XXXII (1935), 598-607.

printed description will perhaps give the reader some notion of its general character.

While the overture is playing the curtain rises and discovers the study of Faustus; he enters with a paper in his hand, which he seems to peruse with concern. He after some time pricks his finger with a pin, drops the blood into a pen, and signs the contract. Immediately thunder and lightning follow, and Mephistophilus flies down upon a dragon vomiting fire. Faustus seems surprised and runs from the spirit, who lays hold of him and embraces him, and after several actions of courtesy from the spirit, he seems to be pleased and receives a wand from him which gives him the conjuring power.

Immediately two countrymen and their wives enter. . . . Faustus (as they are turning to depart) seizes the two women; the countrymen, missing their wives, immediately turn upon the doctor and endeavor to release the women. The doctor waves his wand, it thunders, several devils enter and fright the husbands, who run into the porch of the house for shelter; which on the instant turns with 'em in and in their room a table furnished with a collation comes out. Mephistophilus sets himself down to make one at the table, whose frightful appearance drives the women away; Faustus waves his wand and the spirit is changed into a well-dressed shepherd, who dances to entertain 'em, then bows to the company, and sinks. The two husbands by this time have found the windows up one pair of stairs on the inside of the house, which they open; and perceiving their wives making merry with the doctor, threaten 'em out of the window. The wives, seeing 'em, show 'em to the doctor, who waves his wand and immediately upon both the countrymen's foreheads sprout out a pair of large horns. They still threaten the doctor, though fixed to the window, who goes out with the women, deriding the husbands. Faustus beckons the table, which runs out after him. . . .[7]

The scene changes to the inside of the house and discovers the doctor writing at a table. The usurer enters again with his bag of money, which he puts on the table before the doctor; the doctor offers him a promissory note, which he refuses with contempt and points to his right leg. The doctor offers him his arm or his head, but still he insists on his right leg. At last he complies, puts it on the table, the usurer cuts it off with a knife brought for that purpose, and goes out with the leg, rejoicing and mocking the doctor. The doctor waves his wand, on which enters Mephistophilus, who knowing what he wants, waves his wand, and immediately legs of several colors, sorts, and sizes, both men's and women's, fly in; the doctor chooses one, which is a woman's, and it immediately runs from the rest

[7] John Thurmond, *Harlequin Doctor Faustus, with the Masque of the Deities* (1724), pp. 3-5.

and fixes to the doctor's leg. He jumps on the table and admires his leg, then jumps on the ground and dances to a brisk tune. . . .[8]

The music changes, and the scene draws and discovers a poetical heaven with the gods and goddesses ranged in order on both sides [of] the stage, who express their joy for the enchanter's death (who was supposed to have power over the sun, the moon, and the seasons of the year).[9]

Faustus came out at Drury Lane on November 27, 1723, and on December 20 of the same year a rival pantomime appeared at Lincoln's Inn Fields—*The Necromancer, or Harlequin Doctor Faustus.* It was not issued complete in book form, but one can follow its action fairly closely in Ned Ward's vivacious pamphlet, *The Dancing Devils, or the Roaring Dragon.* Like *Faustus,* it opens in the study of the harlequin-doctor, who sits meditating at his table while good and evil geniuses sing to him.

> Now from a corner of the skies,
> A strange epistle downward flies,
> And shoots itself directly plumb,
> 'Twixt Harle's finger and his thumb.
> The superscription of which letter
> Is turned tow'rds every spectator,
> That boxes, galleries, and pit
> Should see what hand the devil had writ,
> Which to each curious eye appears
> As grand as a commissioner's.[10]

Faustus hesitates, and to tempt him, Mephistophilus resorts to a strange, uncommon expedient.

> And what d'ye think this strange, uncommon
> Expedient proved to be, but woman—
> A tempting devil in Helen's shape,
> On whom young Paris made a rape;
> And by his vile adulterous action
> Brought Ilium into sad distraction:
> Accordingly up starts the shade
> Of this alluring, pretty jade,
> With face so fair and eyes so bright,
> Her breasts so round, her skin so white,
> Her hips so plump, her waist so small,
> Her looks so angel-like withal,

[8] *Ibid.,* pp. 6-7.   [9] *Ibid.,* p. 13.
[10] Edward Ward, *The Dancing Devils, or the Roaring Dragon* (1724), pp. 20-21.

> That not a gazing saint or sinner
> Could guess she had the devil in her;
> Nor had this lovely Grecian ghost
> Alone these soothing charms to boast,
> But sung so sweetly to entice
> The doctor's ears as well as eyes,
> That he was all on fire to board her,
> As soon as e'er he'd seen and heard her.[11]

Faustus, in fact, willingly signs the contract and runs, with extended arms,

> To take possession of her charms.
> [But] young Helen, like a jilting minx,
> From his embraces downwards sinks,
> And when poor Faustus would have kissed her,
> Up starts Beelzebub's own sister—
> An ugly hag, as lean and frightful
> As Envy, and her looks as spiteful.[12]

There follow, as in *Faustus,* conjuring scenes and scenes of the crudest farce. For example, a miller

> Starts up, and with his mealy cap
> Gives Harlequin a dusty flap,
> Which sets the conjurer a-sneezing,
> And to his eyes proves very teasing.
> This pretty jest, in which does shine
> So much contrivance and design,
> Does such a laugh and clap command,
> From every mouth and every hand,
> As if our brightest wits had been
> Projectors of this wondrous scene.[13]

When the harlequin-sorcerer has run his course, a huge dragon appears to swallow him. In olden times, Ward remarks, dragons were not much larger than horses.

> But the bare head of our proud dragon,
> Were it cut off, would load a wagon;
> And when he gapes, his mouth may par
> With Ludgate or with Temple Bar;
> His glaring rainbow-colored eyes
> Give all spectators great surprise,

And shine as dazzling in the night
As any new-rubbed convex-light:
His wings a due proportion bear,
As sails do to a man-of-war,
And through the air convey the creature,
As t'other does the ship through water:
His scaly tail, that's twisted round
To save it from the dusty ground,
Stands always ready cocked to dart
His sting into a giant's heart. . . .
The dragon roaring opens wide
His sparrow-mouth from side to side,
And down he gulps him at one swallow,
As glib as if he'd all been tallow;
Then bellows like a greedy beast,
In pain for such another feast;
New peals of thunder roll aloud
To terrify the gazing crowd,
And render the tremendous scene
More frightful than it need have been;
The dragon roaring mounts up higher,
And gapes to show his mouth's on fire.[14]

To say that the two Faustus pantomimes were successful is to under-
state the case; they were triumphs, so great and so compelling that almost overnight they revolutionized the whole economy of the London
theatres. Read's *Weekly Journal* reports that *Harlequin Doctor Faustus* was the subject of general conversation, particularly, it seems, the
Grand Masque of the Heathen Deities, which is described as the most
magnificent scene of its kind which had ever appeared on the English
stage.[15] The piece was given eighteen times during the season. But
The Necromancer at Lincoln's Inn Fields had an even more impressive record—it was given forty-seven times. At the first performance the
theatre was full long before the curtain went up, and three weeks later
a journalist confessed himself unable to give an account of the entertainment because, he said, the house was so crowded every night that
he could not find a place to see it.[16] Lincoln's Inn Fields became the

[14] *Ibid.*, pp. 64-65, 69.
[15] *Weekly Journal, or British Gazeteer*, December 14, 1723.
[16] *London Journal*, December 28, 1723; *Weekly Journal, or Saturday's Post*, January
11, 1724.

theatre of the hour, and when the run of the Thurmond pantomime was over Drury Lane was on the point of closing its doors.

For the immediate effect of the pantomimes was to reverse the position of the theatres and to establish, for a season or two at least, the supremacy of Rich. In 1724-25 he brought out two spectacular productions—an English opera, *The Prophetess,* and a new pantomime, *Harlequin a Sorcerer.* Both had long runs and we can gauge pretty accurately their success by studying the figures in the company's account-book. Before November 28, the opening night of *The Prophetess,* the company gave only stock plays and old pantomimes; the receipts ranged from £12 (*The Spanish Friar,* November 20) to £135 (*The Recruiting Officer* and *The Necromancer,* September 30), though the average was about £50. But when *The Prophetess* came out the figures immediately soared; the opera brought in £164 (November 28), £105 (December 3), and £125 (December 7); and by the end of the month it was still playing to audiences of about £75. The company's new afterpiece, the *Sorcerer,* was even more profitable; it began at £174 (January 21, 1725) and brought in £156 (February 2), £154 (February 18), and £113 (February 23).[17] Small wonder that Lun liked pantomimes when, with a few new scenes and a few tricks of legerdemain, he could draw such vast audiences to his theatre!

During the same season the actor-managers had, as one can easily imagine, extremely bad luck. Their second pantomime, *Harlequin Sheppard* (November 28, 1724), ran only seven nights—it expired, Mist assures us, in a universal hiss [18]—and in December they were so hard hit by the popularity of *The Prophetess* at Lincoln's Inn Fields that they seriously considered selling their patent.[19] In the spring of 1725, however, they were encouraged by a moderately successful *Apollo and Daphne,* given eighteen times. The seasons of 1725-26 and 1726-27 were on the whole less disastrous, principally because Rich had only one good entertainment to run against them, and by 1727-28 they were again able to compete with their rival on nearly even terms. Two plays in particular helped to restore prosperity at Drury Lane—*Henry VIII,*

[17] Frederick T. Wood, "The Account-Books of Lincoln's Inn Fields Theatre, 1724-1727," *Notes and Queries,* CLXIV (January-July, 1933), 220-24, 256-60, 272-74, 294-98.
[18] *Weekly Journal, or Saturday's Post,* December 5, 1724.
[19] Aitken, *Steele,* II, 303.

revived after a lapse of three years, and *The Provoked Husband,* a new comedy begun by Vanbrugh and finished by Cibber.

Henry VIII owed its success primarily to the pantomime coronation ceremony in Act IV, which was made to resemble as closely as possible the real ceremony which had just taken place at Westminster Abbey, and indeed the imitation seems to have been scarcely less impressive than the original. Choir boys and privy councillors, aldermen and knights of the garter, earls, dukes, and bishops followed one another over the stage, and finally in regal robes the Queen herself appeared under a canopy supported by the four barons of the Cinque Ports.[20] "Pageants on pageants," wrote Pope describing the spectacular performance,

> Pageants on pageants, in long order drawn,
> Peers, heralds, bishops, ermine, gold, and lawn.[21]

The whole production was indeed a triumph of pantomime, but owing to an unfortunate accident the first performance (October 26, 1727) ended in disaster. The theatre was crowded and the applause loud until, in the fifth act, some one—possibly with malicious intentions—raised an alarm of fire and "put the audience in a consternation for almost half an hour." [22] Spectators from every part of the house rushed toward the doors and in the scramble several men were injured and a woman was crushed to death. Wilks immediately offered a large reward for the discovery of the offenders, and Rich, who seems to have been under suspicion himself, offered a second reward two days later. But as far as we know, the offenders were never found.[23]

Despite this inauspicious opening the play proved so popular that the managers were soon encouraged to provide it with "additional decorations" and to add a second interlude in pantomime—"The Ceremony of the Champion in Westminster Hall," [24] for which, it is said, they borrowed armor from the Tower.

[20] See Shakespeare, *Henry VIII* (1762), which describes Garrick's revival of the 1727 pantomime.
[21] Pope, *Works,* ed. Elwin and Courthope, III, 368.
[22] *Daily Post,* October 27, 1727.
[23] *Daily Journal,* October 28, 1727; *Weekly Journal, or British Gazeteer,* October 28, 1727.
[24] *Daily Post,* October 30, 31, November 27, 1727.

> The champion too! and to complete the jest,
> Old Edward's armor beams on Cibber's breast— [25]

such was Pope's malicious comment. Rich hastily brought out *A new grotesque farce called Harlequin Anna Bullen, it being a burlesque upon the Coronation of Anna Bullen and the Ceremony of the Champion,* but the burlesque failed and the Drury Lane pantomime, detached from *Henry VIII* and acted as an afterpiece, had some seventy-five performances before the end of the season.[26]

The Provoked Husband was in some ways an even more significant triumph, for it was a play not a pantomime—it marked an important revival of the legitimate drama; and at the same time it helped to re-establish the reputation of Cibber, whose series of failures during the previous decade had been extremely humiliating. It was his first successful play since *The Non-Juror,* his first important one since *The Careless Husband;* hence particularly reassuring both to Cibber himself and to Drury Lane, whose fortunes were so closely connected with his own.

The unfinished comedy left by Vanbrugh at his death and later published by Cibber under the title of *A Journey to London* concerns two groups of characters—Lord Loverule and his wife Lady Arabella, and the family of the country squire Sir Francis Headpiece.[27] The Loverules are a typical Vanbrugh couple who bicker throughout the play, chiefly about Lady Arabella's late hours and passion for hazard, until finally—though Vanbrugh did not live to write the scene—the husband turns his wife out of doors. The Headpieces move to London bag and baggage because the booby squire Sir Francis has bought a seat in Parliament and hopes to live, as he imagines most Members of Parliament do, at the expense of the Ministry. The party includes a loutish son, a pert hussy of a daughter, and a whole retinue of servants as well as the foolish and extravagant Lady Headpiece, who wants only encouragement to cuckold her husband. Accidents happen, sharpers appear, and the contrast between the manners of London and the country is brilliantly portrayed. Vanbrugh, in fact, had rarely written more

[25] Pope, *Works,* III, 368 and note.
[26] Chetwood, *General History of the Stage,* p. 68. Cibber says "forty days together" (*Apology,* II, 206).
[27] See Croissant, *Studies in the Work of Colley Cibber,* pp. 25-26, 55-56.

entertaining or more realistic scenes. One notices no decline in his powers and one feels that, had he lived, the play would have taken its place beside those two masterly productions of another age, *The Relapse* and *The Provoked Wife*.

When at Vanbrugh's death the fragment came into Cibber's hands, he undertook to finish it in the style of his friend. "My inclination," he says, "[was] to preserve as much as possible of Sir John." [28] But as he worked—as he cut, added, and rearranged—he unconsciously stamped his individuality upon almost every scene. He gave the story of Lord Loverule and Lady Arabella, now called Lord and Lady Townly, a moral and sentimental twist. "I thought such violent measures," he says—that is, turning a wife out of doors, "I thought such violent measures, however just they might be in real life, were too severe for comedy, and would want the proper surprise which is due to the end of a play. Therefore with much ado (and 'twas as much as I could do with probability) I preserved the lady's chastity, that the sense of her errors might make a reconciliation not impracticable." [29] And at the same time he pruned away the coarse humanity of both characters and left them—just persons of quality.

The Lord and Lady Townly scenes are, indeed, especially illuminating, for by studying them and comparing them with the corresponding scenes in the *Journey to London,* we learn a good many of the tricks of Cibber's trade. A few touches here and there, a few changes in phraseology, and the singularly depraved Lady Arabella becomes the elegant Lady Townly. The transformation is almost miraculous, but it takes place before our eyes. In one scene, for example, Lady Arabella says to a friend:

Thou art a most contemptible creature.... You'll make me sick of you.[30]

Lady Townly makes the same remark, but how much more genteelly she puts it!

Well, my dear, thou art an astonishing creature.... I am sure it will give me the vapors.

[28] Vanbrugh and Cibber, *The Provoked Husband, or a Journey to London* (1728), preface "To the Reader."
[29] *Ibid.*
[30] The quotations in this paragraph are from Vanbrugh, *Works,* ed. Dobrée and Webb, III, 149-50, and from Vanbrugh and Cibber, *Provoked Husband,* III, i.

Again Lady Arabella says,

How I detest that word *tolerable!*

and Lady Townly repeats, with significant changes and additions,

Tolerable? Deplorable! Why, child, all you propose is but to endure life: now I want to enjoy it.

Lady Arabella dotes on cards, assemblies, and masquerades, but she goes to sleep at the opera. Lady Townly, on the other hand, is more catholic and even more fashionable in her tastes. "At an opera—" she says, "I expire!" Examples might be multiplied but one need scarcely give more: the difference is immediately apparent. Lady Arabella belongs to the family of Lady Fidget and Mrs Frail; Lady Townly to that of Hillaria, Maria, and Lady Betty Modish. The former can safely be turned out of doors, but the latter—certainly not! She would never survive so horrid an experience. And so when her husband threatens to separate from her, she must come to her senses and repent, and with a proper display of emotion the couple must become reconciled to one another.

A less interesting but scarcely less significant transformation takes place in the character of the husband. The Lord Loverule of the *Journey to London* is a man who has undergone a profound disillusionment. "The pleasure is so great in believing women to be what we wish them," he says to his friend Sir Charles, "that nothing but a long and sharp experience can ever make us think them otherwise. That experience, friend, both you and I have had; but yours has been at other men's expense; mine—at my own." [31] There is a suggestion of finality in his words; we know that a realist is speaking; and at the end of the scene we are not surprised to learn that he has decided, or almost decided, to live apart from his wife. The Lord Townly of *The Provoked Husband* is also disillusioned, but emotionally rather than intellectually. He suffers throughout the play, he freely complains of the anxiety and disappointment of his "heart," but he never reconciles himself to the idea of separation, never admits that in his case it is not only desirable but inevitable. Lord Townly, in short, is a sentimental character who lives in a world where there is no such thing as inevitability. Nearly everyone is fundamentally good, and a wife can

[31] Vanbrugh, *Works,* III, 153.

always atone for a lifetime of frivolity by the simple expedient of bursting into tears, renouncing her follies, and giving her husband a reassuring embrace. But there is another striking difference between the husbands of Vanbrugh and Cibber. Lord Loverule is obviously rich, for he pays his wife's debts without (apparently) inconveniencing himself and he later gives her, through his steward, £200. But Lord Townly is considerably richer, for he gives *his* wife, not £200, but £500—merely to discharge her "trifling" debts of honor—and he does so without having recourse to an intermediary, without doing anything in fact but putting his hand into his pocket. Lord Loverule's guests enter his house without ceremony; Lord Townly's, on the other hand, are usually careful to announce themselves through the servants. Thus where Vanbrugh says simply, "Enter Clarinda," Cibber substitutes:

Enter, a Servant.

SERVANT. Mr Manly, my lord, has sent to know if your lordship was at home.
LORD TOWNLY. They did not deny me?
SERVANT. No, my lord.
LORD TOWNLY. Very well; step up to my sister and say I desire to speak with her.
SERVANT. Lady Grace is here, my lord.[32]

Lord Townly, in fact, is a very superior person made up of tinsel; quite as annoying and quite as offensively genteel as the husband in the *Second Mrs Tanqueray.*

Sir Francis Headpiece and his family are quite different from the other characters even in Vanbrugh—they are too earthy to be capable of good breeding, too incorrigibly comic to furnish opportunities for rhetoric and tears; and for this reason no doubt Cibber leaves them much as he found them in the manuscript. He changes the name to Wronghead, he breaks up Vanbrugh's long expository soliloquies, he improves the construction (at the same time making the plot more conventional), and he occasionally omits daring lines and farcical scenes. Thus when Colonel Courtly is about to visit Lady Headpiece, the bawd Mrs Motherly threatens to expose him. "Do," says the Colonel, "that will make her every time she sees me think of what

[32] Vanbrugh and Cibber, *Provoked Husband,* I, i.

I'd be at." [33] The speech was not used by Cibber. Later Colonel Courtly, Lady Headpiece, and her retinue set out for the playhouse, but the coachman is so drunk that he wrecks them in the kennel. They return "in disorder, some dirty, some lame, some bloody." "We rolled so," the Colonel reports, "that my poor hands were got once—I don't know where they were got. But her ladyship, I see, will pass by slips." [34] In Cibber the same characters set out on an expedition but the accident does not occur. They remain abroad all day, they buy an ocean of fine things, and at night the coach safely returns. But Cibber's changes in this part of the play are seldom so radical. On the whole, he accepts Vanbrugh's characters and point of view, and limits himself to rearranging and filling out scenes which, as they came to him, were admittedly "irregular" and "undigested."

When the play appeared (January 10, 1728) Cibber apparently had some misgivings about its reception, for he provided it with a prologue almost certainly designed to conceal his own share in the authorship. He suggested, deliberately no doubt, that the Townly scenes with their sentimental conclusion were largely Vanbrugh's, an attempt on Vanbrugh's part to atone for the licentious passages in his early works. "This play," the prologue says,

> This play took birth from principles of truth,
> To make amends for errors past of youth.
> A bard that's now no more, in riper days,
> Conscious reviewed the license of his plays;
> And though applause his wanton muse had fired,
> Himself condemned what sensual minds admired.
> At length he owned that plays should let you see
> Not only what you are, but ought to be:
> Though vice was natural, 'twas never meant
> The stage should show it but for punishment.
> Warm with that thought, his muse once more took flame,
> Resolved to bring licentious life to shame.

This stratagem, if stratagem it was, proved entirely effective, for on the first night the audience was misled into the fatal error of applauding the Townly scenes, which they supposed to be by Vanbrugh, and damning the Wronghead scenes, supposed to be by Cibber.

The first scene in Act I was a triumph for Mrs Oldfield, who, it is

---

[33] Vanbrugh, *Works*, III, 146.   [34] *Ibid.*, III, 161.

said, had never appeared to better advantage. Lady Townly was "her *ne plus ultra* in acting," Davies says. "She slided so gracefully into the foibles, and displayed so humorously the excesses, of a fine woman too sensible of her charms, too confident of her power, and led away by her passion for pleasure, that no succeeding Lady Townly arrived at her many distinguished excellences in the character." [35] On the first night she "electrified the whole house" with her speech about the liberties of a married woman, and the "applause was so unbounded that when Wilks, who played Lord Townly, answers 'Prodigious!' the audience applied that word as a compliment to the actress and again gave her the shouts of their approbation." [36] It was a different story when the Wronghead scenes began—the part of the play attributed to Cibber—and several times the hisses were so loud that the actors had to stand still and wait for silence.[37] But the Townlys were again well received in Act V, and the reconciliation scene, brilliantly acted by Wilks, "wrought so effectually upon the sensible and generous part of the audience that the conclusion was greatly and generously approved. Amidst a thousand applauses Mrs Oldfield came forward to speak the epilogue; but when she had pronounced the first line,

> Methinks I hear some powdered critic say,

a man of no distinguished appearance, from the seat next to the orchestra, saluted her with a hiss. She fixed her eye upon him immediately, made a very short pause, and spoke the words 'Poor creature!' loud enough to be heard by the audience, with such a look of mingled scorn, pity, and contempt that the most uncommon applause justified her conduct in this particular, and the poor reptile sunk down with fear and trembling." [38] The epilogue proceeded without further interruption, and when first Wilks and then Cibber stepped forward and addressed the audience, it became evident, even to the poor reptile in the pit, that the play was destined to be successful.[39]

---

[35] Davies, *Dramatic Miscellanies* (1783-84), III, 438-39.
[36] William Cooke, *Memoirs of Charles Macklin* (2d ed., 1806), pp. 23-24.
[37] Victor, *History of the Theatres*, II, 105.
[38] Davies, *Dramatic Miscellanies*, III, 438.
[39] *Daily Journal*, January 12, 1728: "After the entertainment was over we were very much surprised to hear ourselves called to account by a brave Hibernian, who told us with a sneer that the same would be acted again tomorrow and, he hoped, without any interruption. This bravo was seconded by another who, with a great deal of modesty, acquainted us that we were all fools, that we were prejudiced against

The journalists, indeed, commented unfavorably, Mist noting:

On Wednesday last a most horrid, barbarous, and cruel murder was committed at the Theatre Royal in Drury Lane upon a posthumous child of the late Sir John Vanbrugh by one who for some time past has gone by the name of Keyber. It was a fine child born and would certainly have lived long had it not fallen into such cruel hands.[40]

The *Daily Journal* was more specific, suggesting that Cibber had all but ruined the play by introducing the sub-plot of the Wrongheads:

The reputation of the late Sir John Vanbrugh drew me last night to see a play he left behind him, which was intrusted to the care of an ingenious gentleman. We are told in the prologue that the author designed, by the morality of this performance, to make amends for the licentiousness of his former productions, and I was wonderfully delighted to see this good design so well executed. But I could not help expressing my concern to find it intermixed with obscenity, ribaldry, and nonsense. I need not enlarge on the beauties and faults of this play: they were both so *judiciously* distinguished by the audience that no exceptions could be made to their dislike or applause.[41]

But when the Vanbrugh fragment was published,[42] these strictures were blasted and the play continued its run for nearly a month. It left off, Cibber says, "at a receipt of upwards of £140, which happened to be more than in fifty years before could be then said of any one play whatsoever." [43]

But though *The Provoked Husband* succeeded despite the efforts of Mist and his friends, it at least furnished them with an excellent joke at Cibber's expense—the joke about *paraphonalia* and *outdid her usual outdoing.* In the preface to the play Cibber had praised his fellow actors Wilks and Mills, and had ended with a warm tribute to the inimitable Mrs Oldfield.

I will venture to say of Mr Wilks [he had written] that in the last act I never saw any passion take so natural a possession of an actor, or any actor

everything that passed through his hands, and that we had hissed several things of *undeniable merit;* and I wish when he went on to say that this performance was hissed only by the mob, he had considered that persons of the first distinction fell under his censure."

[40] *Mist's Weekly Journal,* January 13, 1728.

[41] *Daily Journal,* January 12, 1728.

[42] *Daily Post:* "Jan. 31, 1727/8. This day is published for the satisfaction of the curious, *A Journey to London....*"

[43] *Apology,* II, 190.

take so tender a possession of his auditors. Mr Mills, too, is confessed by everybody to have surprised them by so far excelling himself. But there is no doing right to Mrs Oldfield without putting people in mind of what others of great merit have wanted to come near her. 'Tis not enough to say, she *here outdid* her usual *outdoing*.[44]

He had then given a theatrical character of Mrs Oldfield, in the course of which he had said:

The qualities she had *acquired* were the *genteel* and the *elegant*. The one in her air and the other in her dress never had her equal on the stage, and the ornaments she herself provided (particularly in this play) seemed in all respects the *paraphonalia* of a woman of quality.

Cibber's unhappy blunders were at once noticed by Mist, who commented at length:

We must take a little notice of Mr C[ibber]'s preface; not that I intend to make an exact critique upon it, for to tell the truth, it is above my capacity, unless some person of learning would be so good as to translate it into English for me; for I own it is written in a language of which I understand no part of speech; however, I have been informed by some that have consulted the players upon it that he designed it as a panegyric upon himself as an author and upon his brethren as actors. He calls it a picture in which Mrs Oldfield stands the principal figure, and truly his character of her has something in it very peculiar. . . . He goes on to assure us that *she outdid her own outdoing;* which expression people maliciously explain into a scandalous reflection upon that lady's reputation, but for no other reason but because they don't understand it. . . . But the master stroke is not yet taken notice of, it is there Mr C[ibbe]r has shown his fine parts; for before he has done with this lady, he tells us that *the ornaments she herself provided (particularly in this play) seemed in all respects the* PARAPHANALIA [sic] *of a woman of quality.* There's a noble word! Let the admirers of Dryden, Otway, or Wycherley show me where any of them have written so fine a word. The critics, indeed, pretend he meant *paraphernalia,* but that objection will appear idle when it can be proved that one is as much to the purpose as the other.[45]

In the second edition Cibber changed *outdoing* to *excellence* and spelled *paraphernalia* correctly, but the damage had already been done —the blunders furnished material for parody as long as he remained on the stage.

[44] This quotation and the one which immediately follows are from Vanbrugh and Cibber, *Provoked Husband,* preface.
[45] *Mist's Weekly Journal,* February 24, 1728.

Before *The Provoked Husband* had finished its run at Drury Lane, *The Beggar's Opera* was produced at Lincoln's Inn Fields. It was, of course, amazingly successful—so successful, in fact, that it helped rather than injured the play at the rival theatre. On February 8 a writer in the *Daily Journal* notes: Gay's piece "meets with that universal applause that not one third part of the company that crowd thither to see it can get admittance; which occasions a new run to *The Provoked Husband* at Drury Lane and so proves an equal advantage to both houses." But *The Beggar's Opera* continued to be acted long after *The Provoked Husband* had been withdrawn, and when autumn came both theatres began preparing operas of the new type. Gay worked on *Polly* for Rich, while Cibber wrote *Love in a Riddle* for his fellow managers at Drury Lane.

In the *Apology* Cibber briefly points out what he tried to do in his ill-fated opera. "After the vast success of that new species of dramatic poetry, *The Beggar's Opera*," he says, "the year following I was so stupid as to attempt something of the same kind upon a quite different foundation, that of recommending virtue and innocence, which I ignorantly thought might not have a less pretense to favor than setting greatness and authority in a contemptible, and the most vulgar vice and wickedness in an amiable light." [46] Virtue and innocence are indeed the subjects of *Love in a Riddle*. The scene is Arcadia, and with one or two exceptions, the characters are love-sick swains and artless maidens. Ianthe is in love with Iphis, but because he has stolen a kiss from her, she will not have him until he solves a riddle proposed by the oracle of Diana. Driven almost to madness, he himself consults the oracle, learns the solution, and wins his bride. Pastora's virtue is tried by her father, who offers to let her marry Philautus, "a conceited Corinthian courtier." To her father's delight, she rejects the offer and gives her hand to her shepherd-lover Amyntas. Phillida loves Damon, "an inconstant," who returns her affection but refuses to marry her. Her father, Corydon, urges her to forget Damon and choose between the "simple brothers," Cimon and Mopsus. Fortunately, however, Damon reforms and Phillida too is happily married.

Wit never intrudes into this pastoral romance; the pace is slow and

---

[46] *Apology*, I, 243-44. For a recent discussion of *Love in a Riddle*, see Edmond Mc-Adoo Gagey, *Ballad Opera* (New York, 1937), pp. 79-81.

the dialogue is carried on in inflated blank verse. In his songs Cibber
is closer to Gay, though even here he is always careful to recommend
virtue. A good example is:

> Virgins, beware how you fix on a lover!
> Beds of flowers may harbor a snake;
> Gold and silver gaily may cover
> Heads that wander and hearts that forsake.[47]

Too often we are reminded of *Myrtillo* and *Venus and Adonis;* but
occasionally a stanza is neatly turned, as in Phillida's complaint:

> I caught him once making love to a maid,
> When to him I ran.
> He turned and he kissed me, then who could upbraid
> So civil a man?
> The next day I found to a third he was kind,
> I rated him soundly, he swore I was blind;
> So, let me do what I can,
> Still—still he's the man.[48]

The men's parts were prepared for Mills, Harper, Williams, Ray, and
Mrs Thurmond; the women's for Mrs Lindar, Mrs Theophilus Cibber,
and a young actress who was just becoming popular—Mrs Raftor, the
future Mrs Clive. Despite his shrill voice, Cibber himself undertook to
act and sing Philautus.

The fate of *Love in a Riddle* was apparently settled at least six
months before the first performance took place. As early as the spring
of 1728 it was probably known that Cibber had rejected *The Beggar's
Opera,* which had first been offered at Drury Lane, and when, in the
autumn of the same year, it appeared that he himself was writing a
similar opera, the newspapers at once began printing frivolous notices
about it. In his issue of September 7-14 Mist announced:

The *very ingenious* Mr Cibber, who has so often obliged the town at *his
own expense,* will, we hear, very speedily present the public with an entertainment entitled *The Egyptians'* (*or Gypsies'*) *Opera;* being supposed to
be a sequel of his last celebrated performance called *Caesar in Egypt.*

Six weeks later the *Daily Journal* made a similar announcement:

We hear the company of players at the old house intend to entertain the
town shortly with a new comedy written by a celebrated hand, noted for

[47] Cibber, *Love in a Riddle* (1729), II, ii.   [48] *Ibid.,* II, i.

malignancy to his brethren of the quill and for his ill success hitherto in dramatical performances.[49]

In December a different tone is noticeable, for in that month *Polly* was suppressed. The newspapers undoubtedly suspected that Cibber had influenced the Lord Chamberlain, and in any case they knew that he stood to gain if *Love in a Riddle* were the only ballad-opera of the season. The *Craftsman* wrote:

The sequel to *The Beggar's Opera,* which was going into rehearsal at the theatre in Lincoln's Inn Fields, is suppressed by *authority* without any particular reasons being alleged; but we doubt not that the public will be soon made acquainted with the *exceptions* to it, which must be very strong since the *properties* of so many people are concerned in this affair. It is hoped, from *this circumstance,* that the celebrated Mr Cibber's opera (which we are assured is perfectly *inoffensive*) will be now acted with great success.[50]

The *Craftsman's* appeal was answered, for on the night of the first performance—January 7, 1729—hostile groups appeared in every part of the house. They hissed and jeered during the first act, stopped during the second to encourage Mrs Raftor, and then damned the play in the third when Cibber himself was on the stage.[51] "I remember," says a spectator, "Mrs Thurmond, who played some shepherdess or other in this piece, came on to attack Philautus with a boar spear, and as she held it level to his person, some ill-natured persons cried out from the pit, 'Kill him, kill him!' at which Philautus started back a good deal frighted. . . . [The audience] called aloud several times to have the curtain dropped; but Philautus came forward and humbly petitioned that they would hear him one song more. They granted his request and then damned his new-fangled innocent performance." [52]

The second night was a repetition of the first, even though Cibber, to intimidate his enemies, had induced the Prince of Wales to be present. "The audience," says another observer, "without any regard to who was there, made such a scandalous noise of hissing, talking, and catcalling that for two acts not a word could be heard"; [53] and in

[49] *Daily Journal,* October 22, 1728.
[50] *Craftsman,* December 14, 1728; also *Apology,* I, 246-48.
[51] Whincop, *Scanderbeg,* p. 197; Chetwood, *General History of the Stage,* pp. 127-28.
[52] *The Laureat,* p. 46.
[53] *Historical MSS. Commission, Diary of the Earl of Egmont* (1920-23), III, 325.

the third act Cibber himself finally realized that the play could never survive.

I therefore quitted the actor for the author [he says] and stepping forward to the pit, told them that since I found they were not inclined that this play should go forward, I gave them my word that after this night it should never be acted again; but that in the meantime I hoped they would consider in whose presence they were and for that reason at least would suspend what farther marks of their displeasure they might imagine I had deserved. At this there was a dead silence, and after some little pause a few civilized hands signified their approbation. When the play went on, I observed about a dozen persons of no extraordinary appearance sullenly walked out of the pit; after which every scene of it, while uninterrupted, met with more applause than my best hopes had expected. But it came too late: peace to its *manes!* I had given my word it should fall and I kept it by giving out another play for the next day, though I knew the boxes were all let for the same again. Such then was the treatment I met with.[54]

It was left for Mist to provide an epitaph for the play, which he did with more than his usual wit:

On Tuesday night last a ridiculous piece was acted at the theatre in Drury Lane which was neither comedy, tragedy, opera, pastoral, or farce; however, no thief or robber of any rank was satirized in it and it could be said to give offense to none but persons of sense and good taste; yet it met with the reception it well deserved and was hissed off the stage. However, it may serve to bind up with the rest of Keyber's works.[55]

But the fury of Gay's partisans was not entirely spent, and when the managers attempted to produce another piece of the same type—*The Village Opera* by Charles Johnson—they encountered similar difficulties. The *Craftsman,* indeed, urged the town to "give it a favorable reception and show that their late treatment of *another piece* did not proceed from any prejudice against *that company* in general"; [56] but this time the *Craftsman's* appeal was ignored. On the second night "some persons in the gallery were so clamorous that the play could not go on, but a constable, assisted by a sergeant and the guards, prevailed on them to walk out. One of them was carried before a justice

[54] *Apology,* I, 248-49; also Whincop, *Scanderbeg,* p. 198; *Craftsman,* January 11, 1728. As a matter of fact an abbreviated version of the opera—called *Damon and Phillida*— appeared at the Haymarket in 1729. Whincop says (*Scanderbeg,* p. 198): "Not coming out as a new piece, nor known by everybody to be Cibber's, [*Damon and Phillida*] was much applauded and has continued to be frequently acted to this day."

[55] *Fog's Weekly Journal,* January 11, 1729.

[56] *Craftsman,* January 25, 1729.

of the peace and confessed what he had done. It is to be observed that
this person had *The Scornful Lady* lately acted for his benefit, in consideration of his withdrawing a play which was offered by him to be
acted there; which play, we hear, is since carried to the other house." [57]
But despite the constable's vigilance, the opera was interrupted on each
of its subsequent appearances, and Johnson felt obliged to insert a
notice in the *Craftsman,* entreating forbearance on the benefit night.

Several persons of quality and others having tickets for the sixth night of
The Village Opera, they desire (and it is humbly hoped by the author)
that it may be permitted to be acted *once more only* for their entertainment
and for his benefit.[58]

Love in a Riddle was, with the exception of *King John* in 1745, the
last of Cibber's works to appear on the stage. But his enemies did not
relax their vigilance and for several years continued to attack plays in
which they found, or thought they found, some traces of his hand.
Thus in 1732 they attempted to damn *The Modish Couple* by Charles
Boadens because they had heard that it had been touched up by Cibber before it appeared on the stage. Successful the first two nights,
they were thwarted on the third, when the play was acted "before one
of the finest assemblies of persons of quality" ever seen at Drury Lane.
The fourth performance was "so interrupted that the players ... were
forced to dismiss the audience." [59] Theophilus Cibber's *The Lover* was
also rumored to have been written or revised by the elder Cibber, and
though Theophilus sent a denial to the *Daily Post,*[60] his play, too, was
attacked. The first performance saw bloodshed in the pit and "the success was so dubious that it was uncertain whether the hisses or the
claps were more numerous." [61] The epilogue, however, was unusually
well received, the audience not seeming to realize that it was the only
part of the play written by Cibber.[62]

[57] *Daily Post,* February 8, 1729.
[58] *Craftsman,* March 22, 1729.
[59] *Grub Street Journal,* January 20, 1732, also February 24, 1732; *Fog's Weekly Journal,* January 15, 1732; *Historical MSS. Commission, Diary of the Earl of Egmont,* I,
205, 216.
[60] *Daily Post,* January 9, 1731.
[61] *Grub Street Journal,* January 21, 1731.
[62] *Apology for T ... C ...,* p. 82; Chetwood, *General History of the Stage,* p. 119.

VIII. THE CONTEST FOR THE
LAUREL

MARTYRDOM has its inconveniences but also, in the end, its rewards; and Cibber, who firmly believed himself a martyr to the cause of the Hanoverian succession, was handsomely rewarded in 1730, when he was appointed Poet Laureate of England. The probability is that he owed his good fortune quite as much to his friendship with the Duke of Grafton and other noblemen at court as to his political services, which were indeed negligible; but the fact remains that he himself attributed it entirely to his comedy *The Non-Juror*.

Cibber's appointment seems today distinctly odd, but it is not quite so odd when one realizes that in the eighteenth century the laureate was not necessarily a man of great literary ability.[1] Under the Georges his chief duty was to write odes that could be set to music and sung before the King. But since the Georges were foreigners who scarcely understood English, the odes themselves were not very important; anyone could write them; and indeed one has only to glance at the laureates of the century to become convinced of the truth of this statement. But even before the accession of the Georges the decline had set in. After Dryden there was Shadwell, a gifted playwright but a bad poet; Tate, whose doggerel was notorious; Rowe, who regarded the office as a sinecure and seldom bothered to write his own odes; and Eusden, perhaps the least distinguished of all. And when Eusden died the government apparently limited its choice to Whig authors like Philips, Theobald, Dennis, and Duck, who, whatever their merits, were certainly unable to bring to the office genuine literary distinction. Philips and Dennis were, it seems, scarcely considered; Theobald's chances were only slightly better; and from the first the newspapers confidently predicted that Duck would receive the award.

[1] Here and elsewhere throughout this chapter I am indebted to James Kemper Broadus, *The Laureateship. A Study of the Office of Poet Laureate in England* (Oxford, 1921).

Duck's early career is unusually interesting and, in so far as it throws light on the taste of the period, possibly of some significance.[2] In 1727 he was a thresher in Wiltshire, trying with the help of a dictionary to struggle through *Paradise Lost;* in 1730 he was a favorite at court, by some people considered the best poet of the age and a genius superior to Pope. His appearance at Windsor excited intense interest and a great deal of speculation. Dr Clarke discussed him with Mrs Clayton and made helpful suggestions about his reading. He should be given Burnet's *Sacred Theory of the Earth* and Ray's *Wisdom of God in Creation,* Clarke thought, but he should not see Swift, Montaigne, or even Cowley.[3] Joseph Spence, the Professor of Poetry at Oxford, was even more interested than Dr Clarke; in fact, he took the trouble to become personally acquainted with Duck and to study his behavior with almost scientific precision. On one occasion, for example, he read Duck certain speeches from *Hamlet* and *Julius Caesar* and noted the response. Duck's "countenance changed," "his eye was quick and busy," and Spence was later able to report that he had never seen "applause or the shifting of proper passions so strong in any face." [4] Spence also noticed that music sometimes made him melancholy. The thresher spoke of strange emotions he had felt during the "performances of the little choir of songsters in a country chancel," and when he heard an anthem he would often turn away, "his eyes on a sudden full of tears." "This, no doubt," as the professor remarked, "was a melancholy of the pleasing kind." [5] But what surprised Spence more than anything else was the fact that this thresher from the provinces actually seemed to have a fair command of the English language. He had a dictionary and a grammar, no doubt; still the fact was remarkable and almost without precedent. "Indeed it seems plain to me," Spence wrote, "that he has got English just as we get Latin." [6]

Duck's vogue at court began in the summer of 1730 and his greatest

[2] For Duck's career, see Rose Mary Davis, *Stephen Duck, the Thresher-Poet,* "University of Maine Studies," 2d series, No. 8 (Orono, 1926).

[3] Katherine Thomson, *Memoirs of the Court and Times of King George the Second* (1850), I, 187, 191-92.

[4] Joseph Spence, *A Full and Authentic Account of Stephen Duck, the Wiltshire Poet* (1731), p. 24.

[5] *Ibid.,* p. 10.

[6] *Ibid.*

triumph came on September 11, when he presented a poem to the Queen, stood by while the Earl of Macclesfield read it, and received from Her Majesty a pension of £30 a year and a small house in Richmond Park.[7] A month later Eusden's illness was reported and Duck at once came forward as the leading candidate for the laurel.[8] For several weeks he was heavily favored, and by October 30 his appointment seemed almost certain. "We are credibly informed," said the *Daily Post* in announcing Eusden's death, "that [Mr Eusden] will be succeeded as poet laureate by Mr Stephen Duck." [9] But a few days before this notice appeared Duck was called to Wiltshire by the death of his wife, and his rivals, steadily urging their claims at court, seemed to gain at his expense. His absence was certainly un-fortunate—more unfortunate indeed than he had anticipated, for shortly after he left Kew, another candidate appeared in the field— Colley Cibber.[10]

But though it was admitted that Cibber had entered the contest at exactly the right moment, and though it was known that he was a friend of the Duke of Grafton, in whose hands the award ultimately lay, it was not generally supposed that his chances were as good as Duck's. In Ireland Swift reported, "The vogue of our few honest folk here is that Duck is absolutely to succeed Eusden in the laurel"; [11] and Pope, nearer the court, was probably of the same opinion. But Pope had no favorite among the candidates, and in the pages of the *Grub Street Journal* he twice ridiculed the contest and everyone in-volved in it. In the issue of November 12, 1730, he mentioned Cibber, Theobald, and Duck:

> Shall royal praise be rimed by such a ribald,
> As fopling C——r or attorney T——d?
> Let's rather wait one year for better luck,
> One year may make a singing swan of Duck.
> Great G——! such servants since thou well canst lack,
> Oh! save the salary and drink the sack!

---

[7] Duck, *Poems on Several Subjects* (1730), title-page; *British Journal*, September 26, 1730; etc. In October Duck apparently again waited on the Queen; see *Fog's Weekly Journal*, October 10, 1730.

[8] *Daily Journal*, October 9, 1730.

[9] *Daily Post*, October 30, 1730.

[10] *St James's Evening Post*, October 29-31, 1730.

[11] Swift, *Correspondence*, ed. F. Elrington Ball (1910-14), IV, 180.

And in the issue of November 19 he had something to say of Dennis as well as of the more favored candidates. He considered the ancient ceremonial of the laureateship, pointing out that the crown of the successful poet was "to be mixed with vine-leaves, as the vine is the plant of Bacchus and full as essential to the honor as the butt of sack to the salary ... I would recommend a large mixture of the brassica if Mr D[enni]s be chosen; but if Mr Theobald it is not so necessary, unless the cabbage be supposed to signify the same thing with respect to poets as to tailors, viz. stealing. ... In the next place, a canticle must be composed and sung in laud and praise of the new poet. If Mr C[ibbe]r be laureated, it is my opinion no man can *write* this but himself, and no man, I am sure, can *sing* it so affectingly." The new laureate, Pope continues, should triumphantly enter the town upon a large mule or ass; "unless Mr C[ibbe]r be the man, who may with great propriety and beauty ride on a dragon if he goes by land, or, if he choose the water, upon one of his own swans from *Caesar in Egypt*."

In the meantime the contest went on; the Duke of Grafton considered the various candidates, weighed their achievements and listened to their patrons, and at last, in the third week of November, announced the appointment of Cibber.[12]

It was at once evident that the appointment pleased no one; some observers were indignant, some amused, and some frankly incredulous. The *Grub Street Journal,* for example, at first resolutely refused to believe that Cibber had been chosen. Its editor carried but denied the report from the daily papers,[13] and when the report was confirmed he admitted complete bewilderment:

> But guessing who would have the luck
> To be the b[irth]day fibber,
> I thought of Dennis, Theobald, Duck,
> But never dreamt of Cibber.[14]

Less sceptical than his fellow journalist, Mist believed the news at once, but instead of printing it, inserted the following note in his paper:

[12] *Grub Street Journal,* November 19, 1730; *British Journal,* November 21, 1730; *Daily Post,* November 28, 1730.
[13] *Grub Street Journal,* November 19, 1730.
[14] *Ibid.,* December 31, 1730.

There is a report that the renowned Keyber is learning to spell, and that he will himself transcribe the next comedy he steals. If this be true he will certainly *outdo his usual outdoings.*[15]

In a later issue he continued the joke:

We are informed that Keyber comes on pretty well in his spelling, and by that time he begins to read a little he will be initiated into the society of political authors. . . . As he has the happiness to be provided with all the *paraphonalia* of a Whig hackney, it is everybody's opinion he will do his patron as much honor and service as the best of them.[16]

Swift and Pope, though perhaps less deeply concerned than Mist, were equally angry. Pope at once sent a stinging epigram to the *Grub Street Journal:*

> Tell, if you can, which did the worse,
>   Caligula or Gr[afto]n's gr[a]ce?
> That made a consul of a horse,
>   And this a laureate of an ass.[17]

And Swift privately expressed his annoyance in letters to his friends. "If it was the Queen and not the Duke of Grafton that picked out such a laureate," he first wrote, "she deserves his poetry in her praises"; [18] and a few weeks later, when he realized that the Duke had been solely responsible: "If I had any inclination to excuse the court, I would allege that the laureate's place is entirely in the Lord Chamberlain's gift; but who make Lord Chamberlains is another question. I believe if the court had interceded with the Duke of Grafton for a fitter man, it might have prevailed." [19]

In the meantime the contest and its outcome were ridiculed in a special scene introduced, on November 30, into the second act of Fielding's *Tom Thumb.*[20] The characters are Flail (Duck), Sulky Bathos (Dennis), Noctifer (Ralph), Comment Profound (Theobald), and Fopling Fribble (Cibber), the five candidates for the laurel who enter a contest before the King and rime it out on subjects of their own choosing. Sulky Bathos and Comment Profound are the first

---

[15] *Fog's Weekly Journal,* December 12, 1730.
[16] *Ibid.,* January 9, 1731.
[17] *Grub Street Journal,* December 24, 1730.
[18] Swift, *Correspondence,* IV, 200.
[19] *Ibid.,* IV, 220.
[20] "Scriblerus Tertius," *The Battle of the Poets, or the Contention for the Laurel* (1731).

to be considered, but they are easily surpassed by Fopling Fribble, the next entry. Fribble's extemporary verses,

> The most diminutive Tom Thumb
> Is a very great man, Gad strike me dumb,

are obviously well received, and when Flail has been given a short hearing the Lord Chamberlain announces the royal selection. Fribble is led to the front of the stage, Dismal and Dangle follow with laurels, and a servant comes in with a tankard of "potent ale." The oath of office is administered, the tankard is thrust into the new laureate's hand, and the wreath is gravely placed upon his head. Fribble then lifts up his cracked voice and sings, to the tune of "What a pox would you be at?" a canticle not unlike the one which Pope had suggested:

> Sure no wretch will dare
> With me to compare,
> Nor meagre grim satirist flout me;
> For the highest degree
> Of quality see
> The *paraphonalia* about me.
>
> Since now of good sack
> I shall ne'er know the lack,
> The flights of my fancy pursuing,
> With surprise you shall view
> The laureate *outdo*
> His wonderful usual *outdoing.*

This boisterous burlesque was followed during the next few weeks by court ceremonies which, to such contemptuous observers as Pope and Swift, seemed hardly less fantastic and absurd. On December 3 Cibber was officially notified of his appointment. He was presented to His Majesty at St James's Palace, and had the honor to kneel down and kiss the royal hand.[21] The remaining four weeks of the old year were devoted to the preparation of the ode which at court was to usher in the new. Cibber ground out the fulsome compliments that royalty demanded; his halting verses, once finished, were set to music by Eccles; and the singers, Hughes and Gates, and the Chapel Royal learned the parts for the great occasion. On the last day of

---

[21] *Daily Post,* December 4, 1730. But see *Grub Street Journal,* December 10, 1730; *Daily Courant,* December 5, 1730.

December a final rehearsal was held at the Sun and Bell Tavern in King Street, Westminster. Many of the nobility and gentry were present, and the ode, it is said, was received with "universal applause." [22] And finally on New Year's Day the laureate appeared at court, mingled with the distinguished throng that had come to pay tribute to His Majesty, and listened—with what emotions one can scarcely guess—to his own fatuous tribute as it was sung by the Chapel Royal:

Recitativo.

Once more the ever circling sun
Through the celestial signs has run;
Again old Time inverts his glass,
And bids the annual seasons pass:
The youthful spring shall call for birth,
And glad with opening flowers the earth:
Fair summer load with sheaves the field,
And golden fruit shall autumn yield:
Each to the winter's want their store shall bring
Till warmer genial suns recall the spring.

Air.

Ye grateful Britons bless the year,
  That kindly yields increase,
While plenty that might feed a war
  Enjoys the guard of peace;
Your plenty to the skies you owe,
  Peace is your monarch's care;
Thus bounteous Love and George below
  Divided empire share. . . .

Recitativo.

In vain through ages past has Phoebus rolled,
Ere such a sight blest Albion could behold.
Thrice happy mortals, if your state you knew,
Where can the globe so blest a nation shew?
All that of you indulgent heaven requires
Is loyal hearts, to reach your own desires.
Let faction then her self-born views lay down,
And hearts united, thus address the throne:

[22] *Grub Street Journal*, January 7, 1731.

Air.

Hail! royal Caesar, hail!
Like this may every annual sun
Add brighter glories to thy crown,
Till suns themselves shall fail. . . .[23]

The ode, surreptitiously published by one of the singers, was the signal for a second outburst of ridicule. The *Grub Street Journal* devoted a whole page to it, and the other newspapers attacked it for weeks. The anonymous scene in *Tom Thumb* was revived at the Haymarket, and encouraged by its success, scores of writers came forward with squibs, epigrams, and satirical ballads directed either at the ode, the laureate, or the Duke of Grafton. Even Duck, now at Richmond again, may possibly have joined the outcry, for a parody over his name appeared in the *London Evening Post* of January 7, 1731. Philips and Dennis, on the other hand, were silent, and Theobald took his disappointment with commendable stoicism. "The women spurred me up to put in for the withered laurel," he wrote to Warburton. "Accordingly I with Lord Gage attended Sir Robert Walpole; was commanded by him to attend at Windsor; had his warmest recommendations to the Lord Chamberlain; nay, procured those recommendations to be seconded even by His Royal Highness; and yet, after standing fair for the post at least three weeks, had the mortification to be supplanted by Keyber. But as the vacancy has been so supplied, I think I may fairly conclude with Mr Addison's Cato,

"The post of honor is a private station." [24]

The feelings of the new laureate himself are more difficult to analyze. At first, no doubt, he was pleased with his new office primarily because it gave him social standing, because it brought him into close contact with the court and the King. For years he had been trying, as he himself put it, to keep the best company, to associate on terms of intimacy with the Duke of Argyle, the Duke of Grafton, the Duke of Richmond, and other great noblemen of the court. But he had never been entirely successful because he was only an actor, a

[23] *Gentleman's Magazine,* January, 1731.
[24] John Nichols, *Illustrations of the Literary History of the Eighteenth Century* (1817-58), II, 617.

member of a profession which in the eighteenth century occupied a relatively low place in the social scale. Now, however, his position was different; he was a person of some standing in the world—he was indeed almost respectable. He could go to court, he could discuss the plans for the royal birthday, he could attend the exclusive assemblies of Sir Thomas Robinson, he could mingle familiarly with the fine gentlemen at White's. . . . The doors of the beau monde were at last open to him and he took full advantage of his opportunities.

He may perhaps have been disconcerted by the ridicule which the newspapers heaped upon him, but he had too much self-assurance to be deeply hurt or permanently embittered. His critics were, he felt, miserable hacks who earned their bread by writing satire. They had to put well-known names into their verses; otherwise they would fail to attract the attention of the town. He did not blame them, he pitied them; though from time to time he was not above playing practical jokes at their expense. Thus he occasionally wrote verses about himself in the best Grub Street style, "merely," we are told, "for the pleasure of sitting in coffeehouses and hearing them . . . praised and called palpable hits, keen, things with spirit in them, etc." [25] In fact, he himself reports such an incident from the year 1731. For some time his friends had made a practice of showing him the more malicious passages in the newspapers and asking him to read them aloud.

This [he says] was a challenge which I never declined, and to do my doughty antagonists justice I always read them with as much impartial spirit as if I had writ them myself. While I was thus beset on all sides there happened to step forth a poetical knight-errant to my assistance, who was hardy enough to publish some compassionate stanzas in my favor. These, you may be sure, the raillery of my friends could do no less than say I had written to myself. To deny it I knew would but have confirmed their pretended suspicion. I therefore told them, since it gave them such joy to believe them my own, I would do my best to make the whole town think so too. As the oddness of this reply was, I knew, what would not be easily comprehended, I desired them to have a day's patience and I would print an explanation to it.[26]

[25] William Ayre, *Memoirs of the Life and Writings of Alexander Pope* (1745), II, 82.
[26] *Apology*, I, 46-47.

He did so—he sent the *Whitehall Evening Post* a letter and some verses in which he made use of the very arguments advanced by his friends. But to show his indifference to satire he concealed his authorship—concealed it, that is, until ten years later when the *Apology* appeared.

Indifferent Cibber certainly was, but he was nevertheless keenly aware that his odes were bad and he occasionally felt obliged to offer excuses and explanations. Thus in *The Egoist* he pointed out that he had to write too frequently and always upon the same subject. What poet, he asked, could maintain a high level of distinction under these circumstances? Could even Horace himself have frequently come up to the standard of his *Carmen Saeculare?* But there was another difficulty. The odes were intended, not to be read, but to be sung: they needed musical accompaniment and without it they could have only an "adjective merit." For this reason, Cibber added, I have never published my odes, though "they constantly creep into papers without my consent or knowledge. How they come there I do not give myself the trouble to inquire. Probably some poor spy of the press may filch them out of the several parts of the voices at a practice." [27]

But though Cibber freely and publicly admitted that his verse was inferior, one is not to infer, as Broadus has done, that he regarded his office as a sinecure and made no attempt to write well.[28] For the evidence indicates that, on the whole, he took his duties very seriously. He wrote the odes many months in advance, revised and corrected them with the utmost care, sometimes even showed them to friends and asked for suggestions and advice.[29] Once, for example, he read his latest performance to Samuel Johnson, already well known as the author of *London*.[30] He undoubtedly hoped to get acute criticism from so distinguished a poet, but he was disappointed, for Johnson was too rude to be very helpful. "I made some corrections," Johnson later

---

[27] Cibber, *The Egoist, or Colley upon Cibber* (1743), p. 50.

[28] Broadus, *The Laureateship*, pp. 134-35.

[29] Boswell, *Life of Johnson*, ed. Hill (1887), I, 402.

[30] Possibly before 1745 because in the epilogue to *Papal Tyranny in the Reign of King John*, published in that year, Cibber uses the wren-eagle figure correctly. He also uses it in the dedication to *Ximena*, though in this case he quotes from Dryden.

remarked, "to which [Cibber] was not very willing to submit. I remember the following couplet in allusion to the King and himself:

> Perched on the eagle's soaring wing,
> The lowly linnet loves to sing.

Sir, he had heard something of the fabulous tale of the wren sitting upon the eagle's wing and he had applied it to a linnet. . . . I told him that when the ancients made a simile, they always made it like something real. . . . I could not bear such nonsense and would not let him read it to the end; so little respect had I for *that great man* (laughing). Yet I remember Richardson wondering that I could treat him with familiarity." [31]

The remark about the ancients was particularly insulting, for Cibber had opened the conversation by abusing Pindar. But some allowances must perhaps be made for Johnson's manner. He felt, as he later told Boswell, that Cibber was by no means a blockhead; but he was apparently reluctant to encourage the poetaster when only the playwright deserved praise.[32]

[31] Boswell, *Life of Johnson*, I, 402; III, 73; II, 93.
[32] *Ibid.*, I, 402-3.

IX. THE RISE OF THEOPHILUS
CIBBER

- I -

CIBBER's retirement from the management of Drury Lane and his last regular performances on the stage belong to a new period in theatrical history; a period in which the great figures of the early part of the century—Wilks, Booth, and Mrs Oldfield—were no more, and new figures like Quin, Macklin, Mrs Heron, and Mrs Clive had come forward to take their places; but a period not entirely unconnected with the name of Cibber, for the most compelling of all the new figures, in 1732-34 and even later, was Cibber's son Theophilus. This capricious and eccentric young man, in fact, stamps his personality upon that short but not very distinguished age which falls between the retirement of the three great actor-managers and the appearance of David Garrick.

Eccentric certainly, but the word is too colorless to describe the behavior of this bewildering and preposterous person. He was born during the Great Storm of 1703—a fact which was later felt to be significant—and he grew up while his parents were quarreling over the legacies of the Shores. Unruly, undisciplined, and irresponsible, he was nevertheless remarkably precocious, and his father decided to make him either a doctor or a lawyer; but at the age of sixteen he left school and joined the company in Drury Lane.[1] His histrionic ability was undeniable, but for several years he appeared in the taverns and bagnios of the town more regularly than he appeared upon the stage. He associated with young men whose habits were as dissolute as his own, and he became one of the favorite companions of the notorious Duke of Wharton.

The intimacy I had with that unfortunate, mistaken peer [he wrote later] made me pay a sigh to his memory.... I have often when he was alive

[1] John Carteret Pilkington, *Real Story* (1760), p. 167; *Apology for T ... C ...*, pp. 5-6.

rallied him for his foibles, for he had good humor enough to be pleased with a pleasant thing though said of himself. Nay . . . I have sometimes taken an honest freedom of being roundly severe upon his errors. He would hear me with a grave face, swear he would think of his affairs, remember the dignity of his rank, the honor of his family, his allegiance to his monarch, and what he owed to himself; then starting from his dressing room, bounce through a levee of duns who waited in his antechamber, get into his chariot, roll down to the Groom Porter's, lose his money, and after seeking for him three days and nights successively, I have at last found him at a bagnio with a witty wanton, making a jest of morality and perhaps writing a libel against the government.[2]

But Theophilus often took part in the Duke's midnight escapades, and there was perhaps more of coincidence than of design in the meetings at the bagnio.

At seventeen Theophilus gave an earnest of his talent by improving a play of Shakespeare's,[3] and at twenty-one he began to get good minor parts at Drury Lane. He is said to have been well received as Lory in *The Relapse,* as Snap in *Love's Last Shift,* and as Abel Drugger in *The Alchemist.* Judicious critics, indeed, complained that he marred his performances by overemphasis—by "ridiculous squinting and vile grimace," and by a kind of effrontery which was inseparable from everything he attempted.[4] But even his enemies admitted that he made an excellent Pistol in *Henry IV;* the part suited him exactly and he had only to be perfectly natural to give a consummate performance. The "peculiar kind of false spirit" which he displayed—the "uncommon blustering," the "turgid action and long unmeasurable strides," the "loud and grotesque vociferation"—was a triumph, not of histrionic interpretation, but of nature.[5] In fact, Theophilus *was* Pistol, off as well as on the stage, and for years after his first appearance in the part he was known by no other name.

Despite his egotism and his hot-headedness, the young man made rapid progress at Drury Lane. In 1723 he supplanted Mills as manager of the summer company, and in 1727 he made himself assistant to Wilks during the regular season. The young deputy—if one may

[2] Theophilus Cibber, *Country Correspondent,* No. 2 (April 28, 1739).

[3] Theophilus Cibber, *An Historical Tragedy of the Civil Wars in the Reign of King Henry VI* (n. d.).

[4] Davies, *Dramatic Miscellanies* (1783-84), II, 107; *Grub Street Journal,* January 6, 1737; etc.

[5] Davies, *Dramatic Miscellanies,* I, 294.

believe his own account—was always farsighted and diplomatic, and he soon began to regard himself as the chosen successor of the triumvirate. He asserted in public that the patent was his "birthright," and he impatiently waited for the time when the aging managers should retire and should invest him, and him alone, with their authority.[6]

For several years he waited, and at last as the new decade opened changes began to take place. In 1730 the managers applied for a patent to replace the one which was to expire three years after the death of Steele. In November they were assured that their application would find favor at court, and in April, 1732, the new patent actually passed the Great Seal.[7] Booth, who had not been able to appear on the stage since 1727, was by this time ready to retire, and in July, 1732, he arranged to sell half his share in the company to John Highmore, a wealthy young man who had recently acted at Drury Lane as the result of a wager. The negotiations were conducted by Victor and the price fixed was £2,500. Two months later Wilks fell ill, and realizing that he would not recover, he begged Cibber to look after his interests in the company. Cibber kindly offered to do so without charge, but when, a few days later, Wilks died, his wife rejected the offer and appointed the painter John Ellys as her representative. Annoyed by this slight and still further annoyed by "the chimerical notions" of his new colleagues, Cibber himself retired from the management. On October 29, 1732, he assigned his share to Theophilus for the rest of the season at a rent of £442, and at the same time engaged himself as a hired actor in the company at the handsome salary of twelve guineas a week.[8]

The new arrangements were not of course entirely satisfactory to Theophilus, who had hoped for more—who had, in fact, tried to rent the share of Mrs Wilks as well as the share of his father.[9] But as he reviewed his position, as he considered his own wide experience in

[6] Theophilus Cibber, *Lives of the Actors*, pp. 60-64; Theophilus Cibber, *Letter to John Highmore* (1733).

[7] *Daily Journal*, November 3, 1730; *Grub Street Journal*, May 4, 1732. See also *Apology*, II, 257, note.

[8] Victor, *History of the Theatres*, I, 3-10; *Grub Street Journal*, July 20 and November 2, 1732; *Apology*, II, 255-56; Theophilus Cibber, *Letter to Highmore*.

[9] Unless otherwise noticed, information and quotations in the following paragraphs come from Theophilus Cibber, *Letter to Highmore*.

the theatre and the inexperience of his colleagues, he came to the conclusion that he had not made such a bad bargain after all. He was an *actor,* Highmore and Ellys were only *gentlemen;* surely he was qualified to overrule their ill-considered opinions, surely if he were firm he could make himself sole master of the company in fact if not in name. But when he actually met his colleagues in the office of the theatre and began discussing with them questions of general policy, he discovered that they were less easily influenced than he had anticipated. Indeed he found that they had notions of their own, and after a few unsatisfactory conferences he began to realize that he would have to use all his skill to prevent them from actually putting their notions into practice.

During the first part of the season of 1732-33, however, he had comparatively little difficulty. He took a firm stand, he resisted interference, and on point after point the gentlemen gave way before him. He raised the salaries of several actors and actresses, he brought Joe Miller back into the company and reimbursed him for his loss,[10] he gave Mrs Clive a present of ten guineas for her performance as Lappet. . . . The list of his benefactions is indeed impressive. At the same time he pushed forward new plays and revivals, and began getting up a pantomime founded on *The Harlot's Progress.* But unfortunately—at a critical point in the season—his health broke down, and during his absence from the theatre the gentlemen were able to undo his work. They dropped *The Harlot's Progress* and substituted for it a pantomime by Ellys—a pantomime which, they said, would not cost £5.

Theophilus was naturally infuriated by such duplicity, and ill as he was he at once wrote a letter of protest, sending it to his father and five of the principal actors of the company and directing them to read it before they turned it over to Highmore and Ellys. "Gentlemen," he began, and there was perhaps a sting in the formal word of address,

I once more remind you, you have all positively agreed heretofore to the getting up *The Harlot's Progress and Ridotto al' Fresco* and desired me to forward it accordingly. Once this was agreed to when we were all present at the office; a second time when Mr Ellys, Mr Highmore, and myself were

---

[10] Further information about the Joe Miller case is to be found in C. 11 83/17.

present only. I proceeded accordingly—nay, your letters consent to the thing and approve it. And yet Mr Devoto, etc. are threatened at their peril to make any progress in it at a time when the cruelty of fate constrains me to be absent. Is this harmony? Is this genteel? When have I proceeded so? Mr Ellys's comic may be a very good one, much better than we imagine; but why do you recede from your agreement? . . . If you think mine doubtful, sell me a few nights, according to a proposal I'll make before Saturday, which shall not, I think, be a disadvantageous one to you; I'll take my chance and the entertainment shall afterwards be among us. Or if you think so meanly of me, *gentlemen,* to suppose I have sinister views, if you'll agree to a proposal I'll make you concerning my present share and salary, etc., you'll be at liberty then to pursue your own schemes by yourselves. But let me tell you, through all our present difficulties our season should have been better already had I not been thwarted; several fresh plays and entertainments been revived (notwithstanding my unlucky illness), and other things not less forward than they are. I know what I have done and know what I can do. I shall avoid as much as possible talking upon this subject, because discourse sometimes grows too warm, and offense may be taken when it is not designed. But on this I am determined—at all events to assert my right and to maintain it at all hazards, especially while I have the laws on my side; nor shall I be browbeat out of anything. If any orders are given without my knowledge, I must be obliged to countermand 'em.

Theophilus recovered, the rehearsals of *The Harlot's Progress* were resumed, but almost immediately further differences of opinion developed. In February, 1733, Theophilus had a particularly unpleasant interview with Highmore, after which he apparently retired to his apartment and relieved his feelings by writing a second letter to the gentlemen:

By my discourse with you at Tom's last night, you seem to entertain a jealousy of me and such a sort of opinion as I should be ashamed to have of anyone with whom I was engaged in business without the justest foundation, and you have none yet. Which do you take me for, an unaccountable fool, or knave, or a mixture of both? . . . Methinks things would have carried a better air if a gentleman newly entered into a business (to which I must insist he is a stranger) had consulted the experienced and in a proper manner joined or opposed their proceedings as they fairly appeared reasonable or not. I must add in justice to Mr Ellys, he has appeared more ready than yourself to proceed thus. Sir, I can clearly see who has merit and shall propose their encouragement accordingly; and let me tell you, in our business to save money is very well, but the way to get it is to lay it out. This may appear a riddle, but I can expound it at a proper season. Groundless jealousies are ungenerous and I scorn to have 'em of others, as

I am above deserving 'em myself. While I am guided by justice and well known precedents founded on experience and reason, I shall smile at unreasonable suggestions and proceed properly.

Realizing from such communications as this that Theophilus was incorrigible, the gentlemen began to look for a way of forcing him out of the management. They knew that he had already arranged to rent his father's share in the patent for another year, but they also knew that the articles of agreement, though drafted, had not yet been signed. Seeing their opportunity, they approached Cibber and offered to buy him out for 3,000 guineas.[11] He accepted the offer without even consulting his son, and in March, 1733, his retirement from the stage and his sale of his interest in the patent to Highmore were publicly announced. Theophilus was informed that his connection with the management would last only until June 1.

The gentlemen possibly expected that Theophilus would quietly retire, but of course no such thing was really conceivable. Pistol was still Pistol, still a daring captain who was ready, like another contemporary hero, to ride the whirlwind and wield the thunder. A fortnight after the sale of the patent the young man persuaded the principal actors of the company to appoint him their leader, and to formulate articles of union binding themselves not to act under the gentlemen-patentees until their salaries had been raised.[12] Then, in the name of the union, he took the lease of Drury Lane—the lease that Collier had held for so many years—and approaching the gentlemen, made his startling proposals.[13] "You the gentlemen have the patent," he said in effect, "but we the actors have the theatre. Now we will allow you to use Drury Lane and we will pay you 1,200 guineas a year if you will retire from the management and let us carry on the theatre as we see fit. Otherwise," Theophilus continued, "we will occupy Drury Lane ourselves and force you to get another theatre and another company of actors." But the ultimatum was of course preposterous, and Highmore not only rejected it, but took steps to prevent the actors from getting control of Drury Lane. On May 26, 1733, he armed a band of ruffians and sent them to guard

---

[11] Victor, *History of the Theatres*, I, 8.

[12] The agreement of the actors was kept secret, but their principal grievance seems to have been the "cartel" of 1722; see Add. MS. 12, 201; *Daily Post*, June 11, 1733.

[13] *Daily Post*, June 4 and September 26, 1733; C. 11 778/28.

the theatre doors, providing them at appropriate intervals with strong liquors, "to keep their bloods warm," as Theophilus complained, "and stupefy their senses, lest a little common morality should touch their consciences to the obstruction of their performing any desperate act." [14] Unable or unwilling to take the theatre by storm, Theophilus sued for a writ of ejectment and devoted the summer to the task of getting a license for his company. He wanted a patent, which would make him permanently independent of the gentlemen, and it is said that he persuaded his father to apply for one at court.[15] But a patent was difficult to obtain, and the actors finally had to be content with the title of "Comedians of His Majesty's Revels." Not getting their writ of ejectment as soon as they had hoped, they gave performances at Bartholomew Fair during August and at the Little Theatre in the Haymarket during the autumn. Their audiences were at first extremely good, and they were in a position to wait until Highmore should meet their terms or Drury Lane should fall into their hands.[16]

During September and October Highmore held out, hotly contesting the ejectment suit,[17] and trying with the miserable remnants of his company to draw a few spectators from the Haymarket; but by November his losses were so heavy that he was obliged to change his methods and make a legal attack on the unlicensed companies of the town, which included, of course, the company in Goodman's Fields as well as the company of the Revels. Persuading Rich to join him, he summoned Giffard of Goodman's Fields and Mills of the Haymarket before a justice of the peace and charged them with vagrancy under a statute of the 12th of Queen Anne which included in its description of vagrants strollers and players of common interludes. But the justice, not satisfied with the formality of the summons, promptly dismissed the case.[18] After careful preparation Rich and Highmore selected November 12 for their second attack, for

14 The occupation of Drury Lane is reported less melodramatically in the *Daily Post*, May 29, 1733.

15 Davies, *Dramatic Miscellanies*, III, 474; Davies, *Garrick* (1780), I, 70; see also, Victor, *History of the Theatres*, I, 14-15.

16 *Apology for T . . . C . . .*, pp. 88-89, 95-96; *Grub Street Journal*, August 16, 1733.

17 C. 11 778/28; Chancery Decrees and Orders, 1733 A, pp. 16, 18.

18 *Daily Post*, November 13, 1733; *Grub Street Journal*, November 8, 1733; etc. See also clippings from unidentified newspapers in the Richard John Smith Theatrical Collection (British Museum 11826.r.s.).

on that day the ejectment suit brought by Theophilus was to be heard in the afternoon and *Henry IV*, with Harper as Falstaff, was to be given at the Haymarket in the evening. They thought that by arresting Harper they could divide the counsel for the actors and at the same time break up the performance of *Henry IV*. Accordingly on the morning of the 12th they swore out a warrant against Harper and brought him before Sir Thomas Clarges and other justices of the peace, who ordered him to reappear with counsel at five o'clock in the afternoon. But at five o'clock the actors' counsel were still engaged at Westminster Hall, and after a short hearing Clarges pronounced Harper a vagrant and committed him to Bridewell.[19]

The gentlemen possibly thought that they had won an important victory, but it was not long before they realized their mistake. By imprisoning Harper they had incurred the ill-will of the town; they had shown that they were really oppressors after all and that Theophilus was really a hero fighting in the cause of liberty. By their own ingenuity, in fact, they had brought about their own defeat.

On the evening of the 12th Theophilus came before the audience at the Haymarket, explained the circumstances surrounding the commitment of Harper, and offered to read the part of Falstaff himself. The audience consented, applauded him generously throughout the play, and the next night went off to Drury Lane to break up a performance of Highmore's. During the following week the newspapers warmly attacked the gentlemen-patentees, compared Harper to Prynne and Sacheverel, and described his commitment as the most "dangerous act of power" since the Revolution.[20] And when, on the 19th of the month, the imprisoned actor was granted a hearing before the Court of King's Bench, a large crowd gathered at Westminster Hall to make sure that the cause of liberty was defended. The decision was entirely satisfactory to them, for the Lord Chief Justice not only released Harper on his own recognizances, but strongly censured the patentees for imprisoning one actor on a charge that was aimed at two whole companies. He ordered that all further proceedings in the case should be conducted on the basis of a feigned issue agreed to by both sides, so that the liberty of no actor or actors should be

[19] *Daily Post*, November 13, 1733.
[20] *Ibid.*, November 13, 14, and 16, 1733.

jeopardized by the decision ultimately rendered. Harper stepped down from the bar a free man, and the case of the patentees almost immediately collapsed.[21] Theophilus took possession of Drury Lane,[22] and Highmore sold his share of the patent to another gentleman, John Fleetwood, and severed all connections with the theatre.[23]

The victory of Theophilus was so complete that when he met Fleetwood to discuss a union of the two companies, he was able to dictate his own terms. He demanded that each of his followers should receive a salary of £200 a year; that Mills and Mrs Heron should have benefits free of all charges; that the other actors should have benefits subject only to the charges of the house; and that Fleetwood should pay all the outstanding debts, buy all the scenes and costumes of the Haymarket Company, and permit the actors to keep the lease of Drury Lane as a security for the fulfillment of their conditions. Fleetwood accepted these hard terms so meekly that Theophilus at once made them a little harder. He insisted that his benefit and the benefit of Milward should also be free of charges; that the benefit of Johnson should be charged only £25; that Mrs Heron should be allowed £100 a year for clothes; and that he himself should be given a special salary of £50 a year for the work he was to do as manager. Fleetwood accepted everything, for indeed he had no alternative, and on March 12, 1734, Theophilus led his followers back to Drury Lane.[24]

– 2 –

Colley Cibber had not played an entirely creditable part during these tempestuous seasons; he had first encouraged Theophilus and then thrown him out of the management, sold his share in the patent to Highmore and then (according to one story) tried to destroy its value. But his conduct had at least been thoroughly consistent,

[21] Eg. MS. 2,320; Theophilus Cibber, *Two Dissertations on the Theatres* (n. d.), Part III, p. 41; *Grub Street Journal*, December 6, 1733; etc.

[22] *Gentleman's Magazine*, November, 1733, and March, 1734; Eg. MS. 2,320; Fitzgerald, *New History of the English Stage*, II, 86-87, 91.

[23] *Daily Journal*, February 1, 1734; C. 11 778/28. Fleetwood paid £2,250 for Highmore's half share, and £1,500 for Mrs Wilks's third share; Giffard bought the sixth share of Mrs Booth. Fleetwood later bought out Giffard (*Daily Journal*, February 7, 1737).

[24] C. 11 778/28; Victor, *History of the Theatres*, I, 26-27; *Apology for T ... C ...*, p. 98.

for he was chiefly interested in making good bargains for himself. He had turned over his share to Theophilus because it brought him a handsome income—£442 rent, twelve guineas a week salary, and a benefit play besides; and he had sold out to Highmore for a similar reason—3,000 guineas was an excellent price to get for a third share in a company already approaching disaster.

Cibber's benefit play in 1733—*The Provoked Wife* with *The Mock Doctor* as an afterpiece—has interesting associations with his social life. Three weeks before it was given he called at the Duke of Richmond's house in Privy Gardens, Whitehall, to invite the Duchess to take the first box upon the stage. But neither the Duke nor the Duchess was at home, and after announcing his visit Cibber sent his invitation to Goodwood.

Knocking last week at your unguarded gate in town [he wrote to his grace] behold! it was surprisingly opened to me by a female porter, from whom I received the unwelcome news of your being gone (not very well) into Sussex. Upon which I sighing said to myself, "Alas, poor Cibber! what a dull audience art thou like to have at the benefit play if the Duchess of Richmond is not to shine at the head of thy circle!" Upon this I ordered my two-legged hacks to amble to court, and there it was my better fortune to hear from Mr Hill that you had resolved to bring up your body and dear soul to the birthday. This gave me again some distant hope. "For is it not possible," said I, "that to make the finest woman in the world still finer, it may be necessary for her to take two or three days in town beforehand to regulate her proper ornaments for so seldom a festival?" ... Therefore my dear, dear, good lord, be so kind in your next to Mr Hill to let me know your pleasure, whether I shall still keep the first box upon the stage for her grace or, in case her filling it is impracticable, whether I may give it to some other lady—that I hold six to four, let her be who she will, will not be quite so handsome.[25]

The Duke's answer has not been preserved, but a little later we find him suggesting that Cibber pay a visit to Goodwood. "The ladies are tempting," the politic Cibber answered, "and I will so far make use of the opportunity you offer me that I will bring myself down in hopes to enjoy them two or three days without you: but I am a little busy at present about purchasing a house to hide my head in and cannot conveniently come till the middle of next week. But then! good gods! how I will rejoice with you! For who can want

[25] The Earl of March, *A Duke and His Friends*, I, 210-11.

spirits at Goodwood? Such a place and such company! In short, if good sense would gratify a good taste with whatever can make life agreeable, thither she must come for a banquet." [26]

Cibber's contract at Drury Lane lasted only one year, and when the Haymarket secession took place he conveniently refused to act at either theatre. But in 1734 he made another contract with Fleetwood, binding himself to appear in his favorite parts at a salary, it is said, of 50 guineas a night.[27] During the season of 1734-35 he acted Bayes, Lord Foppington, Sir John Brute, Sir Courtly Nice, Sir Fopling Flutter, and Fondlewife (for the benefit of his old friend Swiney). During the following season his contract and his parts seem to have been much the same; but he retired in 1736, only to return to the stage in 1738-39 as Shallow in the second part of *Henry IV* and as Richard III in his own play. Both of these performances have been described for us, the first by Tom Davies, the second by Davies and Victor. Davies says:

Whether he was a copy or an original in Shallow it is certain that no audience was ever more fixed in deep attention at his first appearance or more shaken with laughter in the progress of the scene than at Colley Cibber's exhibition of this ridiculous justice of peace.... Whether it was owing to the pleasure the spectators felt on seeing their old friend return to them again, though for that night only, after an absence of some years, I know not, but surely no actor or audience were better pleased with each other. His manner was so perfectly simple, his look so vacant when he questioned his cousin Silence about the price of ewes and lamented in the same breath with silly surprise the death of old Double, that it will be impossible for any surviving spectator not to smile at the remembrance of it. The want of ideas occasions Shallow to repeat almost everything he says. Cibber's transition from asking the price of bullocks to trite but grave reflections on mortality was so natural and attended with such an unmeaning roll of his small pig's eyes, accompanied with an important utterance of tick, tick, tick not much louder than the balance of a watch's pendulum, that I question if any actor was ever superior in the conception or expression of such solemn insignificancy.[28]

The performance of *Richard III* was less successful, for Cibber was never a great tragic actor and besides he was too old—his "strength

[26] *Ibid.*, I, 211-12.
[27] *Biographia Dramatica, or a Companion to the Playhouse* (1812), article Colley Cibber.
[28] Davies, *Dramatic Miscellanies*, I, 306-7.

and spirit failed him." [29] "His cracked pipe could not give force to
the animated scenes," [30] and in the third act he whispered to his
friend Victor that he wanted nothing so much as to be at home in
his easy chair before the fire. After this unfortunate experience he
again retired, though he was later persuaded to act comic parts
for a few years more.

Society, the court, and his friends interested Cibber much more at
this period of his life than the theatre; but he had another favorite
diversion—the opera. He was extremely fond of music; he frequently
sang in company, even—he himself admits—in the presence of
Handel; [31] and once at least, in 1735, he contributed to the fashionable
entertainment by providing an English text for the Italian opera of
Polifemo. His knowledge of Italian, however, as well as his knowledge of classical literature, was regrettably deficient, and he garbled
the central incident of the story in which Ulysses tells, or should tell,
Polyphemus that his name is No-man. The Italian phrases are "Niun
m'appello" and "Ah Niun traditor!" which Cibber translates "I take
no name" and "Where's this nameless traitor?" The blunder was duly
noticed by Pope and described in the variorum notes to the *Dunciad*. [32]

[29] Victor, *History of the Theatres*, II, 48.
[30] Davies, *Dramatic Miscellanies*, II, 222.
[31] Cibber, *Egoist*, p. 34.
[32] Pope, *Works*, ed. Elwin and Courthope, IV, 182, note.

X. DOMESTIC PROBLEMS

THUS BETWEEN 1730 and 1740 Cibber gradually withdrew from the theatre and devoted himself to other affairs, of which the most disquieting, if not perhaps the most important, were those of his family. After 1730 he had trouble with his daughter Charlotte, who was just beginning her adventurous career, and after 1733 he was again drawn into the scandalous escapades of Theophilus, whose disgraceful lawsuit with Sloper was extremely unpleasant for the whole family as well as for the persons immediately concerned. Both children deserve some attention, for by following them throughout the decade we learn a good deal about Cibber himself.

Cibber's family was a large one, and something is known about each of his children. His daughter Anne, for example, worked at Bagshaw's, at the Blackamoor's Head in Leadenhall Street, and later set up a china house at the Golden Jar in Charles Street, Covent Garden. She sold "all sorts of China and Japan ware; the best tea, as pekoe, congon, bohea, hyson, green, and imperial; likewise coffee, sago, and chocolate; also fine hollands, cambrics, and most sorts of millinery goods." [1] Between 1727 (when she moved to Charles Street) and 1734 she married a certain John Boultby. Elizabeth, the favorite of the Shores, married Dawson Brett,[2] and after his death, Joseph Marples. Her life is described as singularly unfortunate, though just what her misfortunes were we have no means of knowing. At the age of fifty-five she opened a "neat, well-accomodated" eating house in Fullwood's Rent near Gray's Inn, where she dressed "flesh, fish, and poultry . . . in an elegant manner at reasonable rates." [3] On more intimate terms with Cibber himself was the eldest daughter Catherine, who married a certain Colonel Brown but who apparently lived with her father during the last years of his life and helped him bring up his two granddaughters (the children of Theophilus). Catherine is

[1] *Daily Post*, November 1, 1727.
[2] Chancery Decrees and Orders, 1733 A, p. 183.
[3] Charke, *Narrative* (1929), p. 120; also pp. 59-60.

the she-dragon, the "cruel monitor," whose "rancorous disposition" and "malice prepense" are so frequently and so spitefully mentioned in her sister Charlotte's autobiography.[4]

Anne, Elizabeth, and Catherine lived inconspicuously if not happily, leaving the urge of the family genius and the task of keeping the family name before the public to their brother Theophilus and their sister Charlotte, who in fact were quite capable of doing so. In the *Dunciad* of 1728 Pope asked his readers to pay particular attention to Theophilus:

> Mark first the youth who takes the foremost place,
> And thrusts his person full into your face.
> With all thy father's virtues blest, be born!
> And a new C[ibbe]r shall the stage adorn.[5]

Thrusts his person full into your face—the phrase describes both children exactly. They were continually thrusting themselves forward, continually demanding attention, continually washing their dirty linen in public; and incidentally of course they were continually involving their father in bad causes and—what was perhaps even more annoying in his case—continually asking him for money. Charlotte was no doubt less notorious than her brother, and some of her antics may not at once have become public property. But even in her early years it was rather generally known that she was disreputable—if not, indeed, sexually abnormal—and it was felt that she was a distinct reflection upon her father and her family.

She was the youngest of the Cibber children, and long after Catherine and Elizabeth had married and Anne had set up her china house in Covent Garden, she remained at Hillingdon under her mother's care. Eccentric from her earliest years, she was a difficult problem for Mrs Cibber, for she refused to learn sewing, cooking, and housekeeping—refused, in fact, to acquire any of the accomplishments of a young lady. At four she displayed a disquieting fondness for masculine dress, and at five she began to take an interest in the stable. Once from his window her father saw her riding about the streets on an ass, preceded by an urchin scraping on a fiddle and followed by a large and unruly retinue. "Gad demme!" Cibber ex-

[4] *Ibid.*, pp. 101-2.
[5] Pope, *Works*, ed. Elwin and Courthope, IV, 293-94.

claimed. "An ass upon an ass!" But what was to be done? The girl
was clearly unlike her sisters and it seemed plain that she must be
reared in a different way. Accordingly her father put her in school,
had her taught Latin, French, Italian, geography, music, and dancing,
and finally sent her back to her mother in the country. But the experiment failed, for her character remained unchanged. Her interest
in the stable was as intense as ever, and she now took up gardening,
drug-brewing, and shooting. She sometimes hunted from morning
till night, and when a straight-laced neighbor objected to this un-
feminine recreation and insisted that Charlotte's gun be taken from
her, Charlotte stole an old muscatoon that hung over the kitchen
mantelpiece at home and amused herself shooting at the neighbor's
chimneys. As a result of another mad prank, she ran over and almost
killed a child, and her father was distinctly relieved when, soon afterwards, he was able to marry her off to Richard Charke, a violinist
at the theatre. But marriage had no steadying effect on the young
hoyden, and she was as much a problem as she had been before. She
quarreled with her eldest sister, dunned her father for money, and
soon left her husband and went on the stage. Deciding to give her
one last chance to reform, the family summoned her to a conference
at Cibber's house in Charles Street. But she refused advice and
"answered nothing to their purpose," and her father finally left the
house in "a strong fit of impatience," vowing that he would never
return to it till she was gone. After a short consultation her sisters
disowned her, and she too left the house—for ever.[6]

Her subsequent career seemed amply to justify the severity of the
family's methods. Having quarreled with Fleetwood and Rich, she
left the stage, ran into debt, and disguised herself as a man (for
"substantial reasons" which she steadfastly refused to reveal). Her life
during the next twenty years was a series of fantastic and disreputable
adventures. She kept a tavern in Drury Lane; she was a waiter in
Marylebone; she acted, on alternate nights, men's and women's parts
in strolling companies; she was a pastry cook in Wales, a puppet-
show manager, a performer at the fairs, a conjurer's assistant in Petti-
coat Lane.... The catalogue is endless. Despite her break with the
family, she continued to dun her father, her uncle, her brother, and

[6] Charke, *Narrative*, pp. 17-104.

even her sisters, and she was not to be put off with curt refusals. It
was reported that she once waylaid her father in Epping Forest. Out-
fitted like a highwayman, "she stopped the chariot, presented a pistol
to his breast, and . . . threatened to blow his brains out that moment
if he did not deliver." [7] The story was no doubt a malicious invention,
but if less sensational, her importunities were no less brazen. Cibber
was known to have a considerable sum of money, and it was imperative that she make her peace with him before he died. She returned to London and took "a wretched thatched hovel situated on
the way to Islington, in the purlieus of Clerkenwell, Bridewell, not
very distant from the New River head, where at that time it was
usual for the scavengers to leave the cleansings of the streets and the
priests of Cloacina to deposit the offerings from the temples of that
all-worshipped power." [8] From this squalid retreat she sent to the
booksellers installments of her remarkable *Narrative of the Life of
Mrs Charlotte Charke,* in which she described her misfortunes and
publicly begged her father to forgive her. But her communications,
public and private, were ignored, and when two years later the old
man died, she was left the "sum of £5 and no more." [9]

Dates in Charlotte's life are difficult to fix, and one cannot even
be sure of the year in which she broke with her father. Dates in
the life of Theophilus, on the other hand, are easily ascertained, for he
was a well-known figure in the theatre and his activities were regularly
reported by journalists and pamphleteers. The first date in what
proved to be the most scandalous episode of his career is 1734.

His first wife, the actress Jane Cibber, had recently died, and on
April 21 he married Susanna Maria Arne, the daughter of an up-
holsterer in King Street, Covent Garden. Miss Arne had been trained
in music by her brother Thomas—not yet quite so famous as he
afterwards became—and had already sung at the Haymarket in opera
and later in *entr'acte* entertainments during the season of 1733-34.[10]

[7] *Ibid.,* p. 95.
[8] *Biographia Dramatica,* article Charlotte Charke.
[9] Cibber's will, Somerset House. Professor Odell has pointed out to me that a Mrs
Harman, described as the daughter of Charlotte Charke and the granddaughter of
Colley Cibber, appeared on the New York stage during the last years of her life and
was buried in Trinity Churchyard (1773); see George C. D. Odell, *Annals of the New
York Stage* (New York, 1927-38), I, 116, 166.
[10] *The Comforts of Matrimony* (1739), pp. 8-10.

From her point of view the match was a very good one, but—possibly she had heard rumors about Theophilus—she insisted upon a rather unusual marriage settlement. All the money she made at the theatre —so read the articles entered into on April 20—was to be strictly her own personal property and was to be turned over to two trustees— Goodwin Washbourne, a wiredrawer, and Charles Wheeler, a surgeon. A hundred pounds of it was to be invested and the rest given to her in small sums as she should require it for her own use. If she should die without children, her savings were to go, not to Theophilus, but to her father and mother, who might by that time be dependent on her for support.[11]

To Theophilus, no doubt, these provisions seemed very odd, and to his father they seemed odder still. For the old man was distinctly disappointed by the marriage, complaining characteristically that his boy might have had a woman with a fortune. But when he saw a little more of his daughter-in-law, he was inclined to take a different view. He became genuinely fond of her and even offered to train her as a tragic actress. Convinced after a lesson or two that she had a good ear and an excellent speaking voice, he recommended her for the part of Zara in the play of that name which Aaron Hill had just adapted from the French.[12] Hill too was particularly kind. He prepared an interlined part in which every accent and inflection, every look and gesture was marked, and he worked tirelessly to make her performance perfect down to the last detail.[13] The play was brought out on January 12, 1736, and the young actress was introduced to the town in a prologue written by Cibber and spoken by Theophilus. "Tonight," Theophilus repeated as he stepped forward on the stage at the opening performance,

> Tonight the greatest venture of my life
> Is lost or saved, as you receive—a wife. . . .
> In you it rests, to save her or destroy;
> If she draws tears from you, I weep—for joy.[14]

And if weeping was in order Theophilus must certainly have wept, for the play was very successful and his wife was recognized, by some

[11] C. 11 1572/14.
[12] *Comforts of Matrimony*, pp. 10-11.
[13] Davies, *Garrick* (1780), I, 137.
[14] Aaron Hill, *The Tragedy of Zara* (1736), prologue.

critics at least, as the most promising tragic actress who had appeared on the stage since the days of Mrs Barry.

The ordeal of the first appearance once over, Theophilus set about finding other parts for his wife. He wanted her to act Amanda, Statira, Indiana, but above all, he wanted to see her as Polly Peachum in *The Beggar's Opera*. He realized of course that Mrs Clive was in "possession" of the part, but he anticipated little difficulty on that score. Mrs Clive, he pointed out, had failed as Polly three years before, and besides, could she not act Lucy in the same revival? Her vivacity would admirably set off the plaintive tenderness of his wife. But Mrs Clive refused to fall in with the scheme, and Theophilus finally had to appeal to the town in the *London Daily Post and General Advertiser*. Mrs Clive sent an even more persuasive appeal to the same journal, Theophilus wrote a violent and abusive reply,[15] and by December, 1736, it was reported that the "contention between the two rival ladies of the theatre" had grown to such a height that the issue was expected "with the same impatience as the evacuation of Tuscany." [16]

For weeks the controversy went on, but Theophilus gained so little ground that he apparently decided to abandon his claim to Polly and bring his wife out in a part which, he felt, would suit her even better—the part of Constance in Shakespeare's *King John*. Accordingly his father's adaptation of the play was brought to the theatre (it was recommended to Fleetwood, we are told, by a group of ladies passionately interested in performances of Shakespeare) and in the winter of 1736-37 the rehearsals began. But as the preparations went forward, difficulties appeared—difficulties which indeed no one could have foreseen but which kept coming up week after week in a most annoying way. In the first place Mrs Clive's friends set up Mrs Butler as a rival for the part of Constance, and though they were not successful in their attempt to dislodge Mrs Cibber, they undoubtedly created much bad feeling and associated the play with

[15] The controversy began when "Spectator" wrote to the *Daily Gazeteer*, November 4, 1736. "A. Z." (probably Theophilus though he later denied it) replied in the *London Daily Post and General Advertiser*, November 13. Mrs Clive replied to A. Z. in the same paper, November 19, and Theophilus wrote over his own name to the *Grub Street Journal*, December 9. There are many other references to the dispute.
[16] *Daily Journal*, December 10, 1736.

quarrels which were still fresh in every memory.[17] A little later, when the rehearsals were well under way, the templars began issuing dark threats, and Cibber finally felt obliged to address them in a public letter. He appealed to their generosity, not so much on his own behalf as on Fleetwood's; for he explained that Fleetwod, having bought the play outright, was the only person financially interested in its success.[18] But the appeal only made matters worse; the threats continued; and the newspapers were soon filled with "letters, epigrams, odes, jokes, and all the ribaldry of Grub Street." Cibber could not at this point legitimately withdraw his play, for "the actors [were] perfect, scenes painted, and much time had been spent which the master of the house would otherwise have been using to his interest. However," continues the same authority, "[Cibber] was resolved it should not be damned; and fearing the master might insist on its being played, what does he but at a rehearsal, seeing his play lying on the prompter's table, he takes up the copy and puts it up into his pocket snug, and decently walked off with it, resolving he would not run the risk of so precarious a fortune." [19] And so for the second time, as Pope was later to remark, *King John* in silence modestly expired.[20]

The loss of two parts in one season was undoubtedly disappointing to Mrs Cibber, but at the moment she was even more disappointed by the behavior of her husband. For Theophilus was now systematically robbing her, and had in fact been robbing her for two years. In 1735 he had taken half her salary, and in 1736 he had taken the present of £50 given her by Fleetwood after her appearance in *Zara*. He had made only the slightest pretense of observing the marriage articles; but in 1737 his conduct became even more outrageous—he took everything he could get. He collected almost all the money his wife made at the theatre; he stripped her of her clothes and even her linen; he paid his creditors with free tickets to her benefit plays; he had himself "colorably" arrested so that he could seize the rest of

[17] Davies, *Dramatic Miscellanies* (1783-84), I, 36.
[18] See Emmett L. Avery, "Cibber, *King John,* and the Students of the Law," *Mod. Lang. Notes,* LIII (1938), 272-75.
[19] *Apology for T ... C ...,* p. 83.
[20] Pope, *Works,* IV, 120.

her personal effects and sell them to raise money.[21] But even these expedients did not enable him to pay for his pleasures, and at the end of the year he took the unusual, though not unprecedented, step of selling his wife to a lover.[22]

The lover was a certain John Sloper, a country squire who had become acquainted with Mrs Cibber during her contest with Mrs Clive. He had seen her from time to time in the greenroom, and he had later paid visits to the house which she and her husband had taken in the country. Theophilus showed no signs of uneasiness at the intimacy which was springing up; indeed he was delighted that his wife had found so charming and distinguished a companion. When Sloper asked if he might teach Mrs Cibber backgammon, Theophilus at once graciously consented. He called Sloper a romp and a good-natured boy, borrowed a few guineas from him, and left for his nightly adventure in Covent Garden. Soon, however, Sloper was not satisfied to play backgammon with his companion; he was in love and he made no secret of the fact; and Theophilus, to his wife's surprise, was as gracious as before. He merely borrowed somewhat larger sums from the squire and contrived to give him even more of Mrs Cibber's company. When Mrs Cibber ignored the hint, it is said that Theophilus led her to Sloper's apartment, drew a pistol, and swore by God she should stay with the squire or he would shoot her through the head. Under such compulsion she could not refuse, and the squire became her lover.

The scandalous relationship was soon accepted by all three, and when, to avoid his creditors, Theophilus took lodgings at Kensington, Sloper went along as a matter of course. The domestic arrangements were necessarily somewhat odd, and Theophilus was finally obliged to take the housekeeper into his confidence. He admitted that his wife was carrying on an affair with Benefit (as he called Sloper), admitted too that his own reputation depended upon his ability to keep

[21] C. 11 1572/14.

[22] The following account of the matrimonial difficulties of the Cibbers is based chiefly upon three works: *Comforts of Matrimony; Benjamin Victor, Original Letters, Dramatic Pieces, and Poems* (1776), I, 21-24; *The Tryal of a Cause of Criminal Conversation between Theophilus Cibber, Gent. Plaintiff and William Sloper, Esq. Defendant* (1739), republished with additions as *The Tryals of Two Causes* (1740). More specific references would perhaps be misleading, since many of the details of the story are almost certainly apocryphal.

it secret. He was about to leave for France, he said, and he urged the housekeeper to remain with Mrs Cibber while he was gone so that no one else might suspect the strange things that were taking place. The woman promised and Theophilus slipped quietly away, taking refuge from his creditors on the other side of the channel.

The weeks passed pleasantly and uneventfully, for Theophilus was beyond the reach of bailiffs and catchpoles, and besides, he received letters from his wife, containing no doubt comfortable remittances from the squire. But suddenly he got a letter in which there was no remittance—a letter, in fact, in which his wife made extremely disquieting disclosures. Sloper, she said, had decided that he could not share her love with any man living, not even with her husband. He advised her to leave the stage and go with him into the country, and she had decided to do so. Theophilus was dumbfounded and—if the letter to his wife which he later published is genuine and if it was written (as it appears to have been) at this time—he abandoned himself completely to paroxysms of grief and remorse.

My dearest Susanna Maria, Not strength of constitution, spirits, resolution, reason, or all I can call to my assistance will, I find, prevent my having a violent fit of illness, which increases daily. If God pleases to dismiss me this life, it will be an act of mercy. My heart trembles, my senses stagger, what a state of despair! I own the hand of Providence and submit to its eternal justice; my condition is greatly terrible: my own faults glare upon me, and self-convicted I own I ought to suffer much; yet sure mine is the heaviest calamity that ever oppressed human nature. How vain were an attempt to express it in words: 'tis not to be conceived; 'tis only to be felt and felt by me alone. Where is the religion, where the unspotted truth, the whitened innocence, that once shone out so brightly in a certain mind? All lost!

But no—this was only a preliminary flourish—all was not quite lost; for Theophilus was prepared to forgive his wife, prepared even to offer her his own loyal heart.

My heart's fondling, my dearest Molly, you may have the sole possession and full command of the heart of a husband that beats to you alone, that wishes the vital blood may no longer warm it than while it flows for you. Take example of heaven and dash not away the tears of penitence: I have been highly to blame and I as truly repent: I will err no more. I here give up all views of idle pleasures, all vanities whatsoever; I will live very near that I may recover my circumstances; I will give up everything but your *heart;* let me recover that treasure and I shall repine at nothing; my heart will be delighted in ecstasy while I can see your countenance smile and wear the looks of cordial affection. . . . Drive me not to despair; insult not my breaking heart; but, my dearest Sucky, my dearest Molly, my dearest Teresa, return to truth and bless me; return to your repentant, fond, forgiving, affectionate, tender, truly loving, though unhappy, husband, T. C.[23]

This appeal was certainly calculated to soften the hardest heart, but Theophilus was too much interested in his wife's salary to trust entirely to correspondence and soon afterwards he returned to London. Unfortunately he found that his wife was adamant, she obstinately refused to go on in the old way. In fact, she had the temerity to suggest that he was using his position to blackmail Sloper—a suggestion which Theophilus found extremely mortifying, since he had never, he felt, even considered a mercenary settlement. Of course, if his wife wanted to leave him, why certainly—he would let her go. He would never speak of her or even think of her again. And as for the money, they could keep it; he would rather starve than touch one penny that came to him in such a way. "A divorce," he wrote to Sloper, "a thorough one, I have learned, is not so excessively expensive as some may have imagined: I expect that of their honor who ought to procure it; and it may be done without prejudice to any or using names that may shock the innocent; 'tis all I want in lieu of a fine lady and her income, which, by my means, may yet be £400 a year; but I would beg rather than share it with her. I think money dirt, sir, as much as anyone; and however necessary an article 'tis in life, I scorn to pick it off dunghills. Pray, sir, what favor do I owe you except one paltry debt, for which you had my bond, and you know might have had stronger security? Did I dream of it e'er 'twas proffered or were any damned terms proposed? No, by my G—d, sir, you know the contrary." But, he pointed out in a postscript, there are some things that my wife ought to return to me: "I insist on her earrings; I have been robbed too much by her already."[24]

A little reflection, however, convinced Theophilus that the earrings

---

[23] *Four Original Letters, viz. Two from a Husband to a Gentleman, and Two from a Husband to a Wife* (1739), pp. 1-10. Theophilus says that he left the letter with his wife when he went abroad, April 16, 1738, and in his second letter he suggests that he went abroad because his wife had confessed her love for Sloper. But this is certainly wrong.

[24] *Four Original Letters,* pp. 19-20.

were not enough, and that articles of separation, which he was now suggesting, should perhaps include some sort of financial settlement after all.

Those articles I mention, madam, ought to leave each as free as we were once fast, if possible; nor is it reasonable I should be liable to a jail for the indiscretions of others whom, I am compelled to say, may not a little have contributed towards the hazard of my being in one. I can make it appear that you have spent me infinitely more than your own income ever amounted to. . . . My few remaining goods, etc., I must part with, for I am ashamed to say it to you but I am in danger of being troubled by some few creditors whose folly has refused my honest proposals; and my whole salary, you know, must go to those good-natured creditors who have complied; though they are all yours, madam, as much as mine, at least. I can't throw away anything where I am sure there's no obligation, nor must my children starve while you riot. . . . After all I know of you—be anything but my wife, and be luxuriously happy if you can—Hell seize me if I wish to interrupt you. And so thou weakest and most worthless of thy sex, farewell for ever.[25]

But it was not really to be farewell, for Theophilus again changed his mind and decided that he must have his wife back at all costs. Since she would not come of her own accord, he must fetch her, by force if necessary; and accordingly he prepared to go to Burnham, where she and Sloper were then staying, and tear her from the very arms of her lover.

The expedition was altogether commensurate with the great task of rescuing a wife from iniquity and bringing her back to the purity of the home. Theophilus assembled three strong, resolute men, rented a coach and four, a saddle horse, and a small arsenal of weapons, and bravely set out on his great mission. The cavalcade reached Burnham about five o'clock in the afternoon. Theophilus left his coach in a lane behind the garden wall, and sent one of the men to summon Mrs Cibber to the door. As soon as she appeared, he seized her by the arm, led her to the coach, and told her that she must now give up all thoughts of Sloper and return with him to London. Sloper ran from the house in bedgown and slippers, but he was too scantily clad to offer much resistance. Still he cursed a good deal and took back to the house a watch which Mrs Cibber gave him. "Well remembered," he was heard

[25] *Ibid.*, pp. 33-37.

to mutter, "the rascal would have had it else." But before he could get dressed, Theophilus had assembled his party and moved off with his captive toward London. Sloper took horse and caught up with them near Slough, where another little altercation took place. Theophilus made a speech and Sloper shot off his pistol in the air, but in the end these turbulent passions were allayed by fatigue and all three passed the night at an inn together, though not perhaps quite so happily as they had done under other circumstances.

Once in London again, Theophilus confined his wife in a house in Wild Court, Great Wild Street, under the care of a candle-snuffer from the theatre. But after a day or two her brother Thomas rescued her by breaking open the door and knocking the candle-snuffer on the head. Theophilus had Arne committed to Bridewell, and Mrs Cibber, who in the meantime had rejoined the squire, swore the peace against Theophilus and had him bound over on good behavior. Sensational events like these could scarcely be kept secret, and Theophilus finally threw all caution to the winds by suing the squire for criminal conversation and demanding damages of £5,000. For Theophilus at last realized that he had been very deeply wounded and could not possibly be expected to recover without a considerable sum of money.

This famous case came to trial on December 5, 1738. The proceedings were opened by the solicitor general, counsel for the plaintiff, who spoke warmly about the grave consequences of crimes against the marriage state. "The crime of adultery," he said, "or depriving a man of his wife, strikes at the root of all society, for it robs a man not only of his ease and peace of mind, but in effect of his fortune or whatever substance by his toil and industry he may have acquired, by tainting his family with a spurious issue." He added that the plaintiff was particulary vulnerable in this respect because he was a member of a distinguished family, lineally descended from William of Wykeham. The solicitor general gave place to Mr Hollings, also counsel for the plaintiff, who spoke well upon the same subject. But Hollings carried the argument a step farther by pathetically calling the jury's attention to "the mischievous consequences of suffering a man to commit such an injury to the married state without being obliged to repair it in damages." The plaintiff, he said, was an Englishman, and as such had rights which ought not to be invaded, particularly in the present instance. He had brought his complaint before a jury of English gentlemen, and Hollings did not doubt that they would award him proper damages, namely £5,000.

The plaintiff's sister, Mrs Brett, was then called to witness the marriage, but as Mrs Brett was not yet in court and as the defense did not seem disposed to doubt that a marriage had actually taken place, the prosecution summoned the plaintiff's father, Colley Cibber. After being duly sworn, Cibber deposed as follows:

QUESTION. Do you know of the plaintiff's being married to his present wife?

MR CIBBER. I was not at the marriage, but I am as well convinced that they were married as that I myself was married. I was against the match.

QUESTION. Why were you against the match?

MR CIBBER. Because she had no fortune.

QUESTION. Did they at first live happily together?

MR CIBBER. They did live happy, very happy, much happier than I expected, for I was averse to the match.

QUESTION. How long did they live thus happily together?

MR CIBBER. About three years; within that time they had two children, which are both dead.

QUESTION. Did Mr Cibber, the plaintiff, during that time support her well and liberally as became an affectionate husband?

MR CIBBER. He did, even to profusion. I often admonished him about it and advised him to retrench his expenses, for I thought them a good deal too large for his condition or what he was able to afford. He made her several valuable presents of rings and jewels.

QUESTION. Is not Mrs Cibber a good actress? And how did she become so?

MR CIBBER. When they married she was a singer, but there were better voices. I thought her voice not the best; and if not the best, 'tis nothing. I thought it might possibly do better for speaking. I asked her husband if he had ever heard her attempt to speak a part; he said he had and that she did it very prettily. I tried her and was much surprised to find her do it so very well.

QUESTION. Did not the husband take pains to instruct her?

MR CIBBER. I believe I was the person who chiefly instructed her; I spent a good deal of time and took great delight in it, for she was very capable of receiving instruction. In forty years' experience that I have known the stage, I never knew a woman at the beginning so capable of the business or improve so fast.

QUESTION. When did you first hear of any disagreement in the family?

MR CIBBER. Soon after he came from France; about last April.

But as to the nature of the disagreement the old man would say nothing, for, as he explained, he was himself in France at the time and he knew of it only by report.

Fleetwood and Rich were then called to testify as to Mrs Cibber's ability as an actress, and when her income—the income which Theophilus had lost—had been fixed at between £300 and £400 a year, the prosecution proceeded to establish the evidence for criminal conversation. A Mr and Mrs Hayes, owners of a lodging house in Leicester Fields, were the principal witnesses. They testified that they had looked through a hole in the wainscot partition, and from this point of vantage had observed incidents which established the criminal conversation beyond any reasonable doubt. The Burnham expedition and the misfortunes of the candle-snuffer were then described, and the prosecution rested its case.

Sergeant Eyre, for the defendant, began by remarking that he believed this to be the first action of its kind which had ever come from the theatre. He had never heard, he said, that the theatre was a place celebrated for virtue. Furthermore he was puzzled by the emphasis on the plaintiff's family tree, and he could not help noticing that, since William of Wykeham was a priest, the plaintiff could not be descended in a right line from him. But Eyre did not press the point. He went on to argue that if criminal conversation had occurred—and he, for his part, sincerely hoped that it had not—it had occurred with the full knowledge and consent of the plaintiff. To establish this important fact, he called the housekeeper, Anne Hopson, who described the relations between her employers, the presents of money given by Sloper to Theophilus, and finally the disposition of beds in the Cibber household. Mr Murray summed up for the defense by saying that if the jury were to bring in a verdict for the plaintiff, there was not in the kingdom a coin of denomination small enough for them to award in damages.

Murray's remarks must have influenced the jury profoundly, for after deliberating half an hour they agreed to follow his suggestions almost to the letter. They decided for the plaintiff—for, indeed, they could scarcely do otherwise—but they fixed his damages not at £5,000 but at £10.

The suit was, of course, disastrous for all the persons concerned.

Mrs Cibber had to leave the stage; Sloper had to live in the country under an assumed name; Theophilus had to endure ridicule and abuse which would have been intolerable to anyone not endowed with his impudence and effrontery. A month after the trial he let it be known that he would continue to act at Drury Lane, and though the templars threatened to hiss him off the stage, he appeared as Lord Foppington in *The Relapse*.[26] "The house was very early crowded," we are told, "and the harmonious discordant concert of catcalls, whistles, etc., etc., began to play before the curtain drew up. Well, though the actors were all frightened, the play began with calmness and applause; but this was only a prelude to the battle. When the scene came in which he was to appear, there was a dead silence, till he popped his poor head from behind the scenes; then at once the hurly-burly began, volleys of apples and potatoes and such vile trash flew about his ears. He retired, the storm subsided; he advanced, it began again. In the most humble gesture and address he made a motion to be heard; it was all in vain and he was once more pelted off. . . . But determined to go through the play, he went through it amidst the greatest uproar that ever was heard so long a space in a theatre, and by a confident heart he surmounted what many of less resolution would have sunk under." [27] Indeed he acted again a few days later—acted so many times, in fact, that the templars finally gave in and stopped baiting him.

But though he could usually appear on the stage without causing a riot, he could seldom command applause, and his influence with Fleetwood rapidly declined. Macklin replaced him as director of rehearsals at Drury Lane, and in a rage he went over to Covent Garden. But after two seasons he quarreled with his new employer, Rich, and returned to Drury Lane.[28] In 1742-43 he was at Lincoln's Inn Fields during the winter and at the Smock Alley Theatre in Dublin during the summer; in 1744 he was at his own theatre in the Haymarket, where he had the bad taste to attempt the part of Othello; in 1745 he was back at Covent Garden. But though he continued to change theatres with the greatest regularity and was always ready to act parts which he had

[26] *The Wentworth Papers* (1883), p. 541.
[27] *Apology for T . . . C . . .*, pp. 63-64.
[28] Victor, *History of the Theatres*, I, 31; *Apology for T . . . C . . .*, pp. 108-9.

never attempted before, he failed to reëstablish himself in the good graces of the town.

For several years he conducted a sort of guerilla warfare against Sloper and his wife, but fortunately he was never quite able to get possession of his wife's income. His greatest triumph came in 1739, when, suing Sloper for trespass and assault in taking, leading away, detaining, and beating his wife, he recovered £500 damages of the £10,000 that he asked. But Mrs Cibber charged him with incontinence in the ecclesiastical court and pestered him with suits in Common Pleas and Chancery until he was finally thrown into the Fleet for debt. After his release he promised that he would no longer molest her, but he was never very careful to keep his word. In 1746, for example, he precipitately left Covent Garden for Drury Lane because he had learned that Mrs Cibber was to play Monimia there for her brother's benefit. Alarmed by his presence, Arne threatened to have the benefit at another theatre, and Theophilus was obliged to defend himself in a public statement, printed and circulated on twenty-four hours' notice.[29]

As [my wife] has sought every occasion to disturb my peace of mind, to stab my reputation and prejudice my circumstances, I should undoubtedly be justified by all mankind in any act of severe justice towards her that would not debase my manhood or shock my humanity. But low as she has reduced my fortune (and that she has been the source of my calamities I will presently and concisely make appear), my mind has never sunk low enough to seek a mean revenge, even against the most faithless, artful, and ungrateful woman that ever imposed on a good-natured world or disturbed the heart of a weak man. I doubt my greatest fault towards her has been too much lenity: this I defy any partial friend of hers or worst of my foes to disprove. I apprehend the foundation of the aforementioned report was grounded on her own conscious fears, which told her such usage she ought to expect; having given some late instances of her heart being entirely shut against him to whom alone it ought to be open.[30]

But these protestations were not to be taken too seriously, for a few years later Theophilus announced his intention of starting another suit against Sloper and preventing his wife from acting at either

---

[29] Theophilus Cibber, *Romeo and Juliet. Revised and Altered from Shakespeare. To which is added a Serio-Comic Apology for Part of the Life of Mr Theophilus Cibber, Comedian. Written by Himself* (n. d.), pp. 94-95.

[30] *Ibid.*, pp. 95-96.

theatre.[31] By this time, however, Mrs Cibber was too well established to fear the malice of a maniac, and the fury of her husband spent itself in threats and imprecations.

Theophilus was now irretrievably ruined, and disappearing into the purlieus of Covent Garden—the scene of his earliest exploits—he sank swiftly into oblivion. During the last years of his life he is seen only at rare intervals—as author of *The Lives of the Poets,* as lecturer at the Haymarket Theatre, as occasional performer on the London stage (usually in benefit plays for himself). But from time to time stories about him are told and his character is burlesqued. Thus in 1756 he appears as Squint-Eyed Pistol in a farce attributed to Arthur Murphy. He is sitting in an elegant apartment in Newport Street, with a fur cap upon his head and a nose and set of false teeth lying on the table beside him. He rises, puts on the nose, clamps the false teeth in his mouth, and spits on the leg of a guest, who later considerately offers to pick up the nose when it falls on the floor.[32] At another time he appears in the greenroom of the theatre, dressed in black satin coat and breeches, with white satin apparaments, and a waistcoat trimmed with silver frogs. His father, who is also there, comes up to him, looks critically at his dress, and asks him what part he is to act tonight. "No part," Theophilus replies. And the old man leaves him abruptly, saying, "Then I pity you." [33] But another scene from the life of this incredible person is even more curious. Theophilus is writing proposals for Cibber and Company, Snuff Merchants, who will shortly open a snuff warehouse, "where will be sold a most excellent cephalic snuff, whose virtues are of such efficacy as few words cannot easily express." [34] But again the scene changes. Theophilus, hurrying away to keep an engagement at the Smock Alley Theatre in Dublin, is caught in a violent storm, and before the most excellent cephalic snuff can be prepared, is drowned in the Irish Sea.[35]

[31] Victor, *Letters,* I, 201-2.
[32] *The Spouter, or the Triple Revenge* (1756), I, v.
[33] Fitzgerald, *New History of the Stage,* II, 89.
[34] Theophilus Cibber, *Two Dissertations on the Theatres,* Part III, p. 113.
[35] Victor, *History of the Theatres,* I, 249-51; *Biographia Dramatica,* article Theophilus Cibber.

XI. THE APOLOGY

DURING the period of the Sloper trials and the fiasco of *King John,* Cibber was writing the book upon which his reputation with posterity was largely to rest—the *Apology* for his life. It was published on April 7, 1740, in a handsome edition sold at a guinea, and on May 14 of the same year a second and more modest edition appeared at the price of five shillings. The book was exceedingly popular and before 1750, when he disposed of the copyright, Cibber is said to have made royalties of more than £1,500.[1]

The title is not without significance, for the book is really Cibber's answer to his critics. He aims to review his career, to point out his achievements, to show that he had always had the best interests of the stage at heart and had in fact, between 1710 and 1732, helped to bring it to its highest period of perfection and prosperity. But he also aims to sketch his own character, to refute once and for all the malicious misrepresentations of his enemies, to demonstrate that his conduct, stupid and foolish as it may at times have seemed, had never really been "inconsistent with happiness."[2]

The first three chapters give the facts of his early life, but digressions are frequent. His school days at Grantham remind him of the uses and abuses of raillery, of Lord Chesterfield and Giles Earle,[3] of the comforts of folly and the vanity of greatness, of the place of laughter in a happy life. In the next chapter he returns to Grantham only to drift off into another set of apparently irrelevant reflections. But his method is somewhat misleading, for in this part of the book he is chiefly interested in defining his own temper and giving his views about life. He represents himself as a gay and carefree philosopher; a

---

[1] *Notes and Queries,* 11th series, III (January-June, 1911), 266; Davies, *Dramatic Miscellanies* (1783-84), III, 476. Robert Walker apparently attempted to pirate an edition of the *Apology;* see Cibber v. Walker, C. 11 1559/15, and Chancery Decrees and Orders, 1740 A, p. 170.

[2] *Apology,* I, 2.

[3] See *The Laureat,* p. 18; *Notes and Queries,* 11th series, IV (July-December, 1911), 382, 475.

little foolish perhaps but even more distinctly whimsical; devoted to good company and harmless recreation. The word *folly* occurs frequently in his paragraphs, but usually in the plural; *tastes* would perhaps better convey his meaning. "If I can please myself with my own follies," he says, "have not I a plentiful provision for life? If the world thinks me a trifler I don't desire to break in upon their wisdom; let them call me any fool but an uncheerful one; I live as I write; while my way amuses me it's as well as I wish it." [4] True happiness, in short, is to be always in good humor, "to give a constant preference to the business of the day and yet be able to laugh while we are about it"; [5] and Cibber considered himself a truly happy man.

The portrait is highly colored and moderately well drawn, but it is not, one feels, entirely true to life. For Cibber was not only a cheerful companion; he had his full share of the uglier human passions, he could be extremely unpleasant, even deliberately disagreeable. "If I were capable of envy," one of his sentences begins; [6] but we know quite well that he was frequently envious. He is "always repining at the success of others," says a writer in 1702, "and upon the stage makes all his fellow actors uneasy." [7] In an earlier passage Cibber promises that he will reveal himself without reservation and make public every one of his follies. "Why not?" he asks. "I have passed my time very pleasantly with them and I don't recollect that they have ever been hurtful to any other man living." [8] But the second half of the sentence instantly gives him away. He was not prepared for serious recollection; he could justify, but not describe, his behavior. The early chapters are interesting in so far as they reflect Cibber's views about himself, but to get close to the real Cibber we must turn to the narrative sections of the book.

At the end of Chapter III Cibber reaches 1690, the year in which he first appeared on the stage, and in the two following chapters he digresses to describe the actors and actresses who were prominent at that time. It is a particularly happy section, a brilliant review of brilliant figures. Betterton, Kynaston, Underhill, Nokes, Mrs Barry, Mrs Verbruggen—almost all the great names of the Restoration theatre in fact—come to life in these vivid pages. We see Kynaston as

---

[4] *Apology*, I, 21.   [5] *Ibid.*, I, 18.   [6] *Ibid.*
[7] *Comparison between the Two Stages*, p. 199.   [8] *Apology*, I, 2.

Henry IV, whispering to Hotspur the line, "Send us your prisoners or you will hear of it": "He conveyed a more terrible menace in [the whisper] than the loudest intemperance of voice could swell to." [9] We see Underhill as the booby Lolpoop in *The Squire of Alsatia*: "He seemed the immovable log he stood for; a countenance of wood could not be more fixed than his when the blockhead of a character required it." [10] We see Nokes in a favorite comic part, hesitating and trying to make up his mind:

He would shut up his mouth with a dumb studious pout and roll his full eye into such a vacant amazement, such a palpable ignorance of what to think of it, that his silent perplexity (which would sometimes hold him several minutes) gave your imagination as full content as the most absurd thing he could say upon it.[11]

We see the incomparable Mrs Verbruggen as Melantha, reading her father's letter and bewildering her gallant in the second act of *Marriage a la Mode*:

Here now one would think she might naturally show a little of the sex's decent reserve, though never so slightly covered. No, sir; not a tittle of it; modesty is the virtue of a poor-souled country gentlewoman; she is too much a court lady to be under so vulgar a confusion; she reads the letter, therefore, with a careless, dropping lip and an erected brow, humming it hastily over as if she were impatient to outgo her father's commands by making a complete conquest of him at once; and that the letter might not embarrass her attack, crack! she crumbles it at once into her palm and pours upon him her whole artillery of airs, eyes, and motion; down goes her dainty, diving body to the ground, as if she were sinking under the conscious load of her own attractions; then launches into a flood of fine language and compliment, still playing her chest forward in fifty falls and risings, like a swan upon waving water; and to complete her impertinence she is so rapidly fond of her own wit that she will not give her lover leave to praise it. Silent assenting bows and vain endeavors to speak are all the share of the conversation he is admitted to, which at last he is relieved from by her engagement to half a score visits, which she *swims* from him to make, with a promise to return in a twinkling.[12]

Comment is unnecessary. Each actor is caught in a characteristic pose, each picture is fixed so vividly in our minds that we share much of Cibber's enthusiasm for the notable performances of the past.

[9] *Ibid.*, I, 126.
[10] *Ibid.*, I, 154-55.
[11] *Ibid.*, I, 144.
[12] *Ibid.*, I, 168-69.

In the same chapters, as well as later in the book, Cibber briefly describes the more famous actors of the next generation; but his enthusiasm immediately cools, his pictures become much less flattering. Estcourt was a capital mimic, but he could not act; Booth delivered correctly the passionate speeches of Othello, but he was hopelessly wrong in the rodomontades of Morat:

[He] covered these kind of sentiments with a scrupulous coldness and unmoved delivery, as if he had feared that the audience might take too familiar a notice of them.[13]

Wilks was unexcelled as the fine gentleman and the pathetic lover, but his Hamlet was deplorably bad:

You have seen a Hamlet perhaps who, on the first appearance of his father's spirit, has thrown himself into all the straining vociferation requisite to express rage and fury, and the house has thundered with applause, though the misguided actor was all the while (as Shakespeare terms it) tearing a passion into rags.[14]
The half of what he spoke was as painful to my ear as every line that came from Betterton was charming.[15]

After the appearance of the book these passages received unfavorable comment because it was felt that Cibber had been blinded by envy to the merits of his immediate contemporaries.[16] Possibly so, but there is also a more charitable explanation. His vision was clear when he wrote about Wilks and Booth, less clear in the case of Nokes and Mrs Verbruggen, who belonged to a remote and somewhat romantic past.

In Chapter VI Cibber begins his history of the stage during his own time, the subject of the remaining two thirds of the volume. He describes the revolt of the actors in 1694-95, the struggle between Betterton and Rich, the building of the Haymarket Theatre, the companies of Collier and Swiney, the rise of the actor-managers, and finally the fortunes and misfortunes of Drury Lane between 1710 and 1732. His method is discursive, his tone disarmingly chatty, but as one reads one sees a definite thesis emerging. Two companies cannot prosper in London: "two sets of actors tolerated in the same place have constantly ended in the corruption of the theatre."[17] Between 1695 and 1710 there had been a company in Drury Lane and another company in

---

[13] *Ibid.*, I, 122.   [14] *Ibid.*, I, 100.   [15] *Ibid.*, II, 245.
[16] *The Laureat*, pp. 30, 33, etc.; Victor, *History of the Theatres*, II, 15 and note.
[17] *Apology*, II, 179.

Lincoln's Inn Fields or the Haymarket; hence low salaries and uncertain profits, poor discipline and careless management; hence, too, the suicidal competition in operas and entertainments. But in 1710 the actor-managers had emerged; the companies had united; better days were finally at hand. In approaching this significant transition between the old theatre and the new, Cibber becomes almost lyrical:

This then was that happy period when both actors and managers were in their highest enjoyment of general content and prosperity. . . .[18]

But here let me rest a while, and since at my time of day our best possessions are but ease and quiet, I must be content if I will have sallies of pleasure, to take up with those only that are to be found in imagination. When I look back, therefore, on the storms of the stage we had been tossed in; when I consider that various vicissitude of hopes and fears we had for twenty years struggled with, and found ourselves at last thus safely set on shore to enjoy the produce of our own labors. . . .[19]

But it is scarcely necessary to follow to the end these inflated paragraphs.

In Cibber's narrative of prolonged disaster and final triumph two figures occupy the foreground—Christopher Rich and Cibber himself. The first figure stands for everything that is undesirable and disorderly in the theatre; he is the enemy of the drama, the master of opera and entertainments; sinister no doubt, but extremely interesting—in fact Cibber's masterpiece in characterization. We see the disreputable old lawyer laughing with his actors over a bottle and biting them in their bargains; we see him constructing back doors, dark closets, and narrow passages in his theatre ("His genius in nook-building was never out of employment"); [20] we see him resenting but not daring to oppose the vigorous measures of Brett ("If his hat were taken from his head in the street, he would make no farther resistance than to say, 'I am not willing to part with it' "); [21] and finally we see him deprived of his patent but not seriously concerned, for he was at last completely free to supervise the construction of the new Lincoln's Inn Fields. The second figure—Cibber himself—is at first sight less credible. His judgment is too clear, his behavior too obviously correct. He exerts a beneficial influence upon Rich and finally breaks with him; he advises Brett; he adopts exactly the right attitude toward Wilks,

---

[18] *Ibid.*, II, 119.   [20] *Ibid.*, I, 334.
[19] *Ibid.*, II, 115.   [21] *Ibid.*, II, 44.

Booth, the new company in Lincoln's Inn Fields. But as one examines the narrative more closely, shadows begin to appear. Cibber shrewdly prolongs the lawsuit with Doggett; he insults, with obvious relish, the Master of the Revels; he makes a mistake in business transactions with Steele. The figure is almost human after all.

Occasionally one is inclined to suspect the accuracy of the narrative, and there are indeed a few passages that need to be supplemented and corrected. In the early chapters Cibber deliberately underestimates his influence with Rich, chiefly no doubt because he was reluctant to share responsibility for the policies pursued at Drury Lane during the early years of the century. Later in the book he tries to clear the reputation of his old friend Owen Swiney. He assures us that the two Haymarket companies managed by Swiney were successful, though actually—as we learn from legal records and newspapers of the time—both companies failed. But doubtful passages of this sort are neither very numerous nor very important, and on the whole the book can be accepted as an authoritative account of the stage history of Cibber's time.

A more serious weakness is the style, the most frequently and most justly criticized aspect of the book. Cibber can be, and often is, extremely vivid; he has an eye for significant detail. He tells us exactly how actors looked and spoke upon the stage; exactly how his colleagues behaved during a dispute in the office of the theatre:

Mrs Oldfield began to titter behind her fan. . . . [Wilks] threw down the part upon the table, crossed his arms, and sate knocking his heel upon the floor, as seeming to threaten most when he said least.[22]

He is even capable of neat turns of wit, as in the tenth chapter where he discusses the Lord Chamberlain's reasons for suppressing *The Maid's Tragedy* during the reign of Charles II. It was felt, he says, that a repentant mistress who kills a king in the very bed which has witnessed her dishonor might prove a dangerous example "to other Evadnes then shining at court in the same rank of royal distinction."

But [he adds] this I doubt is too deep a speculation or too ludicrous a reason to be relied on; it being well known that the ladies then in favor were not so nice in their notions as to think their preferment their dishonor or their lover a tyrant: besides, that easy monarch loved his roses without thorns; nor do we hear that he much chose to be himself the first gatherer of them.[23]

[22] *Ibid.*, II, 235-36.   [23] *Ibid.*, II, 12-13.

But sentences like this are less frequent than loosely constructed, rambling sentences in which conventions of rhetoric are cavalierly set aside. For on the whole the style is that of an undisciplined, even a slovenly, writer; it is a style generally lacking in strength and incisiveness. In the thirteenth chapter, for example, Cibber thus begins a paragraph about Rich and the reconstruction of Lincoln's Inn Fields:

Having shown by what means Collier had dispossessed this patentee, not only of the Drury Lane house, but likewise of those few actors which he had kept for some time unemployed in it, we are now led to consider another project of the same patentee, which, if we are to judge of it by the event, has shown him more a wise than a weak man; which I confess at the time he put it in execution seemed not so clear a point: for notwithstanding he now saw the authority and power of his patent was superseded, or was at best but precarious, and that he had not one actor left in his service, yet, under all these dilemmas and distresses, he resolved upon rebuilding the new theatre in Lincoln's Inn Fields, of which he had taken a lease, at a low rent, ever since Betterton's company had first left it.[24]

The meaning is clear but the movement is too slow; the sentence staggers under the weight of qualifying clauses. In another passage Cibber indulges in a favorite weakness—he digresses to compare the stage and the court:

Thus we see, let the degrees and rank of men be ever so unequal, nature throws out their passions from the same motives; 'tis not the eminence or lowliness of either that makes the one, when provoked, more or less a reasonable creature than the other: the courtier and the comedian, when their ambition is out of humor, take just the same measures to right themselves.[25]

Nature throws out their passions? their ambition is out of humor? At first one is puzzled by clauses like these, and it is only after careful examination of the sentence that one deciphers the meaning. But it would be unkind to multiply examples when Cibber himself has so freely confessed his own shortcomings.

That I am not a master of my own languge, I too often feel when I am at a loss for expression. I know too that I have too bold a disregard for that correctness which others set so just a value upon. . . . Whenever I speak of anything that highly delights me, I find it very difficult to keep my words within the bounds of common sense. Even when I write too, the same failing will sometimes get the better of me; of which I cannot give

[24] *Ibid.*, II, 100.   [25] *Ibid.*, II, 224-25.

you a stronger instance than in that wild expression I made use of in the first edition of my preface to *The Provoked Husband;* where, speaking of Mrs Oldfield's excellent performance in the part of Lady Townly, my words ran thus, viz.: "It is not enough to say that here she outdid her usual out-doing." A most vile jingle, I grant it! You may well ask me, how could I possibly commit such a wantonness to paper. And I owe myself the shame of confessing I have no excuse for it but that, like a lover in the fullness of his content, by endeavoring to be floridly grateful I talked nonsense.[26]

To this disarmingly frank statement there is little to add.

Cibber's uncertain style has undoubtedly discouraged many readers; but the book has an even more fatal defect—its subject matter is rarely of general interest. There is too little about Betterton and Booth, Mrs Oldfield and Mrs Verbruggen, too much about the problems of management at Drury Lane, about long-forgotten companies in the Haymarket and Lincoln's Inn Fields, about personalities whose names have only the vaguest associations for the general reader. The *Apology,* in short, is not a classic: it is a reference book for students and a source book for scholars. It gives a readable, a comprehensive, indeed an indispensable account of a period in theatrical history; but it is only for those who find theatrical history a subject of absorbing interest.

Shortly after the publication of the *Apology,* Swift got a copy from Faulkener and sat up all night to finish it. When the story was told to Cibber he shed tears of joy.[27] Swift's interest was probably shared by many contemporaries who were more or less familiar with the in-cidents described in the book. But there was also much unfavorable criticism, notably in two pamphlets published within six months of the *Apology* itself—*An Apology for the Life of T ... C ...* and *The Laureat, or the Right Side of Colley Cibber.* The first is connected, as the title suggests, with Cibber's son Theophilus. In 1739 that unfor-tunate young man had tried his hand at journalism, and in 1740, immediately after the publication of his father's book, he had decided to write an apology for *his* life. He had issued proposals and begun collecting subscriptions, when suddenly, early in July, such a book appeared. Its full title was *An Apology for the Life of Mr T ... C ...,* *Comedian. Being a Proper Sequel to the Apology for the Life of* *Mr Colley Cibber, Comedian. With an Historical View of the Stage*

[26] *Ibid.,* I, 50-51.
[27] Davies, *Dramatic Miscellanies,* III, 477.

to the Present Year. Supposed to Be Written by Himself. In the Style and Manner of the Poet Laureate. Theophilus could do nothing but return his subscriptions (which he assures us that he did) and threaten the publishers of the fictitious apology with prosecution. But the publishers begged his pardon; "on which," he wrote later, "my indolence combined with my good nature and prevented my proceeding at law. Who the low rogue of an author was ... I could never learn." [28]

The authorship of the pamphlet, indeed, remains a mystery to this day, but Fielding has not without reason been suspected. After carefully weighing the evidence, Fielding's biographer concludes: "Although Fielding, I think, did not actually write the book, he was doubtless in the secret, and may have lent his aid here and there." [29]

The title is somewhat misleading, for the pamphlet deals as much with the elder Cibber as with his son. It begins as a burlesque on the *Apology* and gradually develops into an orderly résumé, the author obviously intending to offer his readers at two shillings what Cibber himself had offered at five. In his later chapters, however, he supplements Cibber's book with much valuable information about the stage. He describes the early years of Theophilus, the revolt of the actors in 1733, the career of Fleetwood, and the abortive production of *King John*. Indeed he gives a lively and comprehensive history of the theatre during the 1730s.[30]

The second pamphlet appeared on November 29 as *The Laureat, or the Right Side of Colley Cibber, Esq.; containing Explanations, Amendments, and Observations on a Book entitled An Apology for the Life and Writings of Mr Colley Cibber. Not Written by Himself.* The author is on the whole less genial, less amusing, and less accurate than the author of the *Apology for T ... C ...,* but occasionally he too gives valuable information about the stage. He supplements Cibber's account of the first performance of *Richard III,* he describes Cibber's treatment of Fenton and Steele, he sketches—in a remarkable section called *The Life of Aesopus*—the character of Cibber himself.

---

[28] Theophilus Cibber, *Lives of the Actors (Life of Booth),* p. xiii.

[29] Wilbur L. Cross, *The History of Henry Fielding* (New Haven, 1918), I, 284.

[30] The author of the pamphlet also tries to show that in 1739-40 Cibber and his son were attempting to get a license for a new company at the Haymarket. Cibber, the pamphleteer argues, had this scheme in mind when he wrote the *Apology,* and so did Theophilus when he wrote the *Country Correspondent.* But the evidence brought forward in the pamphlet is not very convincing.

The sketch is too obviously malicious to be quite convincing, but it undoubtedly contains information which cannot entirely be ignored.

The other books connected with the *Apology* deserve fuller treatment, and to explain satisfactorily their appearance we must go back several years and consider the origins of Cibber's quarrels with his two famous contemporaries, Fielding and Pope.

XII. POPE

CIBBER and Pope first clashed in the year 1717. Cibber, then forty-five years old, was at the height of his reputation. He was the author of half a dozen successful comedies and the most influential of the three actor-managers of Drury Lane. Pope was seventeen years younger, but he too was already famous; in fact, he was already recognized as the greatest poet of the age. He had published the *Pastorals,* the *Essay on Criticism,* the *Rape of the Lock,* and the first two volumes of the *Iliad,* to which Cibber was a subscriber. Their battle of 1717 arose from the fact that Pope had just assisted his two friends Arbuthnot and Gay in writing the farce of *Three Hours after Marriage.*

The farce is not perhaps a very distinguished piece of work, but it is interesting because it contains caricatures of several contemporaries. Dr Woodward is represented as Fossile, Mrs Centlivre as Clinket, John Dennis as Sir Tremendous and Colley Cibber—for he too appears in this extensive gallery of portraits—as the actor Plotwell.[1] The references to Cibber are indeed quite unmistakable, especially in the scene in which Plotwell is shown sponsoring one of the Clinket's plays. "I look upon a kiss in a comedy to be upon a par with a box on the ear in tragedy," Plotwell says, "which is frequently given and taken by your best authors." [2] The sentence clearly alludes to the *soufflet* in Cibber's adaptation of the *Cid.*

Dennis and Woodward may have been hurt by the satire, but Cibber at least showed no signs of being offended. For he not only accepted *Three Hours after Marriage* when it was read at Drury Lane, but tried to insure its success on the stage by acting the part of Plotwell himself. Despite his efforts, however, the play was not very well

[1] For this play and its reception, see George Sherburn, "The Fortunes and Misfortunes of *Three Hours after Marriage,*" *Modern Philology,* XXIV (1926-27), 91-109. I accept Sherburn's identification of Clinket as Mrs Centlivre, though the case for Lady Winchelsea has recently been revived; see Dane F. Smith, *Plays about the Theatre in England, 1671-1737* (London and New York, 1936), pp. 103-4, note.

[2] Gay, *Three Hours after Marriage* (1717), I, i.

received. It was hissed on the first two nights, withdrawn on the seventh, and subsequently attacked by the pamphleteers. Two weeks later *The Rehearsal* was revived at Drury Lane, and Cibber—following stage tradition—introduced topical allusions into his part of Bayes, one of them at the expense of the now notorious *Three Hours after Marriage*. The audience laughed uproariously, and Pope, who was in the theatre at the time, completely lost his temper. According to a contemporary account, he confronted Cibber, called him a rascal, and threatened to have Gay cane him if he repeated his sauciness.[3] Cibber's own account (1742) is similar though more detailed. After the play was over, he says, Pope

came behind the scenes, with his lips pale and his voice trembling, to call me to account for the insult, and accordingly fell upon me with all the foul language that a wit out of his senses could be capable of—How durst I have the impudence to treat any gentleman in that manner? Etc., etc., etc.... When he was almost choked with the foam of his passion, I was enough recovered from my amazement to make him (as near as I can remember) this reply, viz.: "Mr Pope, you are so particular a man that I must be ashamed to return your language as I ought to do: but since you have attacked me in so monstrous a manner, this you may depend upon, that as long as the play continues to be acted I will never fail to repeat the same words over and over again." [4]

The words were indeed repeated, and on the second night Gay came behind the scenes to carry out Pope's threat. But "Cibber very fairly gave him a fillip on the nose, which made them both roar. The guards came and parted them, and carried away Gay, and so ended this poetical scuffle." [5]

Ended it perhaps as far as Gay was concerned, but Pope's resentment was slow to disappear. In December, 1717, indeed, he apparently took steps to pay off an old obligation, Cibber's subscription to the six-volume translation of the *Iliad*. He sent Cibber a polite note (with four guineas enclosed) requesting four tickets to one of the benefit nights of *The Non-Juror*. But there was certainly, as Cibber himself felt, a suggestion of irony in the request, coming as it did from

[3] George Paston, *Mr Pope, His Life and Times* (1909), I, 197.
[4] Cibber, *Letter to Pope* (1742), p. 19.
[5] Paston, *Mr Pope*, I, 197.

a Catholic and a Tory, and the suggestion was confirmed when, about two months later, Pope's pamphlet ridiculing *The Non-Juror* appeared.[6]

The pamphlet—called in the first edition *The Plot Discovered, or a Clue to the Comedy of the Non-Juror* [7]—is an elaborated piece of irony designed to show that Cibber's play is really an attack on the government. The satire, it is true, is aimed chiefly at Bishop Hoadly, but Cibber is frequently mentioned and always in a tone of withering contempt. Thus in his final paragraph Pope says:

One thing I must observe, which I remember we both took particular notice of. It is that the author, though questionless a great master of style, puts bad English into the mouths of most of his personages, so that indeed scarce any of 'em talk at all like English folks, but perpetually make use of an uncorrect foreign jargon. What his drift is in this I cannot imagine, but the instances of it are obvious to every reader and numerous in every page.

The Plot Discovered was published anonymously, but on February 18, 1718, Curll advertised it as Pope's [8] and in the second edition he set the following couplets opposite the title-page:

To Mr Pope

Be generous, Pope, nor strive to be concealed,
Since your own *Clue* its author has revealed;
Go on the frauds of Cibber to explain,
And prove him what he is, a —— in grain.[9]

Curll possibly wanted to start a public controversy; but if so, his hopes were disappointed, for Cibber had no comment to make.

Ten years passed, Pope turned his attention almost exclusively to satire, and again Cibber found himself the object of the poet's ridicule. In March, 1728, he appears in the *Art of Sinking in Poetry,*[10] and in the first edition of the *Dunciad,* published in May of the same year, he is mentioned five times—once as a plagiarist, once as the Lord Chancellor of plays, once as the father of an infamous son, and once

[6] Cibber, *Letter to Pope* (1742), pp. 24-27.
[7] George Sherburn, *The Early Career of Alexander Pope* (Oxford, 1934), pp. 199-200.
[8] *Ibid.*
[9] *The Plot Discovered, or a Clue to the Comedy of the Non-Juror* (2d ed., 1718).
[10] Pope, *Works,* ed. Elwin and Courthope, X, 361, 390, 392, 405.

as the manager who had countenanced—and acted in—the pantomimes.[11] In 1730 he figures in two epigrams and an article—all published in the *Grub Street Journal*—on the subject of the contest for the
laureateship, and in 1733 his odes are contemptuously mentioned in
the *First Satire of the Second Book of Horace*.[12] But the most unkind
of all Pope's references to Cibber occur in the *Epistle to Arbuthnot*
(1735). In one passage Pope speaks of his own humility. "So humble,"
he says of himself,

> So humble he has knocked at Theobald's door,
> Has drunk with Cibber, nay has rimed for Moore.[13]

The suggestion that Cibber was a person with whom one could only
drink is certainly malicious; but the second passage is even more difficult to defend:

> Whom have I hurt? has poet yet, or peer,
> Lost the arched eyebrow or Parnassian sneer?
> And has not Colley still his lord and whore?
> His butchers Henley, his freemasons Moore? [14]

For though Cibber possibly had his whore as well as his lord at the
time the passage was written, he was by no means a notorious whore-
master. In fact, his name was singularly free from scandal in an age
when scandal was difficult to escape.

Cibber's attitude toward Pope's attacks, even the attack in the
Epistle to Arbuthnot, was apparently one of complete indifference. He
simply refused to be crushed, refused to reply, refused even to become
decently angry. In fact, when he accidentally met Pope at the house
of a common friend, General Dormer, he behaved as though the offensive lines had never been printed. He listened sympathetically
while Pope and Dormer told him about *The King and the Miller of
Mansfield,* gave his advice when it was asked, and later recommended
the play to the patentee of Drury Lane. His conduct was certainly
disarming and one is scarcely surprised to find Pope inserting, in his
next satirical epistle, a couplet in praise of *The Careless Husband*.[15]

[11] *Ibid.,* IV, 277, 293-94, 296, 297.
[12] *Ibid.,* III, 291-92.
[13] *Ibid.,* III, 269.
[14] *Ibid.,* III, 248.
[15] Cibber, *Letter to Pope* (1742), pp. 42-43, 52.

"All this may be," he wrote, "the people's voice is odd";

> It is, and it is not, the voice of God.
> To *Gammer Gurton* if it give the bays,
> And yet deny *The Careless Husband* praise,
> Or say our fathers never broke a rule;
> Why then, I say, the people is a fool.[16]

But of course Pope's feelings toward Cibber had not really changed, and he took care to offset the compliment with a sneer at the birthday odes, a contemptuous reference to *Love Makes a Man*—

> And idle Cibber, how he breaks the laws,
> To make poor Pinkey eat with vast applause—[17]

and a jibe at the pantomime coronation ceremony in *Henry VIII* (which, incidentally, had not been acted for ten years)—

> The champion too! and to complete the jest,
> Old Edward's armor beams on Cibber's breast.[18]

When the satire which contained these lines appeared, Cibber was at work on his *Apology*. He was trying to defend himself against just such attacks as those which Pope had recently made, and he was trying, furthermore, to explain why he had never bothered to answer his critics. The gist of the matter is that he was indifferent to what others might say about him and reluctant to be drawn into public controversies because he felt that in the end truth would always assert itself, no matter what he or his enemies might maintain. "When," he says, "they confine themselves to a sober criticism upon what I write, if their censure is just what answer can I make to it? If it is unjust why should I suppose that a sensible reader will not see it as well as myself? Or admit I were able to expose them by a laughing reply, will not that reply beget a rejoinder?"[19] Furthermore, he argues, malice usually defeats itself.

For my part, I have always had the comfort to think, whenever they designed me a disfavor, it generally flew back into their own faces, as it happens to children when they squirt at their playfellows against the wind. If a scribbler cannot be easy because he fancies I have too good an opinion of my own productions, let him write on and mortify; I owe him not the charity to be out of temper myself merely to keep him quiet or give him

---

[16] Pope, *Works*, III, 355.   [18] *Ibid.*, III, 368.
[17] *Ibid.*, III, 367.   [19] *Apology*, I, 42.

joy. Nor in reality can I see why anything misrepresented, though believed
of me by persons to whom I am unknown, ought to give me any more
concern than what may be thought of me in Lapland. 'Tis with those with
whom I am to *live* only where my character can affect me, and I will
venture to say he must find out a new way of writing that will make me
pass my time *there* less agreeably.[20]

The explanation is almost convincing; almost but not quite; for one
soon realizes that the *Apology* itself is an answer and that in the
course of the book Cibber pays his respects to each of his more formidable critics. He answers Mist, he answers Fielding, and—as early
as the second chapter of the book—he answers Pope. The truth seems
to be that at this period of his life Cibber was deeply concerned about
his reputation, and that this concern took the form of a passionate
interest in himself and a passionate desire to justify his conduct in
long-winded public confessions.

The passage on Pope is particularly interesting because it is so very
good-natured, because in fact it is almost an offer of reconciliation.
Cibber is careful to avoid mentioning the lines in the *Epistle to
Arbuthnot,* careful too to speak of his antagonist with the greatest
respect. He assures us that he reads Pope with particular pleasure, even
when the verses contain reflections upon himself, and he goes on to
insist that he and Pope have no personal quarrel with one another.
"When," he says, "I ... find my name at length in the satirical works
of our most celebrated living author, I never look upon those lines as
malice meant to me (for he knows I never provoked it) but profit to
himself. One of his points must be to have many readers: he considers
that my face and name are more known than those of many thousands
of more consequence in the kingdom; that therefore, right or wrong,
a lick at the laureate will always be a sure bait *ad captandum vulgus,*
to catch him little readers; and that to gratify the unlearned by now
and then interspersing those merry sacrifices of an old acquaintance to
their taste is a piece of quite right poetical craft." [21] The sentence is
not indeed very flattering to Pope, but Cibber immediately becomes
more conciliatory. He argues that satire is a terrible weapon in the
hands of a great genius, always liable to be misused; that the character of Atticus is a case in point. "But," he continues, "the pain which

[20] *Ibid.,* I, 45-46.   [21] *Ibid.,* I, 35-36.

the acrimony of those verses [i.e., the verses about Atticus] gave me
is in some measure allayed in finding that this inimitable writer, as he
advances in years, has since had candor enough to celebrate the same
person for his visible merit. Happy genius!" Cibber exclaims, and he
is never more eloquent in the *Apology,* "happy genius! whose verse,
like the eye of beauty, can heal the deepest wounds with the least
glance of favor." [22]

How easy for Pope to have acknowledged this fine compliment!
How graceful his concession would have been! But Pope was not a
man who made graceful gestures, and in his next work, the *New
Dunciad* of 1742, he inserted a few more satirical lines at the expense
of Cibber. In one passage the laureate is represented as reclining upon
the lap of the goddess of dullness; [23] in another he is given a part in
the education of the Young Aeneas, who has, Pope says,

> As much estate and principle and wit,
> As Ja[n]s[e]n, Fl[ee]tw[oo]d, C[i]b[be]r, shall think fit; [24]

and in still another his name is used adjectivally as a synonym for
shameless:

> But she, good goddess, sent to every child
> Firm impudence or stupefaction mild;
> And straight succeeded, leaving shame no room,
> Cibberian forehead or Cimmerian gloom.[25]

It was only too clear that the poet had rejected the offer of reconciliation, and four months later the first open *Letter from Mr Cibber to
Mr Pope* was printed and hawked through the town.

It has recently been suggested that Pope's plan to make Cibber the
king of the dunces originated as early as 1741, and there is strong evidence to support this view.[26] At the beginning of the third book of the
Dunciad the hero falls asleep in the lap of Dullness, and in line 20 of
the fourth book—the *New Dunciad* of 1742—Cibber is found sleeping
in exactly the same place. The temptation to suppose that Pope was
already prepared to identify the two is strengthened when one examines the note to line 20. "With great judgment," he says, "is it

[22] *Ibid.,* I, 38-39.   [24] *Ibid.,* ll. 315-16.
[23] Pope, *New Dunciad* (1742), l. 20.   [25] *Ibid.,* ll. 319-22.
[26] The suggestion is made in George Sherburn, *The Best of Pope* (New York, 1931),
pp. xv-xvi.

imagined by the poet that such a colleague as Dullness had elected should sleep on the throne and have very little share in the action of the poem: accordingly he hath done little or nothing from the day of his anointing, having passed through the second book without taking part in whatever was transacted about him and through the third in profound sleep." If Pope means what he appears to mean in this passage, he had already revised or made plans to revise the first books of his poem. It is even possible that Cibber knew of the existence of such a revision, and deciding to anticipate the most crushing of Pope's blows, published his first open letter. But one need not make this inference in order to explain Cibber's behavior. For the *Apology* shows that he was seriously disturbed by Pope's ridicule several years before the poet's ultimate intentions could possibly have been known to him —so much disturbed, in fact, that he had taken the trouble to make a conciliatory gesture. But the gesture had failed, the *New Dunciad* had appeared. In effect Pope had challenged him to a public controversy, and he was almost obliged to accept the challenge and indeed to see the controversy through to the end.

In the letter, it is true, Cibber refuses to admit motives of this sort. He was gratifying a whim, he maintains, engaging in a "frolic," accepting a challenge, not from Pope, but from his friends. "Since the publication of your last new *Dunciad*," he says, "... my friends now insist that it will be thought dullness indeed, or a plain confession of my being a bankrupt in wit, if I don't immediately answer those bills of discredit you have drawn upon me; for, say they, your dealing with him like a gentleman in your *Apology for Your Own Life, etc.,* you see, has had no sensible effect upon him.... But pray, gentlemen, said I ... does he not blacken himself by it? ... Yet they could not but think Mr Pope was too eminent an author to justify my equal contempt of him, and that a disgrace from such a pen might stick upon me to posterity. In fine, that though I could not be roused from my indifference in regard to myself, yet for the particular amusement of my acquaintance they desired I would enter the lists with you." [27]

The explanation may not be accurate, but it sets the right tone for the letter. It suggests at once that Cibber's intentions are not malicious,

[27] Cibber, *Letter to Pope* (1742), pp. 6-7.

that he is not even angry, that he is prepared to give a scrupulously accurate and dispassionate account of the whole quarrel; and indeed, as far as one can tell, he does so. He is critical of Pope's character, but he avoids the exaggeration and scurrility so freely employed by many of Pope's enemies. "What a merry mixed mortal has nature made you," he says, "that can thus debase that strength and excellence of genius she has endowed you with to the lowest human weakness, that of offering unprovoked injuries!" [28] "I am told there is a serpent in some of the Indies that never stings a man without leaving its own life in the wound; I have forgot the name of it and therefore cannot give it you. Or if this be too hard upon you, permit me at least to say your spleen is sometimes like that of the little angry bee, which in doing less mischief than the serpent yet (as Virgil says) meets with the same fate." [29] The language is restrained even though the views expressed are extreme, and in the examination of Pope's satire which follows the same tone prevails. Cibber admits that many of the lines ridiculing himself are brilliant, but he insists that they are so obviously malicious and unjust that they often miss fire. "I own your *Epistle to Dr Arbuthnot* (though I there find myself contemptibly spoken of) gives me more delight in the whole than any one poem of the kind I ever read." Yet, Cibber continues, "I cannot help thinking that your wit is more remarkably bare and barren whenever it would fall foul upon Cibber than upon any other person or occasion whatsoever." [30] These passages, however, are only preliminaries, for Cibber is really prepared to strike back at Pope, and he does so when one least expects it—he pays Pope exactly in kind.

The passage begins innocently enough—indeed one fails to realize what Cibber is about until one has read almost to the end. He has been speaking of the most vindictive of all the Pope allusions—the "lord and whore" of the *Epistle to Arbuthnot*—and he goes on to say: "As to the latter charge, the whore, there indeed I doubt you will have the better of me; for I must own that I believe I know more of *your* whoring than you do of *mine;* because I don't recollect that ever I made you the least confidence of *my* amours, though I have been very near an eyewitness of *yours*." And there follows the scandalous and now famous story of Pope's visit to the bagnio.

[28] *Ibid.*, p. 34.   [29] *Ibid.*, p. 30.   [30] *Ibid.*, p. 41.

He [i.e., Pope] may remember then (or if he won't I will) when Button's Coffeehouse was in vogue, and so long ago as when he had not translated above two or three books of Homer; there was a late young nobleman (as much his lord as mine) who had a good deal of wicked humor, and who, though he was fond of having wits in his company, was not so restrained by his conscience but that he loved to laugh at any merry mischief he could do them; this noble wag, I say, in his usual *gaieté de cœur,* with another gentleman still in being, one evening slyly seduced the celebrated Mr Pope as a wit and myself as a laugher to a certain house of carnal recreation near the Haymarket, where his lordship's frolic proposed was to slip his little Homer, as he called him, at a girl of the game, that he might see what sort of figure a man of his size, sobriety, and vigor (in verse) would make when the frail fit of love had got into him; in which he so far succeeded that the smirking damsel who served us with tea happened to have charms sufficient to tempt the little-tiny manhood of Mr Pope into the next room with her: at which you may imagine his lordship was in as much joy at what might happen within as our small friend could probably be in possession of it. But I (forgive me all ye mortified mortals whom his fell satire has since fallen upon) observing he had stayed as long as without hazard of his health he might, I,

Pricked to it by foolish honesty and love,

as Shakespeare says, without ceremony threw open the door upon him, where I found this little hasty hero, like a terrible tomtit, pertly perching upon the mount of love! But such was my surprise that I fairly laid hold of his heels and actually drew him down safe and sound from his danger. My lord, who stayed tittering without in hopes the sweet mischief he came for would have been completed, upon my giving an account of the action within, began to curse and call me an hundred silly puppies for my impertinently spoiling the sport; to which with great gravity I replied, "Pray, my lord, consider what I have done was in regard to the honor of our nation! For would you have had so glorious a work as that of making Homer speak elegant English cut short by laying up our little gentleman of a malady which his thin body might never have been cured of? No, my lord! Homer would have been too serious a sacrifice to our evening merriment." Now as his Homer has since been so happily completed, who can say that the world may not have been obliged to the kindly care of Colley that so great a work ever came to perfection? [31]

Reports about Cibber's letter reached Pope some time before the letter itself, and he was extremely anxious to know what it contained. But in his correspondence with his friends he betrayed no uneasiness. "God knows when I shall read it when it is published," he wrote to

[31] *Ibid.,* pp. 46-49.

Lord Orrery on July 23, 1742, "and perhaps I may send to ask your
account of it. Your opinion whether or not to answer it I need not
ask. [Cibber] swears he will have the last word with me, upon which
I have seen an epigram." [32] And even when the letter reached
Twickenham, he was still so unconcerned as to offer to read it aloud
to the two Richardsons, who were with him at the time. "These
things are my diversion," he remarked before he began, but as he
read his voice faltered and his features were "writhen with anguish."
Each sentence was painful, and young Richardson later told his father
that "he hoped to be preserved from such diversion as had been that
day the lot of Pope." [33]

Cibber's letter was of course extremely gratifying to Pope's enemies,
and several of them at once hastened into the field to make the most
of his discomfiture. In August, 1742, Lord Hervey published *The
Difference between Verbal and Practical Virtue, with a Prefatory
Epistle from Mr C—b—r to Mr P* (a dull performance, sufficiently
described by the title), and in the same year *A Letter to Mr C—b—r
on His Letter to Mr P—* (containing an elaborate comparison of the
two men entirely to Cibber's advantage). Two other publications hostile
to Pope were *Blast upon Blast and Lick for Lick, or a New Lesson
for P—pe* (*August* 19, 1742) [34] and *Sawney and Colley* (August
31). [35] But from Pope's point of view the most painful of all the
publications were undoubtedly the prints which illustrated the story
of the bagnio. He himself was represented as a bald, wizened hunch-
back, lying upon a bed with his arms about the harlot. Cibber pulled
at his heels while one of the lords entered the room exclaiming,

[32] Pope, *Works*, VIII, 504-5.

[33] Davies, *Garrick* (1780), II, 202; Johnson, *Lives of the Poets*, ed. George Birkbeck
Hill (Oxford, 1905), III, 188 and note (which apparently concerns the same conversation).

[34] The author's pseudonym (Capt. H—s Vinegar) suggests, and was undoubtedly
intended to suggest, Fielding; see Walpole, *Letters*, ed. Toynbee, I, 274-76. But the
parody—originally applied to Pope and Theobald—had appeared in 1729 as *Dean
Jonathan's Parody on the 4th Chap. of Genesis;* see Knox Chandler, "Two 'Fielding'
Pamphlets," *Philological Quarterly*, XVI (1937), 410-12. It was reprinted in *Tunbri-
galia, or the Tunbridge Miscellany for the Years 1737, 1738, 1739* (1740).

[35] Attacks on Cibber were: *A Blast upon Bays, or a New Lick at the Laureat*
(August, 1742); three articles in the *Universal Spectator*, August 7, 14, and 21, reprinted in the *Gentleman's Magazine*, August, 1742, and the *London Magazine* of the
same date; and *The Scribleriad. Being an Epistle to the Dunces. On Renewing their
Attack upon Mr Pope under Their Leader the Laureat* (1742).

"Zounds, Colley, you have spoiled all." But the redoubtable actor
replied over his shoulder, with a self-righteous smirk upon his face,
"Yes, my lord, but I have saved Homer."

The composition of Pope's answer to Cibber—the final revision of
the *Dunciad*—is difficult to date, but it seems clear that Pope rapidly
finished his own share of the work. On November 27, 1742, he wrote
to Warburton, proposing to make him editor of the edition and
pointing out that he was anxious to publish the poem as soon as
possible. "Your next," Pope says, "will find me probably with Bowyer,
who does not quite answer my impetuosity for getting this poem out
of my hands."[36] In December, 1742, the work was apparently complete,[37] but in February, 1743, if not earlier, difficulties developed about
the copyright. Pope had recently sued to recover it from Lintot, his
former publisher, but until Lintot's date expired the new edition
printed by Bowyer could not be distributed.[38] The delay was very
annoying to Pope, especially since it permitted Cibber to write and
publish a second contribution to the controversy—*The Egoist, or
Colley upon Cibber. Being His Own Picture Retouched to so Plain a
Likeness That No One Now Would Have the Face to Own It but
Himself.*

Retouched perhaps, but not greatly changed; for Cibber merely
repeats arguments about his own indifference to satire which he had
used in the *Apology*. His peculiar characteristic, he insists—and the
passage contains almost all that is interesting in the pamphlet—is "an
insensibility to all the displeasures of life that only concern myself.
Any man that has as little ambition for fame as I have may enjoy
the same privilege with as little disturbance."[39] But he also makes a
few incidental remarks about Pope. He reviews the motives which
led him to write the open letter, and touches on the surreptitious
publication of Pope's correspondence.

Pope, still in trouble about the copyright, relieved his feelings by
sending Cibber a copy of the first sheet of the revised *Dunciad*,[40]

[36] Pope, *Works*, IX, 225.
[37] *Ibid.*, IX, 226.
[38] *Ibid.*, IX, 230-31; Sherburn, *Early Career of Alexander Pope*, pp. 22-23.
[39] Cibber, *Egoist*, p. 22.
[40] From Cibber's quotations I infer that it was the first sheet of the new work. See,
however, Spence, *Anecdotes* (1820), p. 348: "The false leaf of the *Dunciad* sent to
Cibber as stolen from the printer's by a friend, mentions the story about Mr Pope in

and Cibber immediately acknowledged it in a second open letter, published February 15, 1743. He begins by quoting from the sheet in question:

> Close to those walls where Folly holds her throne,
> And laughs to think Monroe would take her down,
> Where o'er the gates, by his famed father's hand,
> Great Cibber's brazen, brainless brothers stand.

This is, he argues, very poor stuff, worth answering only with a pun.

First then give me leave to observe that these figures upon the gates of Bedlam do not *stand* but *lie*. Do you observe, sir? I say they are no more *upright* than you are when you *stand* or write, nay they *lie* as flat as you sometimes do when you *write*. . . . And so, sir, if these verses with the note upon them is a specimen of that formidable vengeance I am to tremble at for the insolent dullness and stupidity of my late letter to you, you are heartily welcome to go on with it. But unless you think it worth while to mend your hand upon me, I am in doubt whether I shall give you the trouble of any farther reply. In the meantime, to get out of your debt as fast as I can, though my poetical payments are not made in such golden coin as yours, yet if you will accept of what brass I am master of, the following sum is at your service, viz.:

> Still brazen, brainless! still the same dull chime!
> Is impudence in prose made wit by rime?
> No wonder then thou art so famed in satire;
> Thou needst but rime and leave the rest to nature.
> Thy nature be my champion then—I've done.
> No pen can worse bewray thee than thy own.
> On me thy wit's so worn, so void of smart,
> I read, I yawn, and (by your leave too) f—t.

Pope hastened to explain to his friends that he himself was not responsible for giving Cibber the sample sheet. "You guessed right as to the verses sent that silly fellow," he wrote to Warburton. "It was done by a friend of mine who had your opinion of his impenetrability and judged more truly of him than I confess I did. I begin to be more scrupulous of hurting him and wish him more conscientiously impudent." [41]

Cibber's letter and insinuates that Gay was of the party, and that Cibber, breaking in upon Mr Gay's privacy, found him in company with his own daughter, and therefore pulled him away."
[41] Pope, *Works*, IX, 231.

But Pope's scruples were not to be taken too seriously, for on October 29, 1743, the revised *Dunciad* finally appeared.

The portrait of Cibber in the first book undoubtedly contains many brilliant lines, but as a whole it can scarcely rank as one of Pope's finest achievements. It is patchwork—ingeniously conceived and brilliantly executed patchwork no doubt—but patchwork nevertheless. Pope makes indeed all the familiar points about Cibber, assures us that Cibber was a fop, a rake, a dunce, a gambler, a snob, a coxcomb, a poetaster:

> Bayes, formed by nature stage and town to bless,
> And act, and be, a coxcomb with success.
> Dullness with transport eyes the lively dunce,
> Remembering she herself was pertness once.
> Now (shame to Fortune!) an ill run at play
> Blanked his bold visage, and a thin third day....
> Next o'er his books his eyes began to roll,
> In pleasing memory of all he stole,
> How here he sipped, how there he plundered snug,
> And sucked all o'er, like an industrious bug.
> Here lay poor Fletcher's half-eat scenes, and here
> The frippery of crucified Molière;
> There hapless Shakespeare, yet of Theobald sore,
> Wished he had blotted for himself before....
> "Some demon stole my pen (forgive the offense)
> And once betrayed me into common sense:
> Else all my prose and verse were much the same;
> This prose on stilts, that poetry fallen lame.
> Did on the stage my fops appear confined?
> My life gave ampler lessons to mankind....
> What can I now? my Fletcher cast aside,
> Take up the Bible, once my better guide?
> Or tread the path by venturous heroes trod,
> This box my thunder, this right hand my God?
> Or chaired at White's amidst the doctors sit,
> Teach oaths to gamesters, and to nobles wit?
> Or bidst thou rather Party to embrace?
> (A friend to Party thou, and all her race)....
> What then remains? Ourself. Still, still remain
> Cibberian forehead and Cibberian brain.
> This brazen brightness, to the squire so dear;
> This polished hardness, that reflects the peer:

> This arch absurd, that wit and fool delights;
> This mess tossed up of Hockley-hole and White's;
> Where dukes and butchers join to wreathe my crown,
> At once the bear and fiddle of the town." [42]

Many of the couplets are stinging, many of the phrases pointed and apt; "prose on stilts," for example, is a particularly happy description of Cibber's sentimental style. But on the whole the portrait never quite comes off; the outlines are blurred; one never *sees* Cibber as one sees Sporus, Atticus, and even Theobald. Something is lacking, possibly the ruling passion so effectively employed in the other satires.

Furthermore—the point is obvious when one compares the old *Dunciad* with the new—the portrait of Cibber is not skillfully fitted into the framework of the poem. The hero—the king of the dunces—should be a half-starved poetaster, and he should attract the attention of the goddess of dullness partly because he is poor. For the goddess, Pope says, holds her throne in the cave of Poverty and Poetry, where

> Keen hollow winds howl through the bleak recess,
> Emblem of music caused by emptiness.[43]

But Cibber was not poor, he had enjoyed a comfortable income most of his life. How then could he be represented as sitting "swearing and supperless"—he who had been accustomed to dine only too well? Furthermore the hero should be a pedant, for his eyes must roll over his Gothic library, a library "well purged of Greece and Rome."

> There Caxton slept, with Wynkyn at his side,
> One clasped in wood, and one in strong cowhide;
> There saved by spice, like mummies, many a year,
> Dry bodies of Divinity appear;
> De Lyra there a dreadful front extends,
> And here the groaning shelves Philemon bends.[44]

The lines were of course written to ridicule Theobald; but how absurd, how utterly inconsistent they are when applied to the new hero! For Cibber could by no stretch of the imagination be called a pedant, and he had almost certainly never heard of Wynkyn and de Lyra. Here as elsewhere in the poem Pope has made his revisions too casually. He has, as a distinguished critic points out, gratified his

[42] *Ibid.,* IV, 110-18.   [43] *Ibid.,* IV, 104.   [44] *Ibid.,* IV, 114-15.

personal spleen at the expense of poetic consistency, and he has "produced no effect beyond that of marring one of his most brilliant
poems." [45]

Cibber had sworn to have the last word in the controversy, and
shortly after the appearance of the new *Dunciad* he published still
another open letter to Pope. This piece seems to have been rather
generally admired in its own time. Victor described it as "a very
high-mettled, spirited, humorous epistle"; [46] and Hill was even more
enthusiastic. "Some Minerva has lent the laureate a spear," he wrote
to Richardson, "for there are strokes of no Cibberine hand in this
new sixpenny-worth of scorn." [47] But the truth is that the letter is
distinctly an anticlimax, adding nothing to what Cibber had already
said. He again examines Pope's insane irritability and modestly con-
trasts it with his own Olympian indifference. "In a word, till with
the temper of the laureate thou canst join in the laugh when thou
liest open to the jest, thou wilt only revenge thy enemies upon thyself,
and at best but die an anxious, celebrated, miserable man." [48] He even
retouches the story of the bagnio, comparing Pope to a long-legged
spider making love in a cobweb. But it is scarcely necessary to give
further examples of this heavy-handed raillery, which tells us little
about Cibber and nothing about Pope.

Pope's health was rapidly failing when the third open letter appeared, and he was unable, possibly also unwilling, to reply. In
May, 1744, a friendly author approached Cibber and asked his advice
about the pamphlet against Pope which was almost ready for the
press. Cibber urged him not to print it on the ground that further
controversy might aggravate Pope's illness. [49] Some three weeks later
Pope died in his house at Twickenham.

It is useless to review this singular quarrel for the purpose of de-

[45] Pope, *Works,* ed. Adolphus William Ward (London and New York, 1896), p.
xliii.
[46] Victor, *History of the Theatres,* II, 51.
[47] Richardson, *Correspondence,* ed. Anna Laetitia Barbauld (1804), I, 111.
[48] Cibber, *Another Occasional Letter to Mr Pope* (1744), p. 52.
[49] Victor, *Letters,* I, 93-95. Victor says that the author struck a bargain with Osborne,
but the pamphlet does not seem to have appeared. A pamphlet published by Robbins,
however, is announced in the *Gentleman's Magazine,* February, 1744: *Lick upon Lick;
Occasioned by Another Occasional Letter from Mr Cibber to Mr Pope.* In the June
issue of the same journal a muddled epitaph on Pope is ascribed to Cibber. It is Cibberian in thought and style and may possibly be genuine.

termining who came off victorious, for posterity has already passed
judgment. Posterity has condemned to oblivion the three open letters
to Pope, and has formed its opinion of Cibber almost entirely from
the *Dunciad* of 1743 and from that other well-known work by a man
of genius—*Joseph Andrews.*

XIII. FIELDING

WHEN POPE and his two friends offered *Three Hours after Marriage* to the managers of Drury Lane, it was accepted as a matter of course, for the authors were men of established reputation whose work was certain to be discussed. But when, ten years later, Fielding began offering plays to the managers, he encountered considerable difficulty, for as yet he was almost unknown. He was a young man scarcely out of school who had turned to the stage for a living, and though he soon revealed dramatic ability of a high order, he was not the type of playwright whom the managers liked to encourage. He could brilliantly hit off the absurdities of the contemporary theatre, he could write capital farce and uproarious burlesque; but he was reluctant to cook up the conventional sort of comedy which the managers preferred, with exactly the right mixture of sentiment and wit and exactly the right number of good acting parts. In fact, he was never completely at home in the Drury Lane of Cibber; he was too sure of his genius to submit to the managers' discipline, too fond of ridiculing absurdity wherever he found it, even indeed in the management itself.[1]

His first play, *Love in Several Masques,* is not a really characteristic work. It is amateurish and on the whole extremely conventional; in fact, it owes a good deal to the Cibber tradition in comedy; and partly for this reason, no doubt, it was accepted at Drury Lane. It followed *The Provoked Husband* in February, 1728, and though it failed (in competition with *The Beggar's Opera* at the other theatre), it led to no unpleasantness between Fielding and Cibber. The tone of the preface is friendly, even cordial. "I cannot rest," Fielding says, "till I have been in some measure grateful to the performers. As for Mr

---

[1] Throughout this chapter I have made free use of Cross, *History of Henry Fielding.* The facts about Fielding's relations with Cibber are also reviewed in Houghton W. Taylor, "Fielding upon Cibber," *Modern Philology,* XXIX (1931-32), 73-90. An earlier article on the same subject is C. W. Nichols, "Fielding and the Cibbers," *Philological Quarterly,* I (1922), 278-89.

Wilks and Mr Cibber, I cannot sufficiently acknowledge their civil
and kind behavior previous to its representation. How advantageously
both they and the other personages set off their respective parts at that
time has been spoken of by much politer and better judges than
myself." [2]

The preface must have been extremely gratifying to Wilks and
Cibber, who were seldom praised by ambitious young men. But they
soon found that they had misjudged Fielding's character, for he
proved to be a typical playwright—he was so conceited, a contemporary tells us, that he quarreled with everyone who pointed out his
faults.[3] His second play was rejected at Drury Lane,[4] and he therefore
wrote his next plays for the companies in Goodman's Fields and
the Haymarket, and in one of them—*The Author's Farce*—he put
Wilks and Cibber on the stage. He showed them at the reading of a
play, exposed their bad judgment and reproduced their fatuous
comments.

The scene of the reading is undoubtedly an attempt on Fielding's
part to get even with Wilks and Cibber, but personal animus is not
much in evidence. Fielding is objective, good-natured, and extremely
amusing; indeed the scene deserves to rank as the best of many
satires at the expense of the actor-managers of Drury Lane. The
author Luckless begins by reading from a tragedy he has written,
while Marplay (Cibber) yawns and interrupts, and Sparkish (Wilks)
stupidly echoes the words of his colleague. "With thee," Luckless
reads,

> With thee the barren rocks, where not one step
> Of human race lies printed in the snow,
> Look lovely as the smiling infant spring.[5]

But Marplay proposes to alter the lines "to a much better idea":

> With thee the barren blocks (that is, trees), where not a bit
> Of human face is painted on the bark,
> Look green as Covent Garden in the spring.
> LUCKLESS. Green as Covent Garden!
> MARPLAY. Yes, Covent Garden market: where they sell greens.

[2] Fielding, *Works*, ed. Browne (1871), I, 85-86.
[3] "Scriblerus Tertius," *The Candidates for the Bays* (1730), p. 9 and note.
[4] Fielding, *Works*, III, 59.
[5] The quotations in this paragraph are from Fielding, *The Author's Farce, and the Pleasures of the Town* (1730), II, i and ii.

Luckless, however, is unwilling to accept the alteration, and Marplay suddenly rises from his chair and passes judgment on the play: "Sir, it will not do—and so I would not have you think any more of it." Luckless pleads for reasons, but none are forthcoming until he has gone, when the following dialogue occurs:

SPARKISH. What dost think of the play?

MARPLAY. It may be a very good one for aught I know; but I know the author has no interest.

SPARKISH. Give me interest and rat the play.

MARPLAY. Rather rat the play which has no interest. Interest sways as much in the theatre as at court. And you know it is not always the companion of merit in either.

The passage echoes a frequent complaint that the plays of unknown authors were rarely accepted at Drury Lane.

Cibber may perhaps have been annoyed by this scene and one or two other lines in the play, but his principal reaction was undoubtedly one of interest. He saw that *The Author's Farce* was successful, that Fielding's next play, *Tom Thumb,* was successful too; and conveniently forgetting the Marplay scene, he invited Fielding back to Drury Lane. Between January and June, 1732—his last complete season as manager—he accepted and produced no fewer than five of Fielding's plays—*The Lottery, The Modern Husband, The Old Debauchees, The Covent Garden Tragedy,* and *The Mock Doctor;* and about one of them at least—*The Modern Husband*—he was genuinely enthusiastic, for he not only acted in it himself but honored Fielding by writing the epilogue. His verses, it is true, were so dull that Fielding had to substitute an epilogue of his own at the fifth performance; but even so, it was perhaps an honor.[6] Fielding responded by complimenting Cibber and his son in the preface to *The Mock Doctor,* and Cibber then graciously bestowed another favor on the young dramatist—he wrote the epilogue for *The Miser* (February, 1733). The reconciliation seemed complete, Luckless and Marplay were at last good friends.

But events moved swiftly in the theatre during the spring and summer of 1733, and by autumn Fielding and Cibber were again interested in rival companies. Fielding was still writing for Drury

---

[6] Cross, *History of Henry Fielding,* I, 120.

Lane, now controlled by Highmore and Ellys, while Cibber was giving at least moral support to the company of Theophilus at the Haymarket. The result was a revised and enlarged version of *The Author's Farce* (January 15, 1734), embodying Fielding's most recent observations of management under the Cibbers. Wilks, who died in 1732, is appropriately replaced by Theophilus (Marplay, Junior), who undertakes to advise Luckless about his tragedy. "Alack-a-day!" he exclaims when Luckless shows no enthusiasm for alterations. "Was you to see the plays when they are brought to us, a parcel of crude undigested stuff! We are the persons, sir, who lick them into form, that mold them into shape. The poet make the play indeed! The colorman might be as well said to make the picture or the weaver the coat: my father and I, sir, are a couple of poetical tailors: when a play is brought to us we consider it as a tailor does his coat; we cut it, sir, we cut it; and let me tell you, we have the exact measure of the town; we know how to fit their taste." A character interrupts to inquire about *The Lover,* an unsuccessful comedy by Theophilus himself, and young Marplay obligingly describes its reception at Drury Lane:

I did, as you say, once make a small sally into Parnassus, took a sort of flying leap over Helicon; but if ever they catch me there again—sir, the town have a prejudice to my family, for if any play could have made them ashamed to damn it, mine must. It was all over plot. It would have made half a dozen novels; nor was it crammed with a pack of wit-traps, like Congreve and Wycherley, where everyone knows when the joke was coming. I defy the sharpest critic of them all to have known when any jokes of mine were coming. The dialogue was plain, easy, and natural, and not one single joke in it from the beginning to the end; besides, sir, there was one scene of tender melancholy conversation, enough to have melted a heart of stone: and yet they damned it: and they damned themselves; for they shall have no more of mine.[7]

On the whole, however, Theophilus comes off better than his father, who is again contemptuously treated in the tavern scene of the second act. He is also ridiculed in one of the new passages: he is described as the laureate of the Goddess of Nonsense—"Mr What-d'ye-call-him, the gentleman that writes odes—so finely."[8]

In March, 1734, Theophilus and his followers returned to Drury

[7] Fielding, *Works,* I, 294-95.   [8] *Ibid.,* I, 317, 321.

Lane, and for a year or two Fielding stopped attacking the Cibbers. But in the spring of 1736 he left the patent theatre to produce a series of topical farces at the Haymarket, and in several of them he freely ridiculed his associates of former days. In *Tumble-Down Dick,* for example, he glanced at Theophilus,[9] and in *Pasquin* at the elder Cibber, whose odes were still fair game for the satirist. Thus in the election scene of the latter work Lord Place discusses odes with a group of voters:

> SECOND VOTER. I am a devilish lover of sack.
> LORD PLACE. Sack, say you? Odso, you shall be poet laureate.
> SECOND VOTER. Poet! No, my lord, I am no poet, I can't make verses.
> LORD PLACE. No matter for that—you'll be able to make odes.
> SECOND VOTER. Odes, my lord! What are those?
> LORD PLACE. Faith, sir, I can't tell well what they are; but I know you may be qualified for the place without being a poet.[10]

The allusion became particularly piquant when, on the eleventh night, the part of Lord Place was taken over by Cibber's daughter Charlotte Charke.

But Fielding's most comprehensive satire at the expense of the Cibbers appears in his next play, *The Historical Register,* a review of the principal events of the year 1736. It begins, appropriately enough, with an ode to the New Year, written by the chief character, Medley:

> This is a day, in days of yore,
> Our fathers never saw before;
> This is a day, 'tis one to ten,
> Our sons will never see again.
>   Then sing the day,
>   And sing the song,
>   And thus be merry
>   All day long.

"There, sir," says Medley when the ode has been sung, "there's the very quintessence and cream of all the odes I have seen for several years last past." [11] But other interesting events during 1736 involved the Cibbers—the War of the Pollies, for example; and so in the second act Theophilus appears in regal splendor and petitions the mob on behalf of his consort:

[9] *Ibid.,* III, 447.   [10] *Ibid.,* III, 282.   [11] *Ibid.,* III, 347-48.

Behold how humbly the great Pistol kneels.
Say then, O town, is it your royal will
That my great consort represent the part
Of Polly Peachum in *The Beggar's Opera?*

The mob hisses, and Pistol continues triumphantly:

Thanks to the town, that hiss speaks their assent;
Such was the hiss that spoke the great applause
Our mighty father met with, when he brought
His *Riddle* on the stage; such was the hiss
Welcomed his Caesar to the Egyptian shore;
Such was the hiss in which great John should have expired;
But wherefore do I try in vain to number
Those glorious hisses which, from age to age,
Our family has borne triumphant from the stage? [12]

The fiasco of *King John,* here mentioned incidentally by Pistol, gets a complete scene in the third act. Cibber (Ground-Ivy) discusses his play and Shakespeare's with Apollo and the prompter of the theatre. "It was a maxim of mine," he says, "when I was at the head of theatrical affairs, that no play, though ever so good, would do without alteration. For instance, in the play before us the bastard Faulconbridge is a most effeminate character, for which reason I would cut him out and put all his sentiments in the mouth of Constance, who is so much properer to speak them." But the prompter ventures to express doubts.

PROMPTER. I am only afraid as Shakespeare is so popular an author, and you, asking your pardon, so unpopular—
GROUND-IVY. Damn me, I'll write to the town and desire them to be civil, and that in so modest a manner that an army of Cossacks shall be melted: I'll tell them that no actors are equal to me and no authors ever were superior: and how do you think I can insinuate that in a modest manner?
PROMPTER. Nay, faith, I can't tell.
GROUND-IVY. Why, I'll tell them that the former only tread on my heels and that the greatest among the latter have been damned as well as myself; and after that, what do you think of your popularity? I can tell you, Mr Prompter, I have seen things carried in the house against the voice of the people before today.
APOLLO. Let them hiss, let them hiss, and grumble as much as they please, as long as we get their money.[13]

[12] *Ibid.,* III, 364-65.   [13] *Ibid.,* III, 369-70.

Cibber was in the side-boxes at the Haymarket on the first night of *The Historical Register,* and when, during the Ground-Ivy scene, the audience laughed and looked at him, he laughed too and applauded.[14] But his position was certainly an uncomfortable one, and not many months later he sketched an insulting passage on Fielding for the *Apology.* The reference is not very different from the references to Mist later in the book, for in Cibber's eyes Mist and Fielding were probably men of much the same caliber. Both seemed miserable hacks who made a precarious livelihood by abusing the government and respectable people generally, and both had written much that deserved to be, and had in fact been, suppressed. Of the two Fielding was perhaps the more contemptible, because, as a playwright, he might have trained himself to prepare edifying comedies in the style of *The Conscious Lovers* and *The Provoked Husband.*

The passage on Fielding follows a reference to the small companies which had appeared in London during the 1720s.

These so tolerated companies [Cibber says] gave encouragement to a broken wit to collect a fourth company, who for some time acted plays in the Haymarket, which house the united Drury Lane comedians had lately quitted. This enterprising person, I say (whom I do not choose to name, unless it could be to his advantage, or that it were of importance), had sense enough to know that the best plays with bad actors would turn but to a very poor account, and therefore found it necessary to give the public some pieces of an extraordinary kind, the poetry of which he conceived ought to be so strong that the greatest dunce of an actor could not spoil it. He knew, too, that, as he was in haste to get money, it would take up less time to be intrepidly abusive than decently entertaining; that to draw the mob after him, he must rake the channel and pelt their superiors; that to show himself somebody he must come up to Juvenal's advice and stand the consequence:

> Aude aliquid brevibus Gyaris, et carcere dignum
> Si vis esse aliquis—
>
> Juv., *Sat. I.*

Such then was the mettlesome modesty he set out with; upon this principle he produced several frank and free farces that seemed to knock all distinctions of mankind on the head; religion, laws, government, priests, judges, and ministers were all laid at the feet of this Herculean satirist. This Drawcansir in wit that spared neither friend nor foe, who, to make

14 Cibber, *Egoist,* pp. 27-28.

his poetical fame immortal, like another Erostratus, set fire to his stage by writing up to an act of Parliament to demolish it. I shall not give the particular strokes of his ingenuity a chance to be remembered by reciting them; it may be enough to say in general terms, they were so openly flagrant that the wisdom of the legislature thought it high time to take a proper notice of them.[15]

These last sentences refer to the Licensing Act of 1737, which had been passed shortly after the appearance of *The Historical Register.* Fielding's theatre in the Haymarket had been closed and Fielding himself had turned journalist and pamphleteer. But though he had changed his profession, he had soon shown that he had changed neither his methods nor his views. For in his newspaper the *Champion* he had continued to ridicule, as boisterously as before, the absurdities of contemporary life, without ignoring either the government or Cibber. In the issue of December 25, 1739, for example, he had touched on Cibber's learning:

I know it may be objected that the English Apollo, the prince of poets, the great laureate abounds with such a redundancy of Greek and Latin that, not contented with the vulgar affectation of a motto to a play, he hath prefixed a Latin motto to every act of his *Caesar in Egypt.* . . . Nay, his learning is thought to extend to the Oriental tongues, and I myself heard a gentleman reading one of his odes cry out, "Why, this is all Hebrew!"

But when in 1740 the *Apology* appeared, when Fielding saw himself contemptuously referred to as a broken wit and his plays described as openly flagrant and intrepidly abusive, he devoted even more space in his journal to the laureate-apologist. He made an elaborate analysis of Cibber's style, he singled out examples of bad grammar and faulty diction. Thus in the issue of April 22 he found Cibber guilty of misusing the word *adept:*

This word our great master hath tortured and wrested to signify a tyro or novice, being directly contrary to the sense in which it hath been hitherto used. This spirit of absolute power is generally whipped out of boys at school, and I could heartily wish our adept had been in the way of such castigation.[16]

In the issues of April 29 and May 6 he compiled a list of Cibber's worst phrases:

[15] *Apology,* I, 286-88.   [16] *Ibid.,* II, 54, note.

Satire is angrily particular (angry with a particular person).

Beauty *shines into* equal warmth the peasant and the courtier (he hath made a verb active of *shine*).

The *utile dulci* was of old equally the point.

Public approbation is the warm weather of a theatrical plant.

Mrs Oldfield threw out such new proffers of a genius.

Melts into pangs of humanity.

A man may be debtor to sense or morality.

Our enemies made a push of a good round lie upon us.

So *clear an emanation of* beauty etc. *struck* me into a regard that had something softer than the most profound respect in it.

Some actors heavily drag the sentiment along with a long-toned voice and absent eye.

The strong intelligence of his attitude and aspect drew you into an impatient gaze.

A forward and sudden step into nature.

A spectacle for vacancy of thought to gaze at.

And so forth—there are many more. And in the issue of May 17 he summed up his criticism in a burlesque *Trial of Colley Cibber*. He represents the laureate, Colley Apology, being brought to the bar and indicted for an assault upon the English language. The apologist pleads not guilty, but after his publisher has appeared on the witness stand, and after three numbers of the *Champion* have been read, it is felt that the evidence is pretty conclusive against him.

COURT. Well Mr Col. Apol., what have you to say for yourself?

PRISONER. Sir, I am as innocent as the child which hath not yet entered into human nature of the fact laid to my charge. This accusation is the forward spring of envy of my laurel. It is impossible I should have any enmity to the English language, with which I am so little acquainted; if, therefore, I have struck any wounds into it, they have rolled from accident only....

The prisoner then called several persons to his own and his book's character. As to his own, they all gave him a very good one, and particularly a certain fat gentleman who often told the court that he was a *pleasant companion*....

The captain then summed up the evidence, and just before he concluded Mrs Joan whispered in his ear that the *Apology* was ordered by the author to be twice advertised in the *Champion;* upon which the captain, not from the motive of a bribe, but of the prisoner's submission to his correction, and likewise considering that he had stood already three times in the censorial pillory and been well pelted, directed the jury in his favor and they found it chance-medley.

But Fielding's ridicule of Cibber was not confined to the *Champion*. In 1740, as we have seen, he was possibly concerned in the fictitious *Apology for T ... C ...,* and in 1741 he produced a still more amusing pamphlet, *An Apology for the Life of Mrs Shamela Andrews. By Mr Conny Keyber.* The satire, it is true, is here principally directed at Richardson's *Pamela,* but the pseudonym under which Fielding wrote suggests Cibber (as well as Conyers Middleton) and in the text itself there is at least one pointed allusion to Cibber. Parson Tickletext writes to Parson Oliver, sending him a copy of "sweet, dear, pretty *Pamela,* a little book which this winter hath produced." "This book," he continues—he quotes from one of the introductory letters in the second edition of Richardson's novel—

This book is the "soul of religion, good-breeding, discretion, good nature, wit, fancy, fine thought, and morality. There is an ease, a natural air, a dignified simplicity, and *measured fullness* in it that, *resembling life, outglows it.*"

Parson Oliver replies:

If I had not known your hand, I should, from the sentiments and style of the letter, have imagined it to have come from the author of the famous *Apology,* which was sent me last summer; and on my reading the remarkable paragraph of *measured fullness that, resembling life, outglows it* to a young baronet, he cried out, "C—ly C—b—r, by G—!" [17]

Satire at the expense of *Pamela* with a few incidental jibes at Cibber was obviously to Fielding's taste, and in 1742 he returned to it in one of the most brilliant of his works, *Joseph Andrews.* Quotation from this well-known novel is almost an impertinence, but the reader should perhaps be reminded of the fact that it begins as a burlesque of two books—*Pamela* and the *Apology.* "I pass by these," Fielding says in his famous first chapter—and by "these" he means the histories of Jack the Giant-Killer, Guy of Warwick, and the Seven Champions of Christendom—"I pass by these and many others to mention two books lately published which represent an admirable pattern of the amiable in either sex. The former of these, which deals in male virtue, was written by the great person himself, who lived the life he hath recorded, and is by many thought to have lived

[17] *An Apology for the Life of Mrs Shamela Andrews,* ed. R. Brimley Johnson (1926), pp. 12, 15.

such a life only in order to write it. The other is communicated to us by an historian who borrows his lights, as the common method is, from authentic papers and records. The reader, I believe, already conjectures I mean the lives of Mr Colley Cibber and of Mrs Pamela Andrews. How artfully doth the former, by insinuating that he escaped being promoted to the highest stations in Church and State, teach us a contempt of worldly grandeur! how strongly doth he inculcate an absolute submission to our superiors! Lastly, how completely doth he arm us against so uneasy, so wretched a passion as the fear of shame! how clearly doth he expose the emptiness and vanity of that phantom, reputation!" At this point Fielding introduces his own hero—the virtuous Joseph, brother of Pamela. "I shall only add," he continues, "that this character of male chastity, though doubtless as desirable and becoming in one part of the human species as in the other, is almost the only virtue which the great apologist hath not given himself for the sake of giving the example to his readers." [18]

This first chapter in *Joseph Andrews* is not quite Fielding's final reference to Cibber, but it is the last and the most brilliant of a series of fairly long passages in which he ridicules various aspects of Cibber's work. In *The Author's Farce* he shows us the manager; in *The Historical Register for 1736,* the laureate and the adapter of Shakespeare; in the *Champion,* the prose writer; and here, finally, the apologist, the author of those hopelessly insincere and inaccurate first chapters in the autobiography. Taken together these passages give an extremely amusing caricature of Cibber; much more amusing certainly than the somewhat muddled caricature in the first book of the *Dunciad.* But—one need scarcely point out—it is a caricature after all: the real Cibber was much more complex, much more human, and perhaps even more amusing.

It would be interesting if we knew what Cibber's reactions were when he read *Joseph Andrews* for the first time. Did he at once realize that he was in the presence of a masterpiece? or did he still think that Fielding was openly flagrant and intrepidly abusive, only to revise his opinion later in the light of contemporary criticism? Evidence is lacking, but it is certain that before many years had passed he fully recognized Fielding's genius. In *The Character and*

[18] Fielding, *Works,* V, 22-23.

Conduct of Cicero, published in 1747, he refers to the "fearless, open honesty of a poor Parson Adams." [19] The reference is quite casual, but it comes close to a public admission on Cibber's part that he had once done Fielding a grave injustice.

[19] Cibber, *The Character and Conduct of Cicero* (1747), p. 2.

XIV. OLD AGE

- I -

CIBBER was sixty-eight when the *Apology* appeared, but he behaved—
and continued to behave—like a much younger man. He went to
balls and assemblies, frequented Tom's and White's, paid his addresses
to actresses and court beauties, wrote *The Character and Conduct of
Cicero, The Lady's Lecture,* the *Rhapsody upon the Marvelous....*
He had, it seems, scarcely a moment of leisure; he was too busy to
grow old in the usual way.

Information about him during these last years of his life is not
easy to obtain, but occasionally one catches glimpses of him in characteristic poses. In 1741, for example, one sees him attending an
assembly at Sir Thomas Robinson's. It was a splendid affair at which
a hundred and ninety-seven guests were present; in fact, the doors
of the house had been taken off to accommodate so large a crowd.
"The company," says Horace Walpole, "...was all extremely good;
there were none but people of the first fashion except Mr Kent, Mr
Cibber, Mr Swiney, and the Parsons family, and you know all these
have an alloy." But, he hastens to add, "Cibber and Swiney have
long had their freedom given them of this end of the town." [1] One
sees him again for a moment reciting his own translations from
Horace on a hot day, "till he was in a breathing, and wiped and acted
like anything, and everybody was pleased." [2] Still again one sees
him at Tom's playing whist with an old general. "As the cards were
dealt to him, he took up every one in turn and expressed his disappointment at every indifferent one. In the progress of the game he
did not follow suit, and his partner said, 'What! have you not a spade,
Mr Cibber?' The latter, looking at his cards, answered, 'Oh, yes, a
thousand'; which drew a very peevish comment from the general.
On which Cibber, who was shockingly addicted to swearing, replied,

[1] Walpole, *Letters,* ed. Toynbee, I, 115.
[2] Austin Dobson, *Samuel Richardson* (1902), p. 127.

'Don't be angry, for —— I can play ten times worse if I like.' " [3] On still
another occasion one sees him enjoying a confidential chat with Lord
Chesterfield in the inner sanctum while Johnson waited impatiently
in the anteroom and finally stormed out of the house. The incident
may be (as Johnson later maintained) unauthentic, but even so it
clearly suggests the relative social positions of the lexicographer and
the poet laureate.[4]

Johnson was scarcely acceptable in the circle of Lord Chesterfield;
Cibber, on the other hand, was so good-natured, so vivacious, and so
remarkably entertaining that he was rarely excluded anywhere.[5] He
could maintain his high spirits for hours together, he could adjust
his remarks exactly to the tastes of his companions, he could please
the most fastidious critics of good conversation—even, indeed, Lord
Chesterfield himself. "There was something odd and out o' the way
in his behavior," says the author of *The Laureat*—the account is
somewhat malicious but it is the best one we have—"he had humor
and a kind of wit, but not conducted by any judgment or reflection,
nor seasoned with any tincture of letters. He affected to know much;
and as it must often happen to those who would be thought knowing
when they are ignorant, he frequently got out of his depth and
exposed himself to ridicule and contempt. But the gentlemen who
condescended to be his companions were contented to be diverted
with him as he could divert them. They would delight to hear him
squeak in an eunuch's treble, or mimic Roscius, or rehearse the little
histories of his scenical amours, or invent new oaths at play. . . . He
could be noisy or silent, saucy or well-bred, obscene or modest, the
joker or the jest, the pleasure or contempt of the company, just as
he found they required it." [6] It is worth noticing, however, that he
was rarely at his best in company with men of profound learning.
Dr Johnson, who talked with him several times, later remarked: "It
is wonderful that a man who for forty years had lived with the great
and the witty should have acquired so ill the talents of conversation;
and he had but half to furnish; for one half of what he said was
oaths." [7]

[3] John Taylor, *Records of My Life* (1832), I, 263.
[4] Boswell, *Life of Johnson*, ed. Hill (1887), I, 256-57.
[5] See, for example, John Armstrong, *Miscellanies* (1770), II, 247.
[6] *The Laureat*, pp. 106, 100.   [7] Boswell, *Life of Johnson*, II, 340.

Though he was no longer connected with the management of Drury Lane, Cibber still took a keen interest in the theatre. He attended first nights, he instructed young actors and actresses, he encouraged and sometimes helped the writers of the younger generation. In 1746, for example, he gave advice to his Irish friend Victor, who was interested in sending Barry to London. "I am not a little pleased with the character you give me of Barry," he wrote, "particularly of his discretion in not piquing himself into any sort of rivalship. . . . If he comes over, I should wish him to stand upon his own legs; for if he leans upon another's merit he may be dropped when he is to make a new bargain, and if he has the merit you seem to allow him he will need no better friend to support him. But what's Hecuba to me, or I to Hecuba? I love to speak my mind in matters indifferent to me." [8] But the indifference was largely a pose, for when Barry came, the old man was feverishly excited. Davies reports "that [he] preferred [Barry's] Othello to the performances of Betterton and Booth in that part. . . . I well remember that I saw [him] in the boxes on the first night . . . loudly applauding [Barry] by frequent clapping of his hands—a practice by no means usual to the old man, even when he was very well pleased with an actor." [9]

In 1748 he was equally enthusiastic about a comedy—*The Foundling* by Edward Moore. When he heard it read, he excused himself for criticizing it at all, for it had, he said, only a few little faults here and there. He called it immoderately good, and he went on to remark that he had not seen so good a play for fully fifteen years.[10] After its appearance he described it in glowing terms to his friend Victor; but Victor was somewhat disappointed. "I must own," he replied, "your extravagant encomiums raised my expectations too high. . . . I am charmed, however, with your readiness to be pleased with a dawning genius and to encourage it by your necessary approbation." [11]

But though the old man was warm in his praises of Barry and Moore, he remained indifferent to the greatest genius of the younger generation—David Garrick. In 1741 he went to Goodman's Fields to see Garrick in his first part of Richard, but like Horace Walpole,

[8] Victor, *History of the Theatres,* II, 205-6.
[9] Davies, *Garrick* (1780), II, 239-40.
[10] Spence, *Anecdotes* (1820), p. 349.
[11] Victor, *History of the Theatres,* II, 213-14.

he was not impressed. "He never heartily joined the public voice in the approbation of [the young actor]," Davies says, "he shrunk from it as if he was hurt by it." [12] In 1742 he saw Garrick in another part, that of Bayes in *The Rehearsal,* but he still refused to show the slightest enthusiasm. "The fellow is well enough," he remarked, "but he is not superior to my boy Theophilus." [13] Later, however, he reluctantly admitted that Garrick made an excellent Fribble in his own play, *Miss in Her Teens.* "One night at White's," says Cooke, "when a nobleman was speaking of the merits of Garrick, [Cibber] suddenly turned about—'Pray, my lord, have you ever seen this young fellow in Fribble?' 'No, Mr Cibber.' 'No, my lord? Why then see him by all means—he is the completest, prettiest little doll figure for a Fribble you ever saw in your life.' 'Well, but Mr Cibber, has he not a great deal of merit in other characters?' No answer for some time; at last, as if breaking from a reverie, he exclaimed: 'What an admirable Fribble! Such mincing—ambling—fidgeting! Well, faith, he must be something of a clever fellow too, to write up his *own character* so well as he has done in this part.' " [14]

During the early 1740s Cibber occasionally emerged from his retirement to act such parts as Lord Foppington and Shallow, though he grew more and more reluctant to appear except on very special occasions. Thus in January, 1741, he acted Fondlewife in *The Old Bachelor,* but only because he had promised to do so for the benefit of the old prompter Chetwood. "Not daring to hope that so short a part would be strong enough to fill the house for him," he says in *The Egoist,* "I fancied an epilogue . . . might make people a little more curious to come to it." Accordingly he wrote an epilogue upon himself in which he repeated several timeworn jokes at his expense, including the one about Mrs Oldfield's outdoing her usual outdoing. "I had a mind," he continues in the same pamphlet, "to see if I could not make the town laugh *louder* at me than all the wits that had worried me for above twenty years before." [15] And indeed he did; for the epilogue was so well received that he was able to repeat it twice for his own profit.

[12] Davies, *Dramatic Miscellanies* (1783-84), III, 470.
[13] Davies, *Garrick,* I, 45.
[14] Cooke, *Macklin* (1806), p. 100.
[15] Cibber, *Egoist,* p. 56.

For some time the old man seems to have amused himself sketching scenes and writing dialogue, but when Garrick asked him if he could not finish another play, he was obviously annoyed. "Who have you to act in it?" he asked. "Why," replied Garrick, "there are Clive, Pritchard, myself, and some others." But the old man shook his head. "No," he said, taking a pinch of snuff with his customary nonchalance, "no, they won't do." [16]

But though he would not finish a new play, he at last consented to produce an old one which had not yet reached the stage—*Papal Tyranny in the Reign of King John*.[17] It is an attempt to regularize the Shakespearean chronicle history and at the same time focus attention upon the struggle between John and the Pope. John acquires many patriotic speeches and becomes, in fact, almost a hero, while general odium attaches to the character of his antagonist, the bloody-minded and hypocritical Papal Legate Pandulph. The objectionable scene between Hubert and Arthur remains, and the part of Constance is actually fattened with rhetorical lamentations, but the Bastard—at least as Shakespeare conceived the character—entirely disappears. In the dedication Cibber complains of Shakespeare's coldness, but his own play is Augustan tragedy at its worst. It is a rhetorical exercise in anti-Catholic propaganda, timely no doubt in 1745 but intrinsically worthless.

The play had an unfortunate history, and for that reason no doubt Cibber rehearsed it as quietly as possible and produced it almost unannounced.[18] The cast included Quin as King John, Cibber as Pandulph, Theophilus as the Dauphin, Mrs Pritchard as Constance, and Mrs Bellamy as Blanch. Quin and Mrs Pritchard were well received by the audience while Theophilus and Mrs Bellamy were hissed, principally, it seems, because they followed too literally Cibber's instructions to "tone" their words. But the chief attraction of the play for the greater part of the audience was Cibber's own performance. He was not, it is true, at his best. He had just lost his teeth, he was acting in a theatre larger than the one to which he was accustomed,

[16] Davies, *Dramatic Miscellanies*, III, 471.
[17] For this play, see Genest, *Some Account of the English Stage*, IV, 158-62; Croissant, *Studies in the Work of Colley Cibber*, pp. 13-14; Odell, *Shakespeare from Betterton to Irving*, I, 347-53.
[18] Whincop, *Scanderbeg*, p. 198.

and to many spectators he was almost inaudible. Still his quavering tones—in so far as they could be heard—were tolerated as the survival of another age, and his pantomime was generally admired.[19] A few spectators, however—among whom was Tom Davies—thought his pantomime even more "disgusting" than his speech. "He affected a stately magnificent tread," Davies wrote later, "a supercilious aspect, with lofty and extravagant action, which he displayed by waving up and down a roll of parchment in his right hand; in short, his whole behavior was so starchly studied that it appeared eminently insignificant, and more resembling his own Lord Foppington than a great and dignified churchman."[20]

The play was produced at Covent Garden on February 15, 1745, and on the 20th of the same month Shakespeare's *King John* appeared at Drury Lane, with Garrick and Mrs Cibber in the principal parts.[21] But *Papal Tyranny* seems not to have been seriously affected, for it ran ten nights in all and made for Cibber more than £400, which he later "wisely laid out in a profitable annuity."[22]

Thus in the winter the old man divided his time between the beau monde and the theatre: in the summer he went to the watering places, following society as it moved from Tunbridge to Scarborough, and from Scarborough to Bath. He was a picturesque, even an impressive, figure. He strutted down the walks in a flowing wig and a profusely laced coat; he wrote verses on a window in the Long Room; he courted Miss Banks and Miss Howe; he acted as a sort of clearing house for gossip. . . . What would Scarborough have been without him? What would Bath have been without its Nash and its Cibber? In 1742 Victor was at Tunbridge. "A week before I came away," he wrote later, "Cibber's *Letter to Pope* was brought down there by a gentleman of my acquaintance, who favored me with the reading it that afternoon. In the evening of that day, going on the walks to return the letter to my friend, I had the pleasure of finding him with

[19] Victor, *History of the Theatres*, II, 49, 162-64; Davies, *Dramatic Miscellanies*, I, 35, 40-41, 53; Davies, *Garrick*, I, 297; Arthur Murphy, *The Life of David Garrick* (1801), I, 102.

[20] Davies, *Dramatic Miscellanies*, I, 41.

[21] The Drury Lane revival was deferred at Cibber's request until after his first benefit; see Theophilus Cibber, *Romeo and Juliet*, p. 90.

[22] Victor, *History of the Theatres*, II, 49, note.

the author of it—the gay blooming Colley, just arrived from London. As unexpected as welcome! Well, we passed that night happily together, and the very next morning who should kind fortune add to the party but my worthy, valuable, reverend friend Dr Young?" [23] The fop and the author of the *Night Thoughts* were, one suspects, equally pleased, for they too had much in common.[24]

"What figures do Mr Nash and Mr Cibber make," wrote Richardson from Tunbridge, "hunting after new beauties and with faces of high importance traversing the walks!" [25] "To see Mr W[al]sh at eighty (Mr Cibber calls him papa) and Mr Cibber at seventy-seven hunting after new faces, and thinking themselves happy if they can obtain the notice and familiarity of a fine woman! How ridiculous!" That summer the celebrated Miss Chudleigh was "the triumphant toast: a lively, sweet-tempered, gay, self-admired, and, not altogether without reason, generally admired lady. She moved not without crowds after her. She smiled at everyone. Everyone smiled before they saw her, when they heard she was on the walk. She played, she lost, she won— all with equal good humor. But alas! she went off before she was wished to go off. And then the fellows' hearts were almost broke for a new beauty." For weeks old Cibber was madly, "over head and ears," in love with Miss Chudleigh. "Her admirers (such was his happiness!) were not jealous of him, but pleased with that wit in him which they had not, were always for calling him to her. She said pretty things— for she was Miss Chudleigh. He said pretty things—for he was Mr Cibber; and all the company, men and women, seemed to think they had an interest in what was said, and were half as well pleased as if they had said the sprightly things themselves; and mighty well contented were they to be secondhand repeaters of the pretty things. But once I faced the laureate squatted upon one of the benches, with a face more wrinkled than ordinary with disappointment. 'I thought,' said I, 'you were of the party of the tea-treats—Miss Chudleigh is gone into the tea-room.' 'Pshaw!' said he, 'there is no coming at her, she is so surrounded by the toupees.' And I left him to fret. But he was

[23] Victor, *Letters*, I, 72.
[24] See Henry C. Shelley, *The Life and Letters of Edward Young* (1914), pp. 189, 191, 220, 225.
[25] Richardson, *Correspondence*, ed. Barbauld, II, 206.

called to soon after; and in he flew, and his face shone again and
looked smooth." [26]

– 2 –

In an earlier chapter we have noticed that, for a man with so many
acquaintances, Cibber had remarkably few intimate friends. He was
a lonely figure in the theatrical world; he neither craved nor invited
intimacy. But time, which had mellowed his features and filled out
the lines of his figure, had also left its mark upon his mind. He was
kindlier, more sympathetic, more confiding; and he was now, for the
first time in his life, disposed to enter into those warm personal rela-
tionships which a generation before he had avoided. It is true that he
continued to hobnob with the Duke of Richmond and the Duke of
Grafton, with Lord Chesterfield, Bubb Doddington, and Giles Earle;
but he now also found time for humbler and less fashionable friends—
for Richardson, already the author of *Pamela* but still an obscure
figure, living in his little circle of female admirers; for Henry Jones,
the bricklayer-poet and protégé of Lord Chesterfield's; and for those
two remarkable Irishwomen, Mrs Woffington, the actress, and Mrs
Pilkington, the adventuress and poet. In the case of the women, his
friendship was no doubt tinged with gallantry, but what else could
one expect from a man who at seventy-seven was head over ears in
love with Miss Chudleigh?

His friendship with Mrs Woffington seems to date from about 1740,
the year in which the *Apology* was published. He saw her make her
first triumphant appearance on the London stage, and he at once
became one of her warmest admirers. He danced attendance on her
in the greenroom; he taught her the singing tone of tragedy; he returned to the stage to play Nykin to her Cocky in *The Old Bachelor*.[27]
By a curious coincidence his friend Swiney was in love with her also,
and as the two ancient beings paid their court, men smiled and alluded
to Susanna and the elders.[28] Once when they were dining at her house,
she asked Cibber to repeat a passage from some character that he had

[26] *Ibid.*, III, 314-17.
[27] Davies, *Garrick*, I, 309-10.
[28] *A Blast upon Bays, or a New Lick at the Laureat*, pp. 21-22, quoted *Apology*, II,
266-67; *Universal Spectator*, August 21, 1742. Lowe refuses to identify the Susanna of
the anecdote with Mrs Woffington.

acted, and after much urging he agreed to do so. "Well, you jade," he
said, "if you will assist my memory, I will give you the first speech of
Sir John Brute." He began, and the little group were held spellbound,
for they had never heard the famous lines spoken in so masterly a
fashion. The expression of disgust on the old man's face is said to have
been more strikingly characteristic of a surfeited husband than anything of the kind which had ever been seen upon the stage.[29] Years
passed, but—it was one of the misfortunes of old age—Cibber made
little progress in his amour. With incredibly bad judgment, Mrs Woffington chose to set up house with Garrick, and when, after two years,
the relationship was dissolved, she did something still more foolish—
she allowed herself to be carried off to France by Swiney, who had
promised her an estate of £200 a year. It was really most distressing,
but the old man could not shake himself free; passion still burned in
that aged breast; and when the fair president of the Beefsteak Club
came back from her trip, he was once more at her beck and call.[30]

But the affair was not perhaps after all very serious, for even while
he was courting Mrs Woffington Cibber found room in his affections
for another woman, Mrs Pilkington. She was not, like her compatriot,
famous, nor was she particularly attractive; but she had one very engaging quality—she was considerate of her ancient admirer; in fact
she needed him. She flattered him, she wrote verses to him, she compared him to Swift, and for several years she almost contrived to live
on the money with which he and his wealthy friends at White's supplied her.

Her life up to this time had been remarkably adventurous. She was
the daughter of Dr Van Lewen, a Dutch midwife who had settled in
Ireland, and at the age of eighteen she had married for love. Her husband, Matthew Pilkington, had been unable to support her, and for
several years she had been compelled to live by her wits. She had done
so remarkably well, for she was shamelessly aggressive and she exercised a certain power over men. In the first year of her marriage she
had achieved a notable triumph—she had insinuated herself into the
confidence of Swift; and she had soon become a sort of retainer of his

[29] Taylor, *Records of My Life*, I, 262-63.
[30] Victor, *History of the Theatres*, I, 157; The Earl of March, *A Duke and His
Friends*, II, 650.

—half companion and half amanuensis.[31] The story of this curious relationship has an interest of its own.

She first met Swift at Dr Delany's house at Delville, and a few days later she had an opportunity to renew the acquaintanceship when her husband was engaged to preach at St Patrick's. Husband and wife were invited to dine at the Deanery, and as soon as they had entered the parlor Swift led Mrs Pilkington toward his study. Her husband would have followed but Swift repulsed him, and thrust his wife on before. "Well," he said when they were alone, "I have brought you here to show you all the money I got when I was in the Ministry, but do not steal any of it." He then opened a cabinet and showed a whole set of empty drawers. After dinner Mr Pilkington went to church, and the Dean and the young poetess were again left alone. "Read to me," the Dean said, and he handed her the manuscript of his annals of the last years of the reign of Queen Anne. She read as best she could in a very loud voice so that the Dean might hear distinctly; but at the end of each paragraph he interrupted her and asked if she had understood. "For," he said, "I would have it intelligible to the meanest capacity, and if you comprehend it, 'tis possible everybody may." She bowed and assured him that she did understand. She was not offended—indeed, she seemed instinctively to realize that she should not be offended. And when she left the Deanery she had the satisfaction of observing that she had made a favorable impression on the Dean. He handed her down the steps to her coach, thanked her for the honor of her company, and at the same time slipped into her hand as much money as she and her husband had given that morning at the offering.[32]

She expected to hear soon from the Dean, and she was not disappointed. During one of his periodical fits of deafness he sent for her, and when she reached the Deanery he told her that he had found her employment. "Look," he said, and he showed her a large book, handsomely bound in Turkish leather. "This is a translation of the *Epistles* of Horace, a present to me from the author; it is a special good

[31] *Dictionary of National Biography*, article Letitia Pilkington; Letitia Pilkington, *Memoirs*, English Library (1928), pp. 30-44.

[32] Pilkington, *Memoirs*, pp. 49-57.

cover. But I have a mind there should be something valuable inside it." So saying he took his penknife and cut out all the leaves close to the inner margin. "Now," he said, "I will give these what they greatly want." And he threw all the leaves into the fire. He then brought out two drawers filled with letters, saying: "Your task, madam, is to paste in these letters in this cover, in the order I shall give them to you; I intended to do it myself, but that I thought it might be a pretty amusement for a child, so I sent for you." Mrs Pilkington followed his instructions, reading the letters as she pasted them in; she was surprised to find that they had been sent to the Dean by such celebrated persons as Lady Masham, the Earl of Oxford, Addison, Congreve, Pope, Gay, and Arbuthnot. When she had finished Swift took her for a walk in his garden. But they had not gone very far when clouds appeared in the sky and Mrs Pilkington remarked that it was about to rain. "I hope not," said the Dean, "for that will cost me sixpence for a coach for you. Come, make haste. Oh, how the tester trembles in my pocket!" And he led her back at a great rate. They reached the house just in time to escape a heavy shower and the Dean breathed a sigh of relief, thanking God that he had saved his money. Mr Pilkington was invited for dinner, but before the meal began, the Dean ran up and down stairs very fast finishing his afternoon walk.[33]

Thus Mrs Pilkington established herself at the Deanery; but she was not satisfied—she was too young to live shut up with an eccentric old man. She wanted friends and admirers, she wanted to cut a figure in the literary world outside the liberties; and so, when she was not at work pasting letters in the Dean's book, she began picking up acquaintances in Dublin. But her conduct was singularly indiscreet and before long malicious rumors began to circulate about her. Finally there was a public scandal and even the worst rumors seemed to be verified. Her husband entered their house through the kitchen window at midnight and caught her with a man in her bedroom. To be sure, she had a perfectly adequate explanation of the compromising situation. The man owned a book which she had been especially anxious to read, and since he had been reluctant to let it out of his sight, she had persuaded him—much against his will—to remain with her while

[33] *Ibid.*, pp. 60-64.

she finished it. Her love of learning had indeed betrayed her into an indiscretion.[34] But her husband was so far from being convinced by her story that he immediately started a divorce suit and the newspapers carried a report of the affair to the deaf old man in the Deanery. His rage was terrible. That Pilkington, he wrote to Barber, is "the falsest rogue and [his wife] the most profligate whore in either kingdom. She was taken in the fact by her own husband." [35] The benevolences of this august personage suddenly stopped, and Mrs Pilkington, unable to bear the reproaches which everyone heaped upon her, determined to leave for ever the land of her misfortunes. A few lines of "Expostulation" prepared her for the journey:

> O God! since all thy ways are just,
>   Why does thy heavy hand
> So sore afflict the wretched dust
>   Thou didst to life command?

And weeping until her heart almost "split with sorrow," she drove to the docks, and took ship for England.[36]

But though for a time she escaped her reputation, there was one thing which she could not escape—her poverty. It was imperative that she at once get a patron or employer who could fill the place in her scheme of economy that Swift had filled before. And so it was that she attached herself to Cibber.

About 1740—though the exact date is uncertain—she sent him a copy of her poem "The Trial of Constancy," together with a polite note, in which she described her misfortunes and asked for his assistance and advice. She had not long to wait for a reply. A few days later he came bounding up the stairs to her room "with the vivacity of a youth of fifteen." "You do not know me, madam," he said, making her a courtly bow. "On the contrary," she replied, quoting Milton, *"Not to know you would argue myself unknown."* "And prithee," he said, "why did not you come to my house the moment you came to London?" "Upon my word, sir, that would have been a modest proof of Irish assurance: how could I hope for a favorable reception?" "Pshaw," he replied, "merit is a sufficient recommendation to me. Come, show

[34] *Ibid.*, pp. 133-34; Victor, *Letters*, I, 141.
[35] Swift, *Correspondence*, ed. Ball, VI, 69.
[36] Pilkington, *Memoirs*, pp. 166-67.

me your writings." She gave him her poem called "Sorrow," and as soon as he began reading she knew that he liked it. "He burst into tears," she wrote later, "and was not ashamed to give the flowing virtue manly way." "Who are you?" he asked when he had finished. "You must tell me your story." And he at once suggested that she take breakfast with him the next morning.[37]

She came, and entertained him for three hours. She spoke of her parents, of her childhood, of the Dean, of her husband, and at last of that unhappy evening when she had borrowed the book and made the owner sit at her bedside while she read it. The old man listened to the end without once offering to interrupt her and without showing the least sign of impatience. Mrs Pilkington is very explicit on this point: "[He] neither yawned, scratched his head, beat tattoo with his foot, nor used any such ambiguous giving out to note that he was weary." "Zounds!" he exclaimed, when she had finished. "Write it out just as you relate it, and I'll engage it will sell." [38] And either at this time or later he gave her advice about approaching ladies and gentlemen of quality. "Never write to him or her of a dark, foggy, frosty morning, particularly before breakfast," he said, "at which time it is ten to one they are out of temper; nor, though you send at any time or even receive an unmannerly answer, do not let a rash pride drive you to return the affront, since it is impossible for you to know what at that instant has chagrined their temper. He who will not be your friend at one time may at another; and though you never can bring him to do you any service, yet do not provoke him to be your enemy: a man may have had ill success at play, missed an appointment with a fine woman, or twenty such accidents, which may for the present sour his disposition; whereas if you continue your assiduities, in process of time he might do you more service than you could hope." [39] But the advice was really unnecessary, for Mrs Pilkington was already a past master at getting money from ladies and gentlemen of quality.

Mrs Pilkington took lodgings in St James's Street, exactly opposite White's, and Cibber was continually seeing her. He left no stone un-

[37] *Ibid.*, pp. 175, 207-8. Mrs Pilkington—never a very good authority—has possibly colored her narrative at this point; see Victor, *Letters,* I, 148. Mrs Pilkington's attack on Victor (*Memoirs,* pp. 197-99) should, however, be taken into account.
[38] Pilkington, *Memoirs,* pp. 208-10.
[39] *Ibid.*, pp. 377-78.

turned to get her money from his distinguished friends and patrons. On his first visit he brought her four guineas, but at the same time he told her of a rumor to the effect that her husband was a poet of some distinction, and that all the verses she had to publish were trifles which she had stolen from him. Could she perhaps disprove this malicious insinuation by writing a few verses on some subject which had never before been attempted? Nothing was easier: she dashed off a panegyric on Mr Cibber, and the old man was so pleased with the lines that he inserted them in his pamphlet *The Egoist,* showed them to all the noblemen at White's, and procured for the writer a large number of subscriptions.[40]

After this Cibber apparently suggested the names of men whom Mrs Pilkington might profitably address. She followed his advice, and the guineas began to pour in upon her. The Ministry changed, and she wrote lines "To the Right Honorable Henry Pelham, Esq." The next morning early the old man trotted off to court, and when he returned he placed five guineas in her hand. "Do you think that a sufficient reward for your poetry?" he asked. "Yes, I really do," she replied. "Well, then," said the laureate, "Mr Pelham distinguished thus: 'There are five guineas for the lady's numbers, and five more for the good advice they contain; and tell her, I hope God will always give me grace to follow it.' " And he placed five more guineas in her hand.[41] There followed lines "To His Excellency the Earl of Chesterfield," but the remuneration was neither so prompt nor so liberal. The old man presented the lines just as dinner was brought up, and his lordship put them in his pocket. In the evening he was reminded that he had not read them, and the next day he was reminded again. "Oh," he said, "I forgot; there's two guineas for her, but don't put them into your silver pocket lest you should make a mistake and pay your chair with them." The laureate then sent Mrs Pilkington the following note:

MADAM,
The poetry of poor people, however it may rise in value, always sinks in the price; what might in happier hours have brought you ten guineas for its intrinsic worth is now reduced to two, which I desire you will come and receive from the hand of
            Your old humble servant,
                                        COLLEY CIBBER.[42]

[40] *Ibid.,* pp. 175-80.   [41] *Ibid.,* pp. 205-6.   [42] *Ibid.,* p. 334.

She came, and he told her the story, explaining that if he himself
had not thought the verses beautiful he would never have undertaken
to present them. Mrs Pilkington thanked him and turned her attention
to more liberal patrons, among whom the most dependable, it seems,
was Cibber himself. Once, when he was writing *The Character and
Conduct of Cicero,* she sent him some lines with which he was not
entirely satisfied, and which he ventured to correct; but he paid her
liberally. "Madam," he said, "there are two guineas for your flattery,
and one more for the liberty I took." She would have thanked him,
but he stopped her. "Come," he continued, "I have more good news
for you; Mr Stanhope altered a line, for which he desires you will accept a guinea; Mr Hervey also pays you the same compliment, for
changing one monosyllable for another." Mrs Pilkington was not dis-
pleased to hear that her verses had been corrected; indeed, she was
silently wishing that every gentleman at White's had, on the same
terms, taken the same liberty, till her work, like Admiral Drake's ship,
had been so often mended that not a bit of the original material remained.[43]

For a time, however, Mrs Pilkington was not in dire necessity. The
lodging in St James's Street had proved a sound investment; there was
a continual stream of visitors from White's; and each visitor brought
with him at least a guinea. For months Mrs Pilkington lived the life
she had always wished for; she had only to water the flowerpots in
her window, and the lovely gentlemen saw and came over to her. A
new existence opened up; she had friends, patrons, lovers; she was
supremely happy.[44] But suddenly, with incredible swiftness, summer
came; the clubrooms emptied, the flow of guineas ceased; and again
the adventuress was destitute. She gave up her lodgings opposite
White's and moved to a cheaper part of town; she met gentlemen at
milliners' shops and through procuresses; and at last, it seems, her
necessity was such that she was obliged to pick them up for herself
on holidays at the Temple Gate.[45] This time, indeed, there seemed to
be no end to her misfortunes. Another winter brought her back opposite White's, but her position was not quite what it had been before;
the lovely gentlemen appeared less frequently, the guineas were
harder to come by; and soon the summer—the dismal summer—was

[43] *Ibid.,* p. 381.   [44] *Ibid.,* pp. 180-97.   [45] *Ibid.,* pp. 210, 213, 236-48.

upon her. The limit of her endurance was at last reached; she had been three days without food; and she decided, as she paced the aisles of Westminster Abbey, that she would commit suicide—that she would put an end to her wretched existence that very evening. Accordingly she went to St James's Park, and taking a seat in the moonlight by Rosamund's Pond, waited until she could accomplish her purpose unobserved. But when the time for action came, she was afraid; she approached the water and drew back; and standing there irresolutely, she was soon lost in a maze of vague sentimental reflections. Just at that moment a well-dressed gentleman touched her on the shoulder. "Lord, can this be Mrs Pilkington?" he asked. And when she assured him that it was, he led her to the Royal Vineyard and ordered her some ham, a cold fowl, and a bottle of champagne. Refreshment revived her wonderfully—she conversed with the gentleman until far into the night; and when at last he took leave of her, he slipped a couple of guineas into her hand and promised to see her the next morning. The adventure was indeed so fortunate that her confidence immediately revived. "I once more began to believe myself under the favor and protection of the Almighty," she later noted in her memoirs, "as His hand, though to me invisible, visibly led me through various mazes perplexed with error; and determined, whatever sufferings He was pleased to inflict, to bear them with resignation, and never permit them to triumph over a Christian faith." [46]

It was fortunate, perhaps, that Mrs Pilkington made this resolution, for a few days later she had need of all her fortitude: she was seized by bailiffs on an action of debt and taken to the Marshalsea. What could she do? Mr Cibber was away, and Theophilus, whom she saw and called to from her prison window, walked on without giving her an answer. For days she suffered the most terrible privations; but she refused to lose heart, she prayed to the Almighty—and at last Mr Cibber returned. As soon as he heard that his protégé was in prison, he sent her a guinea all changed into sixpences so that no one would be tempted to pick her pocket, and later he got "sixteen dukes" to contribute a guinea apiece to set her free. She was released on Christmas Eve, 1742, and on the following New Year's Day she published still

[46] *Ibid.*, pp. 248-72.

another panegyric on Colley Cibber, Esq., the superlatives of which, as the old man wittily remarked, could very properly have been applied to an archbishop.[47]

Why did Cibber go on bestowing favors upon this strange woman? How was he repaid for the time and money he spent on one who, as he himself must have realized, could never permanently profit from his benefactions? The obvious answer is that Mrs Pilkington was his mistress; but one cannot be quite sure. Cibber was, like his friend Richardson, extremely fond of feminine society; he was always dangling after someone—Miss Chudleigh, Miss Banks, Miss Howe, it scarcely mattered whom—gallantry and the fashionable world were the passions of his later life. Furthermore he was impressed by Mrs Pilkington's ability; he felt that she was a poetess of genuine distinction, able to confer lasting fame upon her friends and patrons. Her verses to him, he thought, might easily supply the proper corrective to the *Dunciad* and *Joseph Andrews*—might, in fact, have a distinct influence upon his reputation with posterity.

And indeed his confidence in Mrs Pilkington was to some extent justified. After several more years of adventures, misfortunes, and amours, she returned to Ireland and wrote a famous book—her *Memoirs* (1748). In her first volume she carried her history down to the time of her departure from Dublin, devoting many extraordinarily vivid pages to the rude, kind, generous, eccentric old Dean, who had once befriended her. In a second volume she described her adventures in London, and quite naturally she introduced the laureate to fill the Dean's place. He was the second great man who had honored her with his friendship, and she gave him the same attention that she had given the first. This second portrait was indeed without much shadow; the pigment was uniform, the brightness dazzling and unreal; but Mrs Pilkington could scarcely do otherwise—she was rewarding a living benefactor. "The Almighty raised me one worthy friend," she wrote, "—good old Mr Cibber, to whose humanity I am, under God, indebted

[47] *Ibid.*, pp. 272-82. Here again one can compare Mrs Pilkington's suspiciously romantic narrative with another authority. Victor says in the course of a letter to Cibber: "She was almost five years in London in want, and once a prisoner in the King's Bench for a debt of £10, when I prevailed on you to collect that sum from the noblemen at White's—which you did—and when released, I introduced her to you to thank you for your goodness to her" (Victor, *Letters*, I, 149).

both for liberty and life." [48] And she added characteristically: "I dare say nobody will imagine he served me from any carnal views, since

> If truth in spite of manners must be told,
> Why really seventy-six is something old." [49]

The references to Mr Cibber's humanity, kindness, and generosity followed one another in quick succession. He had brought her four guineas, he had introduced her to Colonel Duncombe, he had persuaded the noblemen at White's to subscribe.... But she had forgotten: before recounting the long list of benefactions, she would have to describe the benefactor himself—to give him a place in her memoirs beside his predecessor the Dean. "And I think I cannot do it in a better manner than I have used in describing Dr Swift—that is, to give him to my readers in his words and actions, as near as I can recollect them during the time I had the honor of being known to him." [50] And she proceeded to sketch his character in this way.

Several months later the laureate sat in his easy chair, reading her words and pondering. Cibber and Swift! What a pleasing combination of names. Never before had he been so highly complimented, never before had he heard himself classed with the great literary figures of his time. He was pleased—he allowed himself to be deluded; and that night as he dozed before the fire, his dreams were more pleasant than usual.

– 3 –

The friendship between Cibber and Mrs Pilkington was nourished on verses—on those slight panegyrics which, from time to time, the adventuress sent to her ancient benefactor. The friendship between Cibber and Richardson had an even more distinctly literary flavor. The two men were undoubtedly well acquainted; they often met at North End, possibly also at Berkeley Square; they introduced one another to their respective circles of admirers. But their conversation, one notices with surprise, was almost exclusively about books—their own books, in fact. They discussed *Clarissa, Sir Charles Grandison, The Lady's Lecture, The Character and Conduct of Cicero;* they praised one another extravagantly and uncritically; they were in complete agreement—except, of course, where questions of morality were

[48] Pilkington, *Memoirs*, p. 168.   [49] *Ibid.*, p. 169.   [50] *Ibid.*, p. 207.

concerned, and then the bonds which held them together were strained almost to the breaking point.

The friendship between the two men apparently began in the early 1740s, when Richardson was engaged in the composition of his masterpiece, *Clarissa*. Cibber took a lively interest in the progress of the book, and when he learned that the heroine was to die, he was almost overcome with grief and disappointment. Mrs Pilkington wrote to the novelist in 1745:

I passed two hours this morning with Mr Cibber, whom I found in such real anxiety for Clarissa as none but so perfect a master of nature could have excited. I had related to him not only the catastrophe of the story but also your truly religious and moral reason for it; and when he heard what a dreadful lot hers was to be, he lost all patience, threw down the book, and vowed he would not read another line. To express or paint his passion would require such masterly hands as yours or his own: he shuddered— nay, the tears stood in his eyes. "What," said he, "shall I, who have loved and revered the virtuous, the beautiful Clarissa from the same motives I loved Mr Richardson, bear to stand patient spectator of her ruin, her final destruction? No!— My heart suffers as strongly for her as if word was brought me that his house was on fire and himself, his wife, and little ones likely to perish in the flame. I cannot bear it! Had Lovelace ten thousand souls and bodies I could wish to see them all tortured, stretched on the rack: no punishment can be too bad for him."

In this manner did the dear gentleman, I think I may almost say, rave; for I never saw passion higher wrought than his. When I told him she must die, he said, G—d d—n him if she should, and that he should no longer believe Providence, or Eternal Wisdom, or Goodness governed the world, if merit, innocence, and beauty were to be so destroyed. "Nay," he added, "my mind is so hurt with the thought of her being violated that were I to see her in heaven, sitting on the knees of the blessed Virgin and crowned with glory, her sufferings would still make me feel horror, horror distilled." These were his strongly emphatical expressions.

"I would," said he, "write to him (and showed me a part of a letter to you) but I fear I have been too sincere already: I have gone every evening to Ranelagh in order to find a face or mien resembling Miss Harlowe, but to no purpose: the charmer is inimitable: I cannot find her equal."

Spare her virgin purity, dear sir, spare it! Consider if this wounds both Mr Cibber and me (who neither of us set up for immaculate chastity) what must it do with those who possess that inestimable treasure? [51]

[51] Richardson, *Correspondence*, II, 127-31. Cibber contributed at least one letter to *Clarissa*, but Richardson did not like it because it made his heroine act and reason too passionately; see *Monthly Magazine*, December, 1813.

But despite Mrs Pilkington's anguish, the novelist remained inflexible, and the horrors of Clarissa's tragedy were not averted.

In the meantime Cibber had himself published a book—*The Character and Conduct of Cicero*—and though for a time it escaped the attention of the Richardson circle, it was finally read and discussed by them with appropriate solemnity. Richardson himself had no doubt that it was, if not a masterpiece, at least an important contribution to history. "The present laureate's performance on the same subject of which Dr Middleton's is the foundation," he wrote to Lady Bradshaigh, "is a spirited and pretty piece. . . . I think I can promise you pleasure in reading [it]; he is candid and impartial, and does justice both to Middleton and Cicero." [52] Lady Bradshaigh soon replied that she had read the book and that she had indeed found her time well spent.

What may be thought of Mr Cibber's performance, I know not; but I think it is wrote with great spirit. The more judicious and grave part of his readers may think him rather too flighty sometimes, at others too low, too full of little expressions and conceits, bringing in a piece of an old song, or the like: but as he always apologizes for them, we will suppose they might be looked over, were they really faults, which I do not take upon me to determine. I know he pleases me in the favor he shows to Caesar, which appears to me just. I cannot, indeed, think so gently of his conduct with the abandoned Cleopatra in Egypt as Mr Cibber seems to do; but his thoughts are consistent with his character.[53]

Sympathy with the abandoned Cleopatra was a fault which neither Richardson nor Lady Bradshaigh could possibly overlook; and though in this case they confined their disapprobation to their own circle, there were other cases in which they spoke—and spoke very sharply— with the old man, whose notions about morality they considered so deplorably loose. In 1748, for example, they took him severely to task for his dialogue, *The Lady's Lecture,* in which he had attempted to reconcile paternal authority and filial obedience. They realized at once that his whole undertaking was unsound, that his doctrines, if taken seriously, might actually make children independent of their parents; and they did their best to make him aware that he was playing with fire. When Richardson heard the dialogue read, he expressed his dis-

[52] Richardson, *Correspondence,* VI, 167, 241.
[53] *Ibid.,* VI, 264-65.

approval in the strongest terms. "I can see," he said with cutting emphasis, "that you do not intend to make your girl dutiful; but at least let me entreat you to make her generous." Not unwilling to have changes made, Cibber gave him the work for correction; but after jotting down half a sheet of remarks on the first page, the novelist asked to be excused from the task. The whole subject was utterly distasteful to him; how could he be expected to correct a pamphlet which was so obviously subversive of morality? [54] "In short," he wrote to Miss Westcomb, "the piece is calculated as it stands at present to throw down all distinction between parents and children.—Yet it has met with so much applause among the young flirts that I don't know whether he will not publish it. If he does I had a good mind that Miss Howe (who is pert enough of conscience to her mamma; Clarissa, you know, is dead) should answer it." [55]

Two or three years later an even more disturbing controversy broke out in that little circle. During one of Cibber's visits to North End, the conversation apparently turned on the character of Sir Charles Grandison, the ideal gentleman whose history the novelist had just undertaken to write; and with his usual perversity Cibber insisted that Sir Charles should have a mistress, if only to show his virtue in parting from her when he had fixed upon a lady to whom he could make honorable addresses. A mistress! The novelist and Mr Edwards were profoundly shocked; and they would perhaps have refused to listen to the heresy, had it not afforded them an opportunity to make many delightfully instructive comments. In marriage, Mr Edwards pointed out, purity desires to meet with purity; the husband must be as free from sin as the wife.[56] And a few days later he recurred to the subject in a letter to his friend. You must certainly represent your gentleman as virtuous with regard to women, he insisted—"a character which, notwithstanding Mr Cibber's vivacity, it seems strange that anyone should think ridiculous in a Christian country. Milton, who was as good a poet and as much a gentleman as he, did not think so." [57]

[54] *Ibid.*, II, 204-5; III, 317-18.
[55] *Ibid.*, III, 318.
[56] *Ibid.*, VI, 65; III, 8-10. I assume that Richardson and Edwards refer to the same conversation; but possibly there were two conversations about the character of a good man, one not directly connected with *Sir Charles Grandison*.
[57] *Ibid.*, III, 8.

Richardson prepared a full account of the affair and sent it, somewhat maliciously, to Lady Bradshaigh, who had herself been heard to express dangerous opinions—who had, in fact, suggested that a man might be called a rake without being an abandoned profligate.

Did I ever tell you, madam, of the contention I had with Mr Cibber about the character of a good man, which he undertook to draw, and to whom, at setting out, he gave a mistress? ... A male-virgin! said he—ha, ha, ha, ha! when I made my objections to the mistress, and she was another man's wife, too, but ill-used by her husband; and he laughed me quite out of countenance. And it was but yesterday in company, some of which he never was in before, that he was distinguishing upon a moderate rake (though not one word has he seen or heard of your ladyship's letter or notion) by urging that men might be criminal without being censurable! A doctrine that he had no doubt about and to which he declared that none but divines and prudes would refuse to subscribe to!—Bless me! thought I, and is this knowing the world?—What an amiable man was Mr B—— in *Pamela* in this light!

But I have this comfort, upon the whole, that I find the good man's character is not impracticable; and I think Mr Cibber, if I can have weight with him, shall undertake the arduous task. He is as gay and as lively at seventy-nine as he was at twenty-nine; and he is a sober man who has seen a great deal and always dressed well and was noted for his address and his success, too, on two hundred and fifty occasions—a little too many, I doubt, for a moderate rake; but then his long life must be considered.[58]

Then to test the orthodoxy of his correspondent the novelist deviated for a few lines into the heresy of Mr Cibber. "I wish we could fix upon the number of times a man might be allowed to be overcome with wine without being thought a sot. Once a week? Once a fortnight? Once a month? How shall we put it? Youth will have its follies." [59] But the test was really unnecessary, for Lady Bradshaigh was too much shocked by Cibber's paradoxes to repeat her error. "I absolutely deny," she wrote back "... that I *allow* of moderate rakery. ... How you make me hate and despise old Cibber! ... Where does he find the doctrine that men may be criminal without being censurable? In his own corrupt heart. I believe, indeed, he is a perfect stranger to the most excellent of doctrines. He does not search too narrowly for fear of finding that all crimes are not only censurable but punishable. With what a heart does he stand upon the brink of that

[58] *Ibid.*, VI, 65-67.   [59] *Ibid.*, VI, 67.

grave that is gaping to devour him! *He* draw a good man! A despicable wretch! *He* noted for his address! Yes, he was noted for the
most finished coxcomb that ever humanity produced. . . . Pray, sir, let
me beg, if I have not lost all my interest, that you will never name your
good man again to that irreclaimable sinner of seventy-nine. His vile
opinion will taint the character. Vice in youth is not excusable, but in
old age it is unpardonable." [60]

And so the controversy went on. The irreclaimable sinner was
lashed, the convictions of the little circle were strengthened, and—
what is perhaps more important—Sir Charles Grandison remained a
pure hero. Through the efforts of the virtuous lady, indeed, his character was preserved for posterity without spot or blemish, so that the
modern reader who is in search of edification may still peruse the
history of one truly estimable man.

- 4 -

In the meantime Cibber had become acquainted with another man
of letters, a man who figures less prominently than Richardson in the
textbooks of today, but who in his own time was considered definitely
talented—the bricklayer-poet Henry Jones.

A native of Drogheda, Jones had in 1745 attracted the attention of
the Earl of Chesterfield, then Lord Lieutenant of Ireland, and in 1748
he had followed Lord Chesterfield to London. Shortly after his arrival he had been introduced to the poet laureate, who—with all of
the good nature and some of the naïveté which he had shown in his
relations with Mrs Pilkington—at once pronounced the bricklayer a
genius. In 1749 the old man subscribed—and no doubt also solicited
subscriptions—to a volume of *Poems on Several Occasions,* and in
1753 he helped Jones finish a tragedy, *The Earl of Essex.* The tragedy
was successfully produced and Jones became a famous man. But the
laureate was not satisfied, he had mapped out a still more ambitious
future for his friend; there were to be more tragedies, more volumes of
verse, and at the end, as the crowning glory of a brilliant career, Jones
was to succeed to the laurel. As early as 1750, it seems, he took steps
to make sure of this final consummation. During the winter he was
extremely ill, and when at last he felt that he had no hope of recov-

[60] *Ibid.,* VI, 93-95.

ering, he called Jones to his bedside and gave him a letter to the Duke of Grafton.[61]

May it please your grace [such were the old man's words] I know no nearer way of repaying your favors for these last twenty years than by recommending the bearer, Mr Henry Jones, for the vacant laurel: Lord Chesterfield will tell you more of him. I don't know the day of my death, but while I live I shall not cease to be your grace's, etc.

COLLEY CIBBER [62]

The Duke of Grafton thought the letter so remarkable that he allowed it to be printed in the newspapers, and in the course of time it came into the hands of Horace Walpole. That incorrigible gossip copied it in full, and hurried off to Lord Chesterfield's to get the whole story of the affair. "Who is this Jones?" he asked. And Lord Chesterfield replied that he was a man eminently fitted to succeed Cibber. "A better poet," he said, "would not take the post, and a worse ought not to have it." But in the meantime Cibber recovered from his illness, and Jones had to wait a little longer.[63]

He waited, but—after the appearance of *The Earl of Essex*—he did little to improve his chances with the Lord Chamberlain. He plunged into dissipation, he associated almost entirely with actors, painters, and poetasters, he even allowed himself to be seen in company with the most disreputable of London rakes, Theophilus Cibber. Of his former patrons he remained on good terms with only one—Lord Chesterfield. He took the trouble to collect a stock of anecdotes and witticisms before he dined at his lordship's table, and he remained sober the whole day. But at last even this connection was broken. He kept away from Chesterfield House for two months together, and his lordship, anxiously inquiring about him, discovered that he had borrowed eight guineas from one of the servants in the house. His lordship confronted the servant, and "calling up that air of good breeding which was so natural to him, observed that as the lending of a sum of money to any gentleman that sat at his table was an act of civility that he could not possibly condemn, he would pay him the eight guineas. 'But as to

---

[61] *Dictionary of National Biography*, article Henry Jones; *European Magazine*, April, 1794.

[62] Walpole, *Letters*, III, 29.

[63] *Ibid.*; Victor, *Letters*, I, 177.

Mr Jones (though,' says he, 'I believe you'll never be put to the trial) if ever he knocks at my door, I'm not at home, and this must be your constant answer.' " [64]

Lord Chesterfield was right: the bricklayer-poet did not return, but shrinking from his friends of former days, passed quickly out of sight. His death—which occurred long after the death of his benefactor the laureate—was a sordid tragedy. He was drunk for two whole days, and on the night of the third day he was run over by a wagon in St Martin's Lane. His hat and coat were gone when he was found, and he was taken to the workhouse to die. [65]

History does not record the feelings of the laureate as he watched the disintegration of his chosen successor, but even that lively octogenarian must, momentarily at least, have been disappointed.

- 5 -

In 1750 Cibber had, as we have seen, a severe illness, but it passed without impairing his constitution. "Though Death has been cooling his heels at my door these three weeks," he wrote to Richardson on Christmas Day, "I have not had time to see him. The daily conversation of my friends has kept me so agreeably alive that I have not passed my time better a great while." [66] In 1753 he made his will, drafting it—the gesture was characteristic—in the presence of Lord Waldegrave, Lord Duncannon, and Robert Bertie, son of the Duke of Ancaster. He left £1,000 to each of the daughters of Theophilus, Jane and Elizabeth Cibber, and he remembered his own children in the order in which they stood in his affections. To Anne and Theophilus he left £50 each; to Elizabeth, wife of Joseph Marples, £5; and to the unfortunate Charlotte Charke "the like sum of £5 and no more." The rest of the estate went to Catherine Brown, his eldest daughter, who probably lived with him in his house in Berkeley Square. [67]

In 1755 Horace Walpole met Cibber at White's and was surprised to observe that the old man was "still hearty and clear and well." Walpole remembered examining the wager-book of the club and discov-

[64] *European Magazine,* May, 1794.
[65] *Ibid.,* June, 1794.
[66] Richardson, *Correspondence,* II, 174.
[67] Cibber's will, Somerset House.

ering that, some years before, Lord Mountford had bet Sir John Bland twenty guineas that Nash would outlive Cibber. But now—it was, as Walpole felt, very remarkable—both wagerers were dead and the two ancient beings lived on.[68] The laureate was certainly less active than he had been a few years before, but he was still able to perform his official duties—to write the New Year's and birthday odes, which celebrated with obvious sincerity the virtues of the Hanoverian King. But suddenly—just as another ode was about to be performed—the pulses of life stopped, and the old man wrote no more. It was December 11, 1757. At six o'clock in the morning he was apparently in good health, for he chatted with his servant, and at nine he was dead, lying peacefully on the pillow just as his man had left him.[69]

The end had so long been expected that no one was inclined to mourn. There were no comments in the newspapers, no elegiac verses; one even searches in vain for an obituary notice of more than two sentences in length. Theophilus, indeed, professed to be broken-hearted, but as usual Theophilus was playing for sympathy. He realized that the death of a father, if properly managed, meant money, and he set out to make what he could. On December 12 he wrote to the Duke of Newcastle, asking for permission to act a few nights after Christmas in order to save himself from what, indeed, he was always about to suffer—immediate ruin. "My father also joins the prayer of that petition, and has subscribed it," he added mendaciously. And for the sake of his father, lying dead in the house in Berkeley Square, the petition was granted.[70] Theophilus appeared upon the stage in deepest mourning, and twisting his features into exaggerated grimaces of sorrow, stammered out a prologue on the subject of his father's death. But despite the actor's manifest preoccupation with grief, the performances were not a success,[71] and Theophilus was soon obliged to avert immediate ruin by accepting an engagement in Dublin. The ship

[68] Walpole, *Letters*, III, 362; Algernon Bourke, *The History of White's* (1892), I, 105; II, 33. For other bets on the duration of Cibber's life, see Bourke, *History of White's*, II, 6-30. The earliest records of the club (1736) suggest that Cibber was one of the original members.

[69] Victor, *History of the Theatres*, II, 52; *Public Advertiser*, December 12, 1757; *London Evening Post*, December 13, 1757.

[70] Add. MS. 32, 876.

[71] Aaron Hill, *The Insolvent, or Filial Piety* (1758), preface and prologue.

on which he traveled, however, was wrecked on the Scottish coast, and Theophilus himself was drowned.[72]

In the meantime the last rites of his father had been performed and the remains interred in Grosvenor Chapel, South Audley Street, Grosvenor Square.[73]

[72] *Biographia Dramatica,* article Theophilus Cibber; Victor, *History of the Theatres,* I, 249-51. For Goldsmith's amusing article on the death of Theophilus, see Goldsmith, *Works,* ed. Peter Cunningham (Boston and New York, n. d.), V, 267-69.

[73] *British Chronicle,* December 19-21, 1757; *Notes and Queries,* 8th series, III (January-June, 1893), 131; VI (July-December, 1894), 12.

BIBLIOGRAPHY

I. CIBBER'S WORKS

1695 A Poem on the Death of Our Late Soveraign Lady Queen Mary. By C. Cibber. 4to.

  Published in June (Arber, *Term Catalogues,* II, 559).

1696 Love's Last Shift, or the Fool in Fashion. A Comedy. Written by C. Cibber. 4to.

  Drury Lane about January (*Apology,* I, 213). Published in February (*London Gazette,* February 10-13). Revised text in Cibber, *Plays* (1721), where several passages are bowdlerized and an entire scene is omitted; see Dougald MacMillan, "The Text of *Love's Last Shift,*" *Mod. Lang. Notes,* XLVI (1931), 518-19.

1697 Womans Wit, or the Lady in Fashion. A Comedy. Written by C. Cibber. 4to.

  Drury Lane. Published in March (*Post Man,* March 20-23).

1699 Xerxes. A Tragedy. Written by C. Cibber. 4to.

  Lincoln's Inn Fields. Published in April (*Post Boy,* April 27-29).

1700 The Tragical History of King Richard III. By C. Cibber. 4to.

  Drury Lane; probably acted 3 times (*Ximena,* preface). Published March 16 (*Flying Post*); no date. Revised text in Cibber, *Plays* (1721); see Arthur Colby Sprague, "A New Scene in Colley Cibber's *Richard III,*" *Mod. Lang. Notes,* XLII (1927), 29-32.

1700 Love Makes a Man, or the Fop's Fortune. A Comedy. Written by C. Cibber. 4to.

  Drury Lane, December. December 9 was probably the first performance; the play was still being acted December 18 (Hotson, *Restoration and Commonwealth Stage,* p. 378). Published January 22, 1701 (*Post Man* and *Post Boy*).

1702 She Wou'd and She Wou'd Not, or the Kind Impostor. A Comedy. Written by Mr. Cibber. 4to.

  Drury Lane, November 26; probably acted 6 times (*Ximena,* preface). Published in December (*London Gazette,* December 17-21); imprint 1703.

1702? The School-Boy, or the Comical Rival. A Comedy. 4to.

  Drury Lane; advertised for October 24, 1702, but the performance was not given; first recorded performance April 30, 1703. Published in 1707.

1703? The Rival Queans. With the Humours of Alexander the Great. A Comical-Tragedy. Written by Mr. Cibber. 8vo.
Drury Lane, probably 1703 (*Visits from the Shades,* pp. 21-22). Published in Dublin 1729.

1704 The Careless Husband. A Comedy. Written by C. Cibber. 4to.
Drury Lane, December 7-16 (9 times). Published December 19 (*Daily Courant*); imprint 1705.

1705 Perolla and Izadora. A Tragedy. Written by Mr. Cibber. 4to.
Drury Lane, December 3-8 (6 times). Published January 3, 1706 (*Daily Courant*).

1707 The Comical Lovers. A Comedy. 4to.
Haymarket, February 4, 5, and 8. Published December 5 (*Daily Courant*); no date.

1707 The Double Gallant, or the Sick Lady's Cure. A Comedy. Written by Mr. Cibber. 4to.
Haymarket, November 1-4 (3 times). Published November 8 (*Daily Courant*); no date.

1707 The Muses Mercury, or the Monthly Miscellany. October, 1707. 4to.
"Prologue spoken at Her Majesty's theatre in the Haymarket, on Saturday the 8th of November, by I. B., Esq. Written by Mr. Cibber."

1707 The Lady's Last Stake, or the Wife's Resentment. A Comedy. Written by Mr. Cibber. 4to.
Haymarket, December 13-19 (5 times). Published December 30 (*Daily Courant*); no date.

1709 The Rival Fools. A Comedy. Written by Mr. Cibber. 4to.
Drury Lane, January 11-14 (4 times). Published January 26 (*Daily Courant*); no date.

1709 The Man's Bewitch'd, or the Devil to Do about Her. A Comedy. By Susanna Cent-Livre. 4to.
Epilogue by Cibber, spoken by Mrs Oldfield, December 12, 1709.

1712 Ximena, or the Heroick Daughter. A Tragedy. Written by Mr. Cibber. 8vo.
Drury Lane, November 28 to December 4, 1712 (6 times). Published October 24, 1719 (*Daily Post*).

1714 The Victim. A Tragedy. Written by Mr. Johnson. 12mo.
Epilogue by Cibber, spoken by Mrs Oldfield, January 5.

1715 Venus and Adonis. A Masque. Written by Mr. Cibber and Set to Musick by Dr. Pepusch. 8vo.
Drury Lane, March 12. The advertisement for the first perform-

ance notes: "A printed book of the masque will be given to each
person that pays in the pit or boxes."

1715 Myrtillo. A Pastoral Interlude. Written by Mr. Cibber and Set to
Musick by Dr. Pepusch. 8vo.
   Drury Lane, November 5. Published November 5 (*Daily
   Courant*); imprint 1716.

1715 The Bulls and Bears. A Farce.
   Drury Lane, December 2, 3, and 5. Unpublished. Mentioned as
   Cibber's in *The Confederates* (1717), etc.

1715? The Tell-Tale, or the Invisible Mistress. By Mr. Cibber.
   Advertised among Lintot's publications at the end of Booth's
   Death of Dido (1716), etc., though it does not appear in the
   list of works bought from Cibber by Lintot (John Nichols,
   Literary Anecdotes of the Eighteenth Century (1812-15), VIII,
   294-95). I have not been able to find a copy of this work.

1717 The Non-Juror. A Comedy. Written by Mr. Cibber. 8vo.
   Drury Lane, December 6-27 (16 times). Published January 2,
   1718; 2d edition January 3; 3d edition January 7 (*Daily
   Courant*).

1719 The Invader of His Country, or the Fatal Resentment. A Tragedy.
   By Mr. Dennis. 4to.
   Epilogue by Cibber, spoken by Mrs Oldfield, November 11.

1721 The Refusal, or the Ladies Philosophy. A Comedy. Written by
   Mr. Cibber. 8vo.
   Drury Lane, February 14-20 (6 times).

1721 Plays Written by Mr. Cibber. 2 vols. 4to.
   Contains *Love's Last Shift, Richard III, Love Makes a Man,
   She Would and She Would Not, The Careless Husband, The
   Lady's Last Stake, The Rival Fools, Ximena, The Non-Juror,*
   and *The Refusal*. Published by subscription.

1724 Caesar in Egypt. A Tragedy. Written by Mr. Cibber. 8vo.
   Drury Lane, December 9-15 (6 times). Published December 15
   (*Daily Courant*); imprint 1725.

1728 The Provok'd Husband, or a Journey to London. A Comedy.
   Written by the Late Sir John Vanbrugh and Mr. Cibber. 8vo.
   Drury Lane, January 10 to February 12 (28 times). Published
   January 31 (*Daily Post*).

1729 Love in a Riddle. A Pastoral. Written by Mr. Cibber. 8vo.
   Drury Lane, January 7 and 8. In the first edition the date is
   misprinted 1719.

1729 Damon and Phillida. A Ballad Opera. 12mo.
   New Theatre in the Haymarket, August 16.

1731   An Ode to His Majesty, for the New-Year, 1730/31. By Mr. Cibber, Servant to His Majesty. 4to.

1731   The Lover. A Comedy. Written by Mr. Theophilus Cibber, Comedian. 8vo.
     Epilogue by Cibber, spoken by Theophilus and his wife January 20 (Chetwood, *General History of the Stage,* p. 119).

1731   The London Merchant, or the History of George Barnwell. By Mr. Lillo. 8vo.
     Epilogue by Cibber, spoken by Mrs Cibber (Theophilus Cibber's first wife) June 22.

1731   An Ode for His Majesty's Birth-Day, October 30, 1731. By Mr. Cibber, Servant to His Majesty. 4to.
     The later odes are printed in the *Gentleman's Magazine* and other newspapers.

1732   The Modern Husband. A Comedy. Written by Henry Fielding, Esq. 8vo.
     The epilogue printed before the play is Cibber's, though it bears his name only in the second edition. It was spoken by Mrs Heron, February 14.

1733   The Miser. A Comedy. By Henry Fielding, Esq. 8vo.
     Epilogue by Cibber, spoken by Mrs Raftor, February 17.

1734   The Scarborough Miscellany for the Year 1734. 8vo.
     "To Miss Eger—n singing in the Long Room. By C—y C—r."
     Verses "wrote on a window in the Long Room at Scarborough. By the Poet Laureate."
     Other verses by Cibber in *The British Musical Miscellany* (1734), *Tunbrigalia* (1740), *Poems on Several Occasions* (1749), etc.

1735   Polypheme. An Opera. By Paul Rolli, F.R.S. Composed by Nicholas Porpora, for the British Nobility. 8vo.
     English translation by Cibber; imprint 1734. First performed at the Haymarket, February 2, 1735.

1736   The Tragedy of Zara. [By Aaron Hill.] 8vo.
     Prologue by Cibber, spoken by Theophilus Cibber, January 12.

1740   An Apology for the Life of Mr. Colley Cibber, Comedian, and Late Patentee of the Theatre-Royal. With an Historical View of the Stage during His Own Time. Written by Himself. 4to.
     Published April 7; 2d edition May 14 (*London Daily Post and General Advertiser*).

1742   A Letter from Mr. Cibber to Mr. Pope, Inquiring into the Motives that Might Induce Him in His Satyrical Works, to be so Frequently Fond of Mr. Cibber's Name. 8vo.
     Published July 27 (*Champion*).

1743   The Egoist, or Colley upon Cibber. Being His Own Picture Retouch'd to so Plain a Likeness That No One Now Would Have the Face to Own it but Himself. 8vo.

> Published in January (*Gentleman's Magazine*). Undoubtedly by Cibber despite the ambiguous title; see DeWitt C. Croissant, "A Note on the *Egoist, or Colley upon Cibber*," *Philological Quarterly*, III (1924), 76-77.

1743   A Second Letter from Mr. Cibber to Mr. Pope. In Reply to Some Additional Verses in His Dunciad, Which He Has not yet Published. fol.

> Published February 15 (*Daily Post*).

1744   Another Occasional Letter from Mr. Cibber to Mr. Pope. Wherein the New Hero's Preferment to His Throne in the Duncaid Seems not to be Accepted. And the Author of That Poem His More Rightful Claim to It Is Asserted. With an Expostulatory Address to the Reverend Mr. W. W—n, Author of the New Preface and Adviser in the Curious Improvements of That Satire. By Mr. Colley Cibber. 8vo.

> Published in January (*Gentleman's Magazine*).

1745   Papal Tyranny in the Reign of King John. A Tragedy. By Colley Cibber, Esq. 8vo.

> Covent Garden, February 15-26 (10 times).

1747   The Character and Conduct of Cicero, Considered from the History of His Life by the Reverend Dr. Middleton. With Occasional Essays and Observations upon the Most Memorable Facts and Persons during that Period. By Colley Cibber, Esq., Servant to His Majesty. 4to.

1748   The Lady's Lecture, a Theatrical Dialogue between Sir Charles Easy and His Marriageable Daughter. Being an Attempt to Engage Obedience by Filial Liberty, and to Give the Maiden Conduct of Virtue, Chearfulness. By C. Cibber, Esq., Servant to His Majesty. 8vo.

1751   A Rhapsody upon the Marvellous, Arising from the First Odes of Horace and Pindar. Being a Scrutiny into Ancient Poetical Fame Demanded by Modern Common Sense. By Colley Cibber, Esq., P. L. 4to.

1752   Eugenia. A Tragedy. [By Philip Francis.] 8vo.

> "The epilogue is old Cibber's, but corrected, though not enough, by Francis" (Chesterfield to his son, February 20, 1752).

1754?   Verses to the Memory of Mr. Pelham, Addressed to His Grace the Duke of Newcastle. By Colley Cibber, Esq., P. L. fol.

> No date.

1760   The Dramatic Works of Colley Cibber, Esq. 4 vols. 12mo.

1777   The Dramatic Works of Colley Cibber, Esq. 5 vols. 12mo.
        Contains *Perolla and Izadora, Caesar in Egypt, The School-Boy,
        Xerxes, Venus and Adonis, Myrtillo,* and *Damon and Phillida,*
        which are not in the 1760 edition. *The Contre Temps, or Rival
        Queans* is substituted for Cibber's *The Rival Queans, with the
        Humors of Alexander the Great,* and *Flora, or Hob in the Well*
        for Cibber's (?) *Hob, or the Country Wake.*

II. WORKS ATTRIBUTED TO CIBBER

1711   Hob, or the Country Wake. A Farce. By Mr. Doggett. 12 mo.
        Drury Lane, October 6. Published in 1715. It is an abbreviated
        version of Doggett's *The Country Wake* (1696), used at Drury
        Lane as an afterpiece. Chetwood (*General History of the Stage,*
        p. 117) assigns it to Cibber. Genest (*Some Account of the Eng-
        lish Stage,* II, 487-88) argues that it was more probably Dog-
        gett's because it was brought out while he was still acting and
        printed as his. Chetwood, however, is too good an authority to
        be set aside on *a priori* grounds.

1713   Cinna's Conspiracy. A Tragedy. 4to.
        Drury Lane, February 19. A translation of Corneille's *Cinna.*
        Biographia Dramatica says: "In a pamphlet by Daniel Defoe,
        written about 1713, this play is, and we think not without
        probability, ascribed to Colley Cibber, who spoke the prologue."
        Croissant (*Studies in the Work of Colley Cibber,* pp. 10-11)
        adds another piece of evidence: in John Nichols, *Literary Anec-
        dotes of the Eighteenth Century,* VIII, 294-95, Lintot is shown
        to have paid Cibber £13 for the manuscript of *Cinna's Con-
        spiracy.* But the style of the play is not Cibberian and it seems
        unlikely that Cibber—who had just laid violent hands on the
        Cid—should have been content to translate *Cinna* without
        making radical changes. See Genest, *Some Account of the
        English Stage,* II, 510-11; Canfield, *Corneille and Racine in
        England,* pp. 179-85.

1745   The Temple of Dullness. With the Humours of Signor Capochio
        and Signora Dorinna. A Comic Opera in Two Acts. The Music
        by Mr. Arne. 4to.
        "This," says *Biographia Dramatica,* "we have heard ascribed to
        Colley Cibber." The most careful study of the piece is George
        W. Whiting, "*The Temple of Dullness* and other Interludes,"
        Review of English Studies, X (1934), 206-11. Whiting points
        out that it is partly taken from the *Interlude* ridiculing Italian
        opera in Theobald's *The Happy Captive* (1741). It might, he

thinks, be Cibber's despite the fact that Pope is praised in the preface. But his arguments are unconvincing, particularly when he attempts to show that Cibber had no liking for Italian opera. Whiting is on firmer ground when he argues against Cibber's authorship of another piece—derived not from *The Temple of Dullness* but from the *Interlude—Capochio and Dorinna. An Interlude for Music of Two Acts. Translated from an Italian Intermezzo of That Title, by the Late Colley Cibber, Esq., Poet Laureat. The Music Composed by Dr. Arne* (n. d.).

INDEX